NOT JUST A
BUNNINGS
MAN

ABOUT THE AUTHOR

Joseph Christensen is a Lecturer of History at The University of Western Australia. His other publications include the biography *The game that counts: Irvine Owen Gaze, Antarctic adventurer and airman* (2018).

NOT JUST A BUNNINGS MAN

THE LIFE AND TIMES OF TOM (G.M.) BUNNING

JOSEPH CHRISTENSEN

UWA PUBLISHING

First published in 2026 by
UWA Publishing
Crawley, Western Australia 6009
www.uwap.uwa.edu.au

UWAP is an imprint of UWA Publishing
a division of The University of Western Australia

This book is copyright. Apart from any fair dealing for the purpose of private study, research, criticism or review, as permitted under the *Copyright Act 1968*, no part may be reproduced by any process without written permission. Enquiries should be made to the publisher.

Copyright © Joseph Christensen 2026.

The moral right of the author has been asserted.

ISBN: 978-1-76080-327-8

 A catalogue record for this book is available from the National Library of Australia

Cover image: Gavin Macrae Bunning (Bunning Family Collection)
Back cover photo: Back cover photo: Tom and Margot Bunning (Bunning Family Collection)
Cover design by Upside Creative
Typeset in 12 point Arno by Lasertype
Printed by Lightning Source

UWA Publishing acknowledge we are situated on Noongar land, and that Noongar people remain the spiritual and cultural custodians of their land, and continue to practice their values, languages, beliefs and knowledge. We pay our respects to the traditional owners of the lands on which we live and work across Western Australia and Australia.

 uwapublishing

Contents

Contents   v
Acknowledgements   vii
Foreword by Gavin Bunning   ix

1. An unplanned beginning   1
2. Bonza times   21
3. The younger set   41
4. Officer, husband, father   63
5. Prisoner of war   83
6. Back to work   109
7. Ploughing back the profits   133
8. Hard-headed innovation   159
9. Buying back the farm   189
10. Raiders and white knights   219
11. The end of a dynasty   249

Appendix   Tom's letter on the Selarang Barracks incident, Changi, 1942   269
Notes   277

Acknowledgements

This biography began with an approach made by Gavin Bunning and Sue Hovell to UWA Publishing in late 2018. I have tremendous gratitude to Gavin and Sue for placing their trust in me, for their patience as I juggled writing the biography with teaching commitments at UWA, for the wealth of source materials they made available to me, and for their feedback on draft chapters. I benefited greatly from Gavin's careful and constructive comments on earlier drafts of the manuscript, which enabled it to be considerably improved. Any errors or omissions in the published version are my sole responsibility.

Several people made themselves available during 2019 for interviews on aspects of Tom Bunning's life and career. For their generosity, I thank Ian Smith, Grant and Kerry Wark, Barry Stanley, Herb Williams, Ian Kuba, Richard Alder, Dolph Zink, Albert Brunini, Penny Holmes, Peter Johnston, Bob Bunning, Michael Chaney, Helen Bunning and Clive Hovell. Gavin and Sue also kindly agreed to interviews. Special thanks are due to Rob Bunning, Duncan Bunning, Devika Hovell, Rory Hovell and Kirsty Wood for sharing their memories of their grandparents at North Fremantle in April 2019. I would also like to thank Bill Bunbury for his helpful advice on the conduct of oral-history interviews at an early stage of this biography.

The late Jenny Mills, author of *The Timber People* (1986), graciously made available her collection of papers and notes on the history of Bunnings and Western Australian forest history. I also thank Anitia Cipriano (Cotswold Investments Pty Ltd) and Yasmin McDonald (Scotch College Archives) for their assistance with source materials used in this biography.

Balancing the work of researching and writing the life history of an important figure in Western Australia's twentieth-century economic and social history with teaching commitments and other university work is one that I did not always handle as expertly as I should have. For their support, I owe a special debt to my colleagues Andrea Gaynor, Tony Hughes-d'Aeth, Jeremy Martens and Alexandra Ludewig. The

ACKNOWLEDGEMENTS

collegial environment of UWA's School of Humanities made this workload easier and more enjoyable to manage. For their constant encouragement, I would like to thank Adam Switzer, James Francis Warren, Greg Bankoff, Paul Di Nunzio, Terry Murphy, and Tim and Judith O'Keeffe. Finally, to my son, Jethro Christensen, I owe my everlasting gratitude for giving me so much enjoyment and fulfilment in my work and life.

Foreword

Gavin MacRae (Tom) Bunning, aged twenty, had just taken up his first salaried position as company accountant when he found himself challenged to save the company. The Bank of NSW announced its intention to close the Bunning Bros. account. It was early 1932; the Great Depression of the 1930s had begun. Tom's task was to find a new bank.

This was just one of many challenges faced by Tom during his lifetime. His story is closely interwoven with the challenges as well as the opportunities that confronted Bunnings, but not just those of Bunnings alone, for its fortunes were directly integrated with the development of Western Australia throughout the entire period, from the company's beginnings in the 1880s under his father, Robert, through until and beyond when Tom's story ends in 1991.

Tom thrived upon creating his own challenges. As a youngster he built his own crystal set (radio), taught himself to play the clarinet, snuck onto a small local golf course as a teenager, and within a few years became a scratch handicap golfer. His father would not let him attend university. His response was to achieve accountancy qualifications in record time via a correspondence course. Even during his final few years, his mind was sharp. He became intrigued by the opportunities created by the emergence of the personal computer, digesting any information he could find on programming and processing data.

Other challenges were thrust upon him. Within a few weeks of arriving in Singapore in January 1942 with members of the 2/4th Machine Gun Battalion, which he had developed into a capable fighting unit, his task for the next three and a half years became one of maintaining the morale and self-esteem of those malnourished troops under his command – all in a frustrating environment of potential despair in the Changi prisoner of war (POW) camp. These efforts are recorded in an amazing diary which he maintained and kept secure throughout his incarceration in the form of a letter to my mother Margot.

Soon after the war an important period of Bunnings expansion began, led by Tom and brother Charles as joint managing directors. It was an unusual, normally high-risk, but remarkably successful partnership that continued for more than twenty years. Charles managed the production operations, and Tom sales, distribution and finance. The partnership flourished through mutual respect, with Tom as the younger brother deferring to Charles as the company's senior spokesman, but being the voice of reason when a cool head was needed.

One of Tom's lifelong passions outside business was golf. He particularly loved the challenge of match play, often beating players rated above him. Amateur golf was then quite a big deal, because there were few professionals and few professional events in Australia, let alone in Perth. Whilst not a long hitter, he could be intimidating on the greens, deadly with any putt inside 3 metres. His business commitments limited his participation in major events. However, they did not prevent State representation twice and being its team captain once, plus three Cottesloe championships, the last twenty-seven years after his first win.

Tom also accepted the challenges of non-executive company-directorship roles and leadership of community-based projects and organisations. He continued to be sought after for his wise counsel by organisations such as Scotch College, Cottesloe Golf Club, as well as Bunnings, long after his official leadership roles ended.

What was behind Tom's long and varied career of commitment and leadership in the community? How did he manage to achieve so much? Joseph Christensen explains in these pages how aligned Tom's motivation and personal development were with the opportunities and challenges which accompanied the growth of WA and the national economy. Tom provides an insight into his own principles and aspirations when outlining in his war diary his hopes and expectations of me. They were a direct articulation of his own priorities, some of which circumstances had denied him as a child.

His list of achievements would not have been accomplished without great support from our mother Margot (or 'MumBun' as she was known by the next generation). Margot was widely respected, particularly among the arts community, in the 60s, 70s and 80s, a period when Tom was at the peak of his career. Sue's and my memories as children were of the constant stream of 'significant' people, many from interstate and overseas, passing through our home. Margot could be formidable when expressing her opinions and would ask questions of visitors which Tom and others were not game to ask. We were included in these dinner events as we grew older. They led a very active social life separate from Tom's business life and had many friends at home and abroad especially through their golfing interests.

Gavin Macrae Bunning (Bunning Family Collection)

They travelled together regularly, catching up with their many friends in the USA and the UK.

One of Tom's characteristics that was noticeable to Sue and me as children was his extraordinary self-discipline. The day began with a cold shower throughout all seasons, followed by an exercise routine in his dressing room. Shoes were cleaned, morning breakfast was consumed while reading the day's headlines, car windscreen was wiped. Often, he would hit a few balls at the golf club on his way to or from the office. In the evening, he was home by 6:45 pm after an occasional beer with friends at the Weld Club. Always a whisky with Margot and then dinner, after which he would retire to his study together with Margot reading nearby.

This routine might have been one for a mundane person leading an uninteresting life. For Tom, it was his means of allocating regular family time, dealing efficiently with routine chores, then ensuring that his mind was clear for the working day responsibilities.

In the chapters to follow, Joseph Christensen has followed Tom's life, blending firstly father Robert's, then his activities and achievements into context with major events and periods of Western Australia's development, as the State grew from a tiny colony in 1886 – the year Tom's father Robert and his brother Arthur arrived from England – to the diverse and prosperous community of the late 1980s. Sue and I are indebted to Joe for his exceptional level of research, and for the resulting insight which he conveys about Tom Bunning, who devoted much of his life to the company which bore his name and thrived under his leadership; but who was much more than just a Bunnings man.

Gavin Bunning
March 2025

1

An unplanned beginning

PERTH WAS SHIVERING through a cold and wet winter when, on 20 July 1910, Gavin MacRae Bunning was born to Robert and Helen Bunning at their home, Innerhadden, in the suburb of Mosman Park. There had been hailstorms that day in the Southwest and southern districts of Western Australia and the heaviest snowfalls in living memory.[1] The fireplace at Innerhadden would have provided comfort to Helen in those early days. It was here she decided their second son would be named Gavin, although his father's preference for Tom took hold from the beginning and became the name by which he was known throughout his life. He was Tom to his family and friends, Tom Bunning the well-known golfer in the sporting columns of Perth newspapers, and even 'Mr Tom' – when not the more formal 'Mr Bunning' – in the yards and mills of the family firm, Bunning Bros, across Western Australia.[2]

A successful builder and timber merchant, Robert Bunning (b. 1859) had acquired his riverside estate a few years earlier to cater for his growing family. He now had seven children – five with Helen and two from an earlier marriage that had ended in tragedy in his late twenties. All of it had come from an unplanned beginning in Western Australia. As a young man of twenty-one, he had travelled from England with his younger brother Arthur (b. 1863), aboard the SS *Elderslie*, intending to visit their sister, Jenny, before continuing on to meet other relatives in Melbourne. Their ultimate destination was America's Pacific Coast, where the

London-born brothers would set about making their fortunes. Yet despite its isolation and a meagre settler population of 40,000, with only 8,000 in Perth, there were opportunities available for skilled tradesmen in this corner of the British Empire. A railway from Perth to the inland towns of York and Northam had recently opened, and the announcement of new lines linking York to Albany and Guildford to Geraldton foreshadowed economic development on a scale that had previously eluded the far-flung colony. Gold discoveries at Halls Creek in the Kimberley, followed by those in the Pilbara and Murchison, were helping to open up the colony's vast northern districts. Robert and Arthur had barely stepped ashore when the Western Australian Government called for tenders for additions to the convict-built lunatic asylum at Fremantle. 'Let's have a go', Robert suggested to Arthur. Both had been trained as carpenters by their father, Joseph, and Robert was confident they could handle the job. In November 1886, they were awarded the contract for £555.[3]

The 'Bunning Bros', as they called themselves, had no sooner finished their work on the Fremantle asylum than another successful tender saw them travelling to the remote northwest to construct a new hospital at Roebourne. This was followed by contracts to rebuild the town's post office, which still stands today, and construct a lighthouse keeper's quarters at the adjoining port of Cossack. A new railway station at North Fremantle had been finished on a trip back to Perth in the interim. The requirements of these commissions led Bunning Bros to branch out into the supply of building materials. Perth Sawmills, a small yet busy operation, was established by the end of the 1880s on Goderich Street.[4] A brickworks was acquired in East Perth soon after. They returned north in 1890 to make additions to the Government Resident's quarters at Roebourne and build post offices in the frontier settlements of Fitzroy Crossing and Halls Creek. In 1892, they built a new headquarters for the Weld Club in Barrack Street, where Tom would become president over seventy years later.[5] The rush to the eastern goldfields was underway, and with their reputations as builders established, the brothers were flooded with commissions. These included Trinity Church on St George's Terrace, a soap factory in North Fremantle, the station master's residence at Midland, and additions to the Legislative Assembly, the museum and Perth's main railway station. Hospitals in the new mining towns of Coolgardie and Kalgoorlie followed. Their largest commission yet, for extensions to the Perth Hospital, was completed in 1895. A year later they constructed one of Perth's grandest homes, Tukurua, along Cottesloe's Marine Parade, for the lawmaker Septimus Burt. It was purchased by the mining magnate Andrew Forrest in 2015 to form part of his domestic 'estate'.[6]

In 1889, Robert had married Gena Taylor while on a trip home to England. Their marriage produced Tom's siblings, Gena and Joe. In early 1897, a second son, David, was born. Only a short time later, Gena came down with gastroenteritis and rapidly succumbed, followed two weeks later by their infant child. A typhoid epidemic had swept through Perth that summer, and it was possibly the true cause of both deaths. It was a bitter blow for Robert, who had been carrying the burden of managing his contracting business single-handed and was frequently away from home as a result. Some years earlier, Arthur had been thrown from a horse on a hunting excursion during a visit to the colony's northwest and, badly injured, he had returned to England to recuperate. From this time on, Arthur's role in the business declined. He never fully recovered from his accident and eventually moved to Victoria, leaving the company entirely in his brother's hands.[7]

During the 1890s, Robert had become frustrated by the difficulty of sourcing timber for his building contracts. The local sawmilling industry was dominated by British-owned companies that were content to send their production back to the lucrative home market, much of it for railway sleepers and as blocks for street paving. As a result, many of the houses being built around Perth had roofs framed with Douglas Fir imported from the United States and Canada. This led Robert to look for opportunities to source his own timber. Shortly before Gena died, he had purchased a small sawmill on a concession of two square miles at North Dandalup, in the Darling Range south of Perth. He briefly considered bundling it for sale with Perth Sawmills and began exploring plans to float a goldmine at Boulder. But, unable to secure either buyers for his sawmills or backers for his mine, he instead settled on expanding his investments in the production of building materials. By 1900, he had entered into partnerships that owned brickyards at Claisebrook, Belmont, Bellevue and Glen Forrest, and limekilns in the area around Fremantle. He also owned a yard at Fremantle to handle his firms' timber imports.[8]

Holding on to his sawmills was soon looking like the right move. The Perth operation was so busy it was attracting complaints from neighbouring retailers about all the sawdust it produced, prompting Robert to relocate it to larger premises along Wellington Street. At the beginning, the business had focused on machining joinery products like architraves, mouldings, frames and doors from imported softwoods such as New Zealand kauri, Californian redwood and Baltic pine. With a two-acre yard and the railway adjacent, it was now possible to store structural timber in quantity. The operation had separate yards for imported timber and jarrah (*Eucalyptus marginata*), a mill containing a gangsaw, bandsaw, circular saws and planers, and a workshop with lathes, sharpeners, and benches for the carpenters and joiners. The firm was now able supply its own sawn hardwoods as cheaply as any competitor, with a reputation for fair prices, quality work and reliability.[9] This helped it to win some of the more prestigious contracts on offer, completing timberwork for the new state parliament and His Majesty's Theatre, and winning the right to supply native timbers for a commemorative casket presented to Queen Victoria for her diamond jubilee, and for displays at Western Australia's entries to international exhibitions in Paris and Edinburgh.[10]

With this growing operation to manage, Robert had put any thought of remarriage on hold. But this changed on a trip home in July 1902, when he met Helen MacRae, the daughter of Charles MacRae, the publican and proprietor of 'Bunrannoch' in Kinloch Rannoch, a village in the highlands of Perthshire. The pair wed a month later in Edinburgh, and in October she accompanied Robert back to Perth, WA. The couple's first child, Flora (Bun to the family), arrived the following year. It was at this time that Robert settled on Innerhadden as his family's home. The three-acre property, bounded by Bay View Terrace, Johnston Street and Palmerston Street, where St Hilda's Anglican School for Girls is today, was purchased and renamed by Helen after an estate in her Scottish homeland. Designed by the architect and engineer James William Wright, the house was in the bungalow-style and faced the river, with a tennis court and sunken garden at the front and surrounded by lawns shaded by fig trees and pines. There were stables and outhouses at the rear and paddocks for horses and the family's cow.[11] To one side, they had a farm owned by the family of the Fremantle merchant Lionel Samson, and to the other, the Buckland House residence of the doctor Adam Jameson. There was still plenty of bush around Buckland Hill and the area between the river and the Perth–Fremantle Road, lending their new home a quiet, semi-rural feel. The household included a gardener, a nurse for the younger children, and a cook, housemaid and laundress to assist Helen. In 1905 the couple welcomed their first son, Charles (Charlie).[12]

Innerhadden (Bunning Family Collection)

Innerhadden, taken from St Hilda's Boarding House (Courtesy Sally Campbell)

By this stage, Robert had shut down the mill at North Dandalup. There was no prospect of extending his concession in this district, and after the export market for jarrah fell away in the early 1900s, it was more economical to purchase the hardwoods needed at Perth Sawmills from other producers. It helped that he got along well with many of them. Some were even among his closest friends. Frank Wilson, one-time manager of the Canning Timber Company, was one of them; he had been travelling with Wilson in Scotland when he met Helen for the first time.[13] But he soon regretted his decision to shut the mill. When the market began its downturn, eight local timber companies, each owned largely by British capitalists, merged into a new conglomerate, the Millars' Karri and Jarrah Company. Known as the 'combine', it controlled twenty-seven sawmills and held logging concessions over nearly 400,000 hectares of prime jarrah and karri (*Eucalyptus diversicolor*) forest.[14] Overnight, it had gained a near-monopoly on the supply of hardwoods in Western Australia. Though his own operation was still able to import timber for some applications, Robert had no choice but to accept the combine's terms when it came to obtaining jarrah.[15]

Confronted by a virtual monopoly of the export trade, the state government ordered a royal commission into the timber industry in 1903. As part of a wide-ranging inquiry, it set out to investigate not only the supply of hardwoods but also the long-term management and conservation of forest resources. It also gave Robert an opportunity to speak on behalf of local timber merchants and would eventually create the conditions for his return to sawmilling. He told the commission that small, independent producers could best compete against Millars if more of the state's vast timber reserves were opened to them: 'I think we, as well as the Combine, should have a right to take up land, under restrictions as to working the mill and cutting the timber. The land should not be locked up against us'.[16] To promote private enterprise at the same time as safeguarding forest resources for long-term harvests, the commission recommended a permit system that would grant rights to cut timber in proportion to the production capacity of existing sawmills. Large areas of jarrah and karri forest would be reserved for the industry by preventing agricultural settlement, Millars would keep its expansive long-term leases, and the door would be opened for logging by others under the new permit system.[17]

This was the opening Robert needed to make up for the closure of the mill at North Dandalup. Making bricks was a profitable enterprise, but it was a

AN UNPLANNED BEGINNING

trade crowded with small-scale producers, and it tied up capital he could use elsewhere. During 1905, he and Arthur sold off their brickyards and looked to buy back into timber production. An opportunity soon came at Lion Mill, an old milling town established to cut sleepers for the railway linking Perth to the goldfields that promised a renewed future through the release of surrounding jarrah forest previously owned by the Midland Railway Company. Two small mills had been recently re-established, and Robert now sought to acquire them. With Arthur, he incorporated a new firm, Perth Jarrah Mills, at the end of 1905. In effect, this was a partnership with William Smith, the owner of the mill over which Perth Jarrah Mills now took control. A year later, the syndicate scooped up the second mill before relocating its production to Lion Mill. The consolidated operation employed fifty men altogether and provided work for an additional twenty bush fellers. The accompanying permits covered 30,000 acres of northern jarrah forest.[18] Though not large by the industry's standards, it was nonetheless a significant step up from Robert's initial foray into sawmilling.

Although it was impossible to foresee, these business dealings were to shape Tom's later life in other ways as well. Robert Law, his future father-in-law, was part of the syndicate that purchased Robert Bunning's brickyards. As business associates they had much in common. Both had settled in Western Australia in the 1880s and worked initially as building contractors. In Robert Law's case, this involved moving on from his family's business constructing railways and bridges both in Victoria, where he had been born in 1867, and later in South Australia. He was awarded the construction of part of Perth's sewerage system, but as he was not yet twenty-one, his father had to come from Melbourne to sign the contract on his behalf. During the late 1890s, he and a partner, William Atkins, built jetties at Fremantle, Rockingham and practically every port north of the capital, contributed to new railways between Perth and Pinjarra and Brunswick and Collie in the southwest, and constructed major buildings in the city, including the Perth Mint, the Perth Boy's School, and the emporium of Boan Brothers, one of the colony's largest retailers.[19] As substantial users of bricks and timber, branching into the building-supplies trade was a natural ancillary. The pair acquired a timber mill at Roleystone in the mid-1890s, before purchasing a brickworks at Helena Vale in 1905. Later that year, the purchase of Robert Bunning's four small brickyards was settled.[20] Law and Atkins also bought into a partnership operating a brickworks at Cardup, alongside the Bunbury railway line near Armadale.[21]

Robert Bunning would not live to see his youngest son marry Robert Law's third daughter, though the two nonetheless felt a certain affinity. As migrants that had prospered in the roaring days of the 1890s, they belonged to a business class that stood apart from the propertied descendants of the 'ancient colonists' that had founded the Swan River Colony. Without substantial land or buildings to borrow against, each was obliged to navigate difficult paths to finance their commercial undertakings. Australian banks had been cautious lenders ever since the Depression of 1893, which, despite having largely bypassed Western Australia on account of the gold rush, still cast a long shadow by way of a reluctance to loan depositors' money for anything other than land or buildings.[22] Robert Law experienced this first-hand only a year after investing in the Cardup brickworks, when a slump in residential construction and a fraught relationship between the works' owners and managers induced the state manager of the National Australasian Bank, Robert England, to foreclose on the partnership's account.[23] In contrast, with financial backing for Lion Mill, and sufficient orders from mining and agricultural districts to keep Perth Sawmills running, Robert Bunning was able to survive the downturn. But if there was a lesson for him in his contemporary's experience, it was to keep a careful eye on the overdraft with the bank, lest a similar fate befall his sawmilling and timber-trading businesses.

The priority at Lion Mill was to increase output by working through the valuable stands of jarrah left untouched during the initial phase of logging. To facilitate the movement of logs to the sawmill, a second-hand steam engine was purchased from the Mount Lyell mine in Tasmania. 'Dirty Mary', as the locomotive was soon known, was capable of hauling loads up high grades in the rugged Darling Ranges.[24] (Tom's son Gavin recalls climbing onto Dirty Mary as a teenager after she was laid up at the Argyle Mill site. By the 1950s, it was the only remaining evidence of this mill's existence.) Robert was soon on the lookout for new mills to acquire. Although his Perth timber yard had an adequate supply of jarrah for its needs, there were opportunities to fill small orders for interstate and overseas customers, and he could see potential in the independent and mostly under-capitalised mills he was competing against.[25] With the prospect of cutting loads for export in the offing, he doubled-down on his move into sawmilling. The next acquisition was a mill at Argyle, near Donnybrook, that had been established some years earlier to supply timber to the goldfields. Lyall's Mill, a rather neglected mill near Collie, was taken over in 1907. A railway to the nearby coal mine at Cardiff had recently been completed, and Robert's plan was to survey and build a connecting line to his new sawmill.[26] To help build his activities as a timber merchant, he also purchased a timber yard close to the harbour at Bunbury.[27]

By these steps, Robert consolidated his standing in the timber industry. He was well-liked by his peers and had recently served as president of the state's Timber Merchants' Association. Arthur had largely stepped back from the firm's affairs since his accident, though the pair remained partners as their operations expanded. They employed seventy men at their city operation, eighty at Lyall's Mill and forty at Argyle, in addition to those at the yards in Fremantle and Bunbury, and the workforce at Lion Mill.[28] What they needed now was capital to develop their mills and expand their activities in the manufacture and sale of timber products. In April 1907 they incorporated Bunning Bros Ltd, adopting the name they had first used as building contractors. The firm had a paid-up capital of £45,000 (the equivalent of $8.2 million in 2024) and five investors, with Arthur and Robert being joined by their accountant, Walter Collins, and two silent partners in the local businessmen Frederick Williamson and Joseph White. Robert would be the managing director on a permanent basis. Perth Jarrah Mills would remain a separate entity for the ownership of Lion Mill, and it would carry on its sideline in the supply of firewood to Perth and its suburbs.[29]

The rewards of a flourishing career were accumulating. Robert had assembled a portfolio of properties in Perth, the southwest and the goldfields, vacant land at the edges of suburbia, and shares in some of Western Australia's largest manufacturing concerns.[30] He kept a houseboat moored in the Swan River and owned one of Perth's first motor cars, registered as Cottesloe Beach Road Board No. 1, with a chauffeur employed to drive him about in it.[31]

Robert and Helen welcomed their third child, Jane, in 1906, followed by another daughter, Marion Adelin (better known as Angie), two years later. As his young family multiplied, Robert took out a lease over an orchard in a quiet valley at Bedfordale, in the hills behind Armadale. It was somewhere to escape to on weekends, where the children could pick oranges and help Helen to make marmalade.[32] At Innerhadden, Helen could draw on the assistance of the cook, housemaid and laundress, and the gardener to look after the grounds. She was

Helen and Robert Bunning (Courtesy Sally Campbell)

an accomplished pianist, and Flora had also shown the ability to play. The eldest children, Gena and Joe, had been sent overseas for their schooling: Joe was at Uppingham, one of the best public schools in England. For a self-made man in a remote and still under-developed corner of the British Empire, these were indeed the trappings of success.

The reality, however, was that this success was hard-won. Inevitably, Bunning Bros was encountering growing pains, which were proving difficult to manage. Supplying the local building trades meant timber needed to be let go on credit, to be paid for when the building in question was complete. Exports were generally paid for in cash at the docks, but with almost all timber still carried aboard sailing ships, there was a degree of uncertainty with payment here as well. It left the firm reliant on its overdraft, and their account was at the same bank that had

Jane, Charles, Tom, Helen, Angie and Flora Bunning, c. 1910 (Bunning Family Collection)

recently lost patience with the company running the Cardup brickyard. Before long, Robert Bunning was feeling a similar pressure. At the beginning of 1908, construction began on the railway at Lyall's Mill. It had been a more-complex piece of engineering than anticipated, and the cost in materials and labour would exceed £6,500.[33] Then, mid-year, the firm delivered timber worth £550 for repairs to, and widening of, the jarrah-pile traffic bridge at North Fremantle. Unfortunately, the municipal authority had exhausted its available funds on labour and other materials and couldn't pay the bill. Bunning Bros was forced to issue a writ against the Mayor of Fremantle for the outstanding payment.[34] There was a pressing need for it. Robert's practice had always been to pay his workers monthly, visiting each mill in person to distribute wages in cash. But during 1908 he twice ran late with the men's pay. Clearly, liquidity was becoming a problem.

There were fresh challenges to contend with later that year. Bunning Bros had so far avoided industrial troubles, even as strikes had broken out at other mills over wages and conditions. The industry was, however, becoming better organised, and towards the end of 1908 the Timber Workers Union began pushing for higher rates of pay. The men at Argyle were soon threatening to stand down unless conditions improved. A strike was averted, but their case would go to arbitration. In the meantime, a fatal accident at Lyall's Mill did nothing to quell the tensions that had been simmering.[35] The new railway was proving more expensive than anticipated, after the steam engine Robert purchased for it proved unable to cope with the steep gradients and had to be replaced with a more powerful locomotive. At the bank, the state manager, Robert England, was losing faith. In November 1909, he called in the firm's debts and refused to honour any more of its cheques.[36]

Bunning Bros was in a fraught position indeed. Without finance, the firm would be forced back to its shareholders for additional funds or into selling off the assets it had steadily accumulated. When England foreclosed on his partnership, Robert Law had used his own money to buy out its debts and assume control over the Cardup brickworks. Robert Bunning decided upon a different course of action. He turned instead to the Melbourne financiers Alfred and Emanuel Abrahams for the funds needed to maintain his business operations. Negotiating through Louis, their Perth-based brother and agent, Robert secured a loan for £15,475 against the land, life-insurance policies and other interests that he and Arthur owned. Interest would be charged at ten per cent, falling to eight per cent if the loan was paid quarterly by a specified date, with a provision to increase borrowing up to £21,000 on additional security.[37] Robert was out of his immediate predicament, though it was hardly a desirable position to be in. He could at least take consolation in the fact that, away from the office, Helen had fallen pregnant again. As his fiftieth birthday approached, he was looking forward to welcoming a seventh child.

On the day that Tom arrived into the world, the *West Australian* ran an interview with the state premier, Sir Newton Moore. Just returned from England, he had been among the last Commonwealth statesmen to be received by Edward VII, and he was still in London when the King passed away in May 1910. Moore's purpose abroad had been to attract immigrants and capital to drive economic growth and expand settlement into new districts, as he now reminded his constituents. 'Western Australia wants to become quickly what it must become eventually, the biggest, richest, and most prosperous State of the Commonwealth', he explained. Against the backdrop of expansion stretching back to the mid-1880s, such visions were by no means outlandish and reflected the optimism that was the hallmark of the Edwardian era. The state, he continued, needed immigration and investment from the home country: 'We want capital to open up the country and people to develop it', Moore said, and migration should come first: 'At whatever cost Western Australia must have men and women and I stick to that…we cannot get the money if we haven't got the people'.[38] The settler population stood at 276,000 in 1910, a sevenfold increase since Robert had decided to stay on in Western Australia, and Moore was signalling that his government would make every effort to keep the population growing.

As he read the newspaper that cold July morning, then, there was a reason to feel reassured that he was making the right moves for his family and himself. Resorting to a moneylender was doubtless an expediency he would rather have avoided, and it would be an encumbrance overshadowing Bunning Bros for some time to come. But it was a calculated gamble, and one that resonated with the Premier's outlook for the state. Western Australia was still in the infancy of its economic development and a great future lay ahead. That population growth and capital investment were the keys to unlocking it was never in doubt. If there was any difference in their positions, it was that Moore was looking to London for the finance needed to develop primary industries, whereas Robert had embarked on the more entrepreneurial route of re-invested profits, partnerships and now, courtesy of the Abrahams, an added element of risk. What justified it was the prospects of the industry he was part of. That year, timber worth £918,000 was exported, behind only gold and wool in the state's economy.[39] Sawmilling permits extended across 617,000 acres, in addition to the 1.5 million acres of leases held by Millars, yet these were only partly logged and together accounted for less than a quarter of the southwest's forests.[40] Bunning Bros continued to focus on the supply of timber products to the building and construction trades, although beyond the limited domestic market, Robert had been jostling to vie for export orders. With a new line of credit secured, he had every reason to stay the course.

Business was soon looking up again. At Argyle, road paving blocks were being cut and delivered for the overseas market. Extensions of the mill's railways into untouched sections of forest were soon underway.[41] The industry was bristling with renewed optimism as the state's wheatlands were opening up, fuelling demand for timber in housing and as sleepers in the new agricultural railways. Moreover, the Commonwealth parliament was set to approve construction of

1,000 miles (1,600 km) of the new transcontinental railway.[42] There was talk of building a plant at Bunbury for the powellising treatment of karri against termites and dry rot to enhance its value to the sleeper trade.[43] Early in 1911, Robert renewed his acquaintance with Robert Law when the pair became partners in a new venture. The company, Wilgarup Karri and Jarrah Company, would build and operate a sawmill at Jardanup (later renamed Jardee).[44] There was something of a rush underway for permits in the untouched belt of karri in the districts surrounding the small town of Manjimup, and neither of them wanted to miss out.

For Robert Law, these were also prosperous years. With his business partner Atkins, he established a ceramics factory, the Stoneware Pipe and Pottery Company. Law then won a major contract to supply the mains and drainage pipes that would be required for Perth's first modern sewerage system.[45] To produce these on the scale required, he set up another enterprise, the Monier Patent Propriety Company, in 1911. His standing in the industry was

Robert Law (Courtesy Elizabeth Green)

acknowledged through his election as the first President of the Master Builders and Contractors' Association in Western Australia.⁴⁶ Earlier, in 1903, when aged 36, he had married 18-year-old Pauline Bertha Brooking, and he was now a father of three – a daughter, Muriel (b. 1904), and two sons, Gordon (1906) and Dudley (1908). A second daughter, Kathleen, was born during 1911. At this time, the family moved to the newly built Lexbourne House, along Colin Street in West Perth. This was a palatial residence, with dining and living spaces downstairs and a grand staircase of polished timber leading to the upstairs bedrooms. There was a live-in cook, nanny and two housemaids, and a gardener and chauffeur were regularly on hand. The grounds occupied more than an acre and included a sunken garden and an aviary (both of which remain in place today) and a tennis court. Kathleen died at a young age, though Robert and Pauline would welcome two more children to their new home. Margot – Tom's future wife – was born on 23 May 1914. A final daughter, Mary, arrived in 1923.⁴⁷

Pauline Bertha Law (Courtesy Elizabeth Green)

In brickmaking, Law was going from strength to strength. He had sold off the troubled Cardup works and focused on building capacity at the Helena Vale operation he now operated solo, having dissolved, on amicable terms, the original partnership with Atkins. A modern kiln was soon installed, increasing annual capacity to some eight million bricks. In 1913, he seized on the opportunity to purchase a rival pressed-brick operation at Armadale, capable of turning out another five million each year. With these moves, Law became the largest single manufacturer of bricks in Western Australia, and all of it was a private concern.[48]

For Robert Bunning, on the other hand, the tide was turning in the wrong direction once again. Shortly after Tom's birth, his old and dear friend, Frank Wilson, had succeeded Moore as state premier.[49] Barely a year later, it became clear this would be the last of the Liberal ministries that had held power since the beginning of responsible government more than two decades earlier. In October 1911, a new Labor government, under the leadership of John Scaddan, was swept to power in Western Australia. Since the gold rush, the nexus between state development and free enterprise had underpinned the rise of firms like Bunning Bros and the various enterprises Law was involved in.[50] But the new government had very different ideas about what constituted a level playing field. Its plan was to prevent price-fixing and 'profiteering' and thereby reduce the cost of living for its constituency, the working class of Perth and the goldfields, by establishing 'state trading' concerns, or what amounted to 'state socialism', to compete against free enterprise. This would occur in almost every sector – there would be state hotels, state dairies, a state meatworks, a fishing enterprise, an agricultural equipment manufacturer, a new State Shipping Service, and, in the building materials industry, a state brickworks, state quarry and state sawmills. Scaddan perceived that the latter would achieve a reduction in the cost of timber products for workers' homes, one of his signature policies. The government also had an eye to supplying sleepers for the transcontinental railway.[51] This would help it to enter into sawmilling on a large scale and break up the power held by Millars in Western Australia.

The industry was beginning to look crowded with bigger players. During 1912, the powerful New Zealand-based, Melbourne-controlled timber exporter, Kauri Timber Company, bought a sawmill at Nannup that was attached to a large permit area and had its own railway to the jetty at Busselton. It soon built a second, modern mill between Nannup and Bridgetown.[52] In a stroke, Kauri had acquired permits over an area equivalent to the total area Robert Bunning had accumulated over the past decade, much of it comprising virgin jarrah and karri forest. With an order for well over a million sleepers on the books, the new State Sawmills operation at Deanmill, near Manjimup, began production in December 1913, followed by two further mills at Pemberton early in the new year. For the more speculative enterprises, the writing was on the wall. The Wilgarup Karri and Jarrah Company was duly sold off to Millars.[53] It scarcely mattered to Robert Law, beyond marking the end of his interest in timber. To Robert Bunning, the lesson was to focus on milling jarrah and the small quantities of other native hardwoods for which there were niche markets. There would be no move back into the karri forest until Tom was an adult. Neither his father nor future father-in-law would have taken any consolation when the new Commonwealth Government removed a large portion of the sleeper contract awarded to the State Sawmills and handed it over to Millars.[54]

During 1913, Bunning Bros took over another modest jarrah sawmill at Noggerup, in the Preston Valley east of Donnybrook. A mill was set up along the railway at Muja to cut wandoo (a very hard timber also known as white gum) a short time later.[55] They had become the first local timber company to import a bandsaw, installed at Lion Mill, and the first to experiment with drying kilns, which Robert had insisted be trialled at Lyall's Mill.[56] The operation at Wellington Street remained the company's centre of operations. It maintained about seventy men on the payroll, comprising a small team of clerks and the rest mainly carpenters and joiners, who turned out structural timber, flooring, mouldings, linings and other products for the building trades. These, and the imported softwoods Bunning Bros had always handled, were sold from its city headquarters or the yards at Fremantle and Bunbury. Its main competitors in this market were Millars and Whittaker Bros, a family-run firm of similar size but more diverse in the timber products and building supplies it carried.[57]

It had taken one-quarter of a century to reach this position. Robert's fortunes had varied across this period, as was the way of commerce, though on the whole he had prospered handsomely. But the new year would bring the biggest setback of his career. In the early hours of 21 January 1914, as the family lay asleep at Innerhadden, a fire took hold at Wellington Street. When the alarm was raised at dawn it had become a conflagration as intense as any fire yet experienced in Perth. From 'all parts of the city, tongues of flame and columns of heavy dark smoke could be seen wreathing heavenward', reported the *West Australian*, 'the brilliant reflection of the conflagration illuminating the scene for miles round'.[58] The glare woke residents in the surrounding suburbs, and a crowd of 3,000 people was soon on hand to observe the unfolding drama. The full complement of the city's firefighting service could do little to extinguish the fire, and within an hour the entire premises was ablaze, along with several adjoining cottages. Across the road, St John's Church of England was badly damaged, and the network of telephone lines and power cables running past lay in tangled ruins, adding to the chaos and delaying publication of that morning's newspaper.[59] There had never been anything quite like it, and for days afterwards, Perth's picture theatres displayed photographs of the disaster for those who had missed it first-hand.[60] There was nothing to do but take whatever could be salvaged and relocate it at a vacant lot on nearby Charles Street, where the task of rebuilding began.

Only months later, another crisis sprang up. The company had long put the pay disputes at its sawmills in the past and generally maintained a good relationship with its workers, in contrast to Millars, where industrial relations were far more fraught.[61] Now, however, the entire industry was being dragged into strife. The trouble began in April, when a number of carpenters at Millars refused to work with non-union labour and went out on strike. The rest of the building trades then refused to work with any materials Millars supplied.[62] When, only weeks later, carpenters and joiners at both Bunning Bros and Whittakers looked set to also insist on a closed shop, the three firms caught up in the dispute announced an immediate halt to trading. 'We are closing the yards because we are turning out work and it has ceased to be profitable', Robert explained to the press.[63] Some 500 men were now out of work, and the industry was at a standstill in the metropolitan area. The government, though unsympathetic to the strikers, would not stand for what it viewed as a lock-out, and took the three companies to the Court of Arbitration. Bunning Bros had their case dismissed, and the matter was eventually resolved through arbitration by mid-June, aided by the more-militant unionists leaving for jobs elsewhere.[64] It had been a bitter dispute, and with longstanding calls for a 44-hour working week still unresolved, further trouble could not be discounted. But only days later, the outbreak of war in Europe pushed the issue firmly to one side.

Robert now had new problems to contend with. Large quantities of imported softwoods had been destroyed in the fire, and the immediate shock to

AN UNPLANNED BEGINNING

global trade and the restrictions on shipping made it difficult to rebuild stocks, especially when it came to Baltic pine. Machinery and tools to replace the losses at Wellington Street would also face delays in arriving from overseas. There would be diminishing demand locally for all kinds of timber, and export markets were rapidly drying up as well. By the end of 1914, Bunning Bros was in trouble. There had been as many as 300 men on the payroll, and although the rush to enlist in the military had reduced this slightly, it was inevitable that others would have to be laid off. In the Southwest, the new sawmill at Noggerup was closed down, followed by the mill at Muja, then Argyle.[65] Yet even these cutbacks were not enough for the company to remain solvent. Robert's only option was to turn back to the Abrahams brothers for a new loan. They were willing to lend to him but on terms far less favourable than before. He had now mortgaged the bulk of his assets and was borrowing at a rate of twenty per cent.[66]

Robert was away from home often during Tom's formative years, and even when he wasn't, he was often kept at the office until late in the evening. Tom could go for many days without so much as seeing him, and this likely contributed to the special bond he maintained with Helen for the rest of her life. It was only much later, as he spoke with Charlie or listened to the company's old timers reminisce, that Tom came to understand the risks his father had taken in these years and the obstacles he had navigated to keep his vision for Bunning Bros alive. That his sons would one day inherit the business was something Robert never doubted. From a young age, he made sure that Charlie and Tom would accompany him at least once a year on a visit to one of the sawmills, up the eastern railway through Greenmount to Lion's Mill or down the Bunbury line to Brunswick Junction to change trains for Lyall's Mill.[67] Each occasion was always a memorable affair. A sawmill was a lively and bustling place, with the steam engines hauling logs down the line and the shrill scream of the saws, the men hard at work and the smell of freshly sawn timber heavy in the air. Essential experiences for a timber merchant's son, these were visits that long remained fixed in his mind.

2

Bonza times

Tom Bunning belonged to the generation that spent its formative years growing up under the shadow of the First World War, before an adolescence shaped by the prosperity of the 1920s. Although too young to appreciate the magnitude of the distant conflict, its legacy was inescapable during his early years. Memorials to the fallen were erected everywhere after 1918, figuring prominently as landmarks in the city itself, at suburban centres and in all the timber towns throughout the Southwest. Anzac Day and Armistice Day services were established as annual fixtures just as Tom was starting out at his school, Scotch College, where the dining room was overlooked by an honour board listing the names of nearly five hundred old boys that had served in the war. Seventy-four of them had not returned, at a time when the student body was small and almost all of the boys and their families were acquainted in one way or another. It meant several of his classmates would be growing up themselves as the sons of deceased men. Three of Tom's masters at Scotch were returned servicemen, and the sporting fields where he learnt to play cricket and football had been dedicated to the fallen as 'the Memorial Grounds'. Loyalty and service to the state, the nation and the British Empire would be central to the values the school strove to impart.[1]

The winter of 1915 was an anxious time for the Bunning family, as Robert sought news of Joe's whereabouts after he was reported among the wounded at

Gallipoli.² Gentle by nature and fond of languages and the arts, Joe had been something of an unlikely recruit to the rough-and-ready army that was the Australian Imperial Force. He had nonetheless lost little time in volunteering, enlisting a fortnight after war was declared against Germany. Posted to the 11th Infantry Battalion then being formed at the Blackboy Hill training camp, he embarked in November for further training in Egypt. With his battalion, Joe landed at Anzac Cove on 25 April under fire from the Turkish defenders in the hills above. Over the frenzied days that followed, the battalion held off counterattacks on their positions, until they were relieved from the front lines after losing almost half their ranks as casualties.³ As they were preparing to stand down, Joe sustained a gunshot wound to his left wrist. Hospitalisation in Alexandria was followed by a spell of recuperation in Birmingham, England, where he was finally able to send a telegram home, before a discharge on medical grounds was ordered. After six months away, with the Gallipoli campaign still bogged down in trench warfare, Joe returned to Perth and joined the staff at Perth Jarrah Mills.⁴

The Bunning Family, c. 1913. Back row: Joe, Flora, Helen Charles, Gena. Front Row: Jane, Robert, Tom, Angie (Courtesy Sally Campbell)

Top and bottom: Mill Waste being railed to Perth for sale as firewood by Perth Jarrah Mills (Bunning Family Collection)

This subsidiary remained nominally in control of the operation at Lion Mill and developed its firewood supply trade as a sideline to the main business carried out by Bunning Bros. It had small yards in suburban Subiaco, Cottesloe, Fremantle and Victoria Park, and a workforce of deliverymen, who were still using horse and cart to deliver the firewood that came from mill waste and second-rate timber to the customers. Soon promoted to manager, it was a role Joe was content to remain in, and it became practically a sinecure position for him as the firewood side of the business declined.[5]

For Bunning Bros, the difficulties caused by the war were multiplying. A contract to supply timber for army huts at Alexandria helped greatly, but with the collapse of regular export markets and a protracted downturn in the local building trade, on top of the losses sustained at Wellington Street, Robert was forced back to the Abrahams brothers for the cash he needed to stay afloat. They were not the kind to take pity on clients in distress.[6] Interest on new loans would be charged at twenty per cent. The relationship had already become strained after it was found that a £500 loan from mid-1911 had been recorded in the company's books without any payment ever being received. It was a clerical mix-up that had long gone unnoticed, and when eventually it was, Louis Abrahams refused to cancel it. The matter rankled with Robert, but there was no other solution to

Perth Jarrah Mill's fleet of delivery trucks in the 1930s (Bunning Family Collection)

his shortage of cash than to borrow even more against the company's real estate, timber and sawmilling assets. A restriction on high-interest loans under the *War Precautions Act* provided some relief, by reducing the monthly interest bill. But as the war dragged on, Bunning Bros was drawing closer to the brink of insolvency.

The relationship with his financiers, already fraught, was about to deteriorate even further. Throughout, the company had kept Lyall's Mill running by using the jarrah it produced to replace softwoods in the manufacture of mouldings, flooring and joinery at Charles Street. But in February 1918, a fire took hold at Lyall's Mill and levelled it to the ground.[7] For Robert, the situation was as grim as when his Wellington Street facility was destroyed four years earlier. Once again, he turned to the Abrahams brothers for assistance. On this occasion, however, they were not prepared to help. The mill had been mortgaged to them as security for a past loan and they decided to keep the insurance payout of £2,923 for themselves. Denied the funds needed for rebuilding, he had to look elsewhere for loans to replace the buildings and machinery lost at Lyall's Mill and to reopen and extend his Muja sawmill to produce jarrah for the remainder of 1918 – a bill that came to £10,886, on top of £5,500 in losses through the fire itself. It was a galling situation because the Abrahams brothers retained the mortgage over his mills, the value of which was now enhanced at the cost of substantially higher debt.[8]

Some of his friends feared that Bunning Bros could not hold on for much longer.[9] Yet Robert retained his confidence, even at this darkest hour. The war had reinforced the importance of innovation, and he had even borrowed more than was necessary in order to build a kiln at Lyall's Mill. It was the first of its kind in Western Australia, where hardwoods had long been dried naturally.[10] With an armistice finally on the horizon, his outlook was increasingly well-justified. It would take time for labour markets and overseas shipping to recover, but the industry could look forward to renewed demand on domestic markets and a resumption to the export trade. There were other reasons for optimism in the timber industry as well. In 1916 a professional Conservator of Forests, Charles Edward Lane-Poole, had arrived in Western Australia. He had set out to reform and modernise forest policy, focusing on protecting forested lands from alienation for agriculture and regenerating areas already cut over.[11] These efforts culminated in a new *Forests Act* being introduced to parliament only weeks before the war ended and assented to early in the new year. The *Forests Act* designated almost all the South West's prime jarrah and karri resources as state forest and established a dedicated agency, the Forests Department, to manage it. A new permit system would be introduced alongside existing royalty agreements and would operate on a sustained yield basis. Reafforestation would be carried out by the department's trained silviculturists.[12] This was good for the industry and for Robert's own prospects. During 1919, he persuaded the Bank of New South Wales to take over his consolidated debts via a loan of £27,500. Bunning Bros would now be trading on a sounder footing, and freed of his liabilities to the Abrahams brothers, he could look to settle the matter of the disputed £500.[13]

Tom had by now commenced at Scotch College. With Charlie already enrolled five years ahead of him, it was the obvious choice for his schooling. Whereas Gena and Joe had been sent to England for their education, the war dictated that the younger siblings receive theirs at home. For Tom, this meant receiving his elementary schooling at Miss Annie Nisbett's school, better known simply as 'Miss Annie's', only a short walk from Innerhadden. Such small private schools remained a popular choice in neighbourhoods like Peppermint Grove or West Perth; a few years later, Margot had only to venture a short distance down Colin Street to her first school at St Mary's.[14] (The school would be progressively relocated to Karrinyup between 1966 and 1970.) By the time Tom reached Scotch, it was no longer the lesser choice to an English public school anyway. One of the four major independent boys' schools in Perth, it had a growing reputation after relocating to Swanbourne, where new classroom blocks, dormitories and a science laboratory meant the college had some of the most modern facilities available in Western Australia. In 1919, he became one of just over two hundred boys on roll.[15]

The leading figure at Scotch was its headmaster, Peter Corsar (better known as 'PC') Anderson. His influence was to have a profound effect on Tom across the next five years. Standing at an imposing 6'4", with a background in theology and ecclesiastical history, Anderson was alternately feared and revered within the college. He was admired for his fair-mindedness and love of sports, but he was a strict disciplinarian and was reputed to have had the entire school caned in an effort to stamp out smoking. He led prayers each morning, knew every boy by name, and taught classics, English and Latin in lower school.[16] Most of Tom's other masters were also figures the boys looked upon with equal measures of fear, respect and admiration. In upper school, classes in English and History were

Tom at Scotch College, 1925
(Bunning Family Collection)

taken by GG 'Bull' Campbell, a younger master who had attended Scotch himself before studying education in Melbourne and serving in the war. The science master was AC McKenzie, an Australian trained at the University of Edinburgh. Maths and sports were handled by WA 'Dang' Gardner, an Englishman who had represented his homeland at soccer.[17] Both Campbell and Gardner were still teaching during Gavin's student days at Scotch, thirty years later.

The curriculum was based on the examination system of junior and leaving certificates. For Tom, this meant that any given day might involve classes in English, history and geography, Latin or French, mathematics, physics or chemistry and physiology and hygiene. The boys could also choose from domestic science, woodwork, metalwork, technical drawing or agriculture. Outside of the classroom, there was a strong emphasis on team sports – rowing, cricket and football together occupied much of the calendar – alongside regular carnivals in athletics, swimming, shooting, gymnastics, surf lifesaving and tennis. The school also maintained a cadet corps.[18] Tom was a bright lad and although shy initially, this quickly left him as he settled in at school. More inclined towards maths and sciences than history, the classics or religion, he set his sights on a career in engineering, the occupation Charlie was also intent on following. Like most of his classmates, Tom took up boxing, though he was never one to get caught up in fistfights. ('Learn to defend yourself' was behind his later encouragement of Gavin to participate in the same activity.) He was generally well liked around the school, but he was prone to being headstrong on occasions, enjoying a good argument with his closer friends. The odd prank was not beyond him, and on one occasion he was reprimanded by the headmaster for mixing salt in the dining room's sugar bowl.[19]

In his junior years, the nearby college boatshed attracted his interest. Although not slightly framed, Tom was by no means a large boy for his age, and

Tom in the Coxswain's seat of the Scotch College boat, 1921 (Bunning Family Collection)

being disciplined and intelligent he made an ideal coxswain (four-oared boats were widely used at this time). Located at Freshwater Bay, the shed was admired as 'the best on the Swan', and with one of the state's best coaches in 'Billy' Goland, Scotch was always in contention for the prestigious Head of the River regatta during the early 1920s.[20] In two years with the first crew Tom came close to this ultimate success, finishing a narrow second behind Christian Brothers College on a wet and windy day in 1921, followed by third place a year later. He regularly made the college's swimming team and was also a strong middle-distance runner, among the fastest over a mile in his age group and a place-getter more than once at interschool competitions.[21]

His other sports, unsurprisingly, were Australian rules football and cricket. Charlie excelled at both and captained Scotch's first teams in both sports during 1922. Tom lacked some of his elder brother's talent and flair, but he made up for it with dedication and determination. He worked hard at his cricket and developed into a solid top-order batsman, albeit one not always able to capitalise on a solid start, and was dependable in the field. By the age of fourteen, he was being picked for the first eleven. He kept a diary that year and regularly made a note of his scores and mode of dismissal; for example, 'made 25 1 chance caught 1st slip' on his first appearance in the senior team. In his final year he was appointed captain and had his most consistent season with the bat, scoring several half-centuries.[22] As a footballer his smaller size counted against him, though when he played forward he was often among the goal-kickers: 'played seconds [against] Wesley. Kicked two goals. Did not play badly'.[23] By 1924 Charlie was playing league football for Subiaco and was widely viewed as one of the most-promising young players in Western Australia. Tom attended each game his brother played. That year, Subiaco won the premiership – the club's first since the war (and last for almost another half-century). It was the high point of Charlie's career, as a knee injury forced him to retire prematurely from the game.[24]

In the meantime, Robert had been steadily turning around the performance of Bunning Bros. Two matters in particular had occupied his attention. The first concerned the *Forests Act*. Although promising at first, the new era was not working in the company's interests. The Noggerup mill had been reopened earlier than planned over concerns its permit would be forfeited, only for royalties to be substantially hiked. Months later, when his concession at Argyle expired, Robert was shocked to find them extended by only another year, rather than the usual ten.²⁵ Having already appealed in vain about the higher charges, he now felt the company was being unfairly targeted, and all the more so in light of its investment in buildings, machinery and railways before the war had forced operations to wind down.²⁶ It was not the only complaint against the Forests Department. Although Lane-Poole desired to bring the Millars (now the Millars' Timber and Trading Co.) under his new permit system, the London-based group had used its influence to ensure their existing concessions were renewed by the government for another ten years. The discontent was spreading. Lane-Poole was unhappy with James Mitchell, the premier since mid-1919. Robert was unhappy with Lane-Poole over the treatment of Bunning Bros, and as the incumbent President of the Timber Merchants' Association, shared his concern with other locally based sawmillers. They felt squeezed between the comparative economic and political advantage enjoyed by Millars and the ongoing preference in government contracts accorded to the state sawmills. But Robert had influence too, and in 1922 a royal commission was established to examine the industry's problems.²⁷

The second matter concerned the claim against the Abrahams brothers. During 1922, the Supreme Court ordered that Bunning Bros be reimbursed for the £500 added to their loan account in error, plus accumulated interest – an amount that came to over £1,300.²⁸ These were difficult times for Louis and Emmanuel Abrahams. Their business practises had been attracting strong public censure, with attention lately falling on their systematic rorting of war gratuity bonds through the sale of land at inflated values to ex-soldiers via their parent firm, the Mia Mia Pastoral Company. A special committee of the Legislative Assembly had exposed the practise and ordered the funds to be returned only months before the verdict in favour of Bunning Bros.²⁹ The Abrahams brothers later appealed against the judgement to the High Court of Australia, only to lose again, with a ruling of costs adding to their bill.³⁰ Louis Abrahams left the country permanently a few years later amid a dispute over unpaid taxes.³¹

Later that year, Robert departed on his longest trip abroad since the war. His destination was the west coast of the United States, where the timber industry was at the forefront of technological innovation. The difficulties of the recent past had been mostly settled, and once again he had his mind firmly fixed on expansion. Lane-Poole had resigned as Conservator of Forests, disappointed in the government's acquiescence to Millars and the broader undermining of his management plans that culminated in the royal commission.³² When it did eventually settle on revised royalty and permit arrangements, the net effect for the company was a net saving of £12,000 to 1924.[33] Some of this windfall would now be invested in new equipment: a modern sander and buzzing machine, along with other new machinery to replace the losses at Wellington Street; and for the Southwest, new sawmilling equipment and tractors to haul logs. The company closed Lion Mill, Robert's first acquisition when he entered sawmilling in earnest (the settlement had been renamed Mount Helena by this time). Argyle and Muja were each expanded, and Noggerup was closed down and production relocated to an operation at Yornup, near Bridgetown, recently taken over by Bunning Bros. The company could now push into the export trade. Contracts had soon been won to supply sleepers to railways in Mauritius, New Zealand and India, mining frames for South Africa, a jarrah warehouse for Ceylon, and paving blocks for Melbourne.[34]

Charles Street was now as busy as Wellington Street had ever been. There were more than 120 men on the payroll, with 40 carpenters in the joiners' shop alone. The office staff had grown to twenty, with a telephonist and typist among them. Walter Collins continued to manage the company accounts and provide a measured influence over Robert's more impulsive inclinations. Tall and solidly built, Collins was stern in his demeanour and thorough in his work. During 1925, Robert recruited Arthur Petherick to become the new manager. Petherick had worked for Bunning Bros briefly during the war before leaving to join a rival outfit, the Australian Lumber Company. Honest and straightforward in his demeanour, he now returned with contacts among local shipping agents that would prove invaluable as the company sought to expand into overseas markets. Bruce Johnston, another strong personality, was also appointed at this time to look after the supply of sleepers, which came mostly from hewers working on contract throughout the Southwest.[35] They were men that Tom would all come to know well, though for the time being, his interactions with them were limited to the odd Saturday mornings when Robert brought him along to the office.[36]

Outside of school and these occasional visits to Charles Street, Tom had any number of hobbies to occupy his free time. Bright and curious, he was interested in the technological marvels of the day, aviation and wireless telegraphy among them. Western Australia's first radio station, 6WF, had started broadcasting, and Tom had joined one of the new wireless clubs springing up in the suburbs, putting together his own crystal wireless set from a kit his parents had gifted him. When it was ready, the family would be able to tune in to the evening broadcasts.[37] Picture shows were another preoccupation, especially when sound-on-film or 'talkies' began appearing in the mid-1920s. The *Boy's Own Annual* was his favourite reading material, and he especially enjoyed the stories dealing with science and technology. On the weekends and school holidays, the outdoors also beckoned. The river was barely a stone's throw away and was a constant part of his upbringing, as Robert still kept a boat and would take his children on trips to visit Frank Wilson or another of his close friends in their waterside properties. Tom and his siblings swam regularly in the river or at nearby Cottesloe Beach. An invitation to go yachting with a school friend or one of his father's business contacts was never far away either.[38] He also enjoyed heading out on bike rides, with his friends or on his own. Sealed roads at this time were still confined largely to the inner suburbs or the highway linking Perth and Fremantle, with only rough tracks beyond. These were always tempting to venture down, even at the risk of a punctured tyre and long walk home.[39]

Tom sometimes played tennis, though only on a social basis. Innerhadden had its own court, of course, as did many of the larger houses around Perth. With three children in their teens, it was used frequently for tennis parties in the 1920s. Charlie and Jane, in particular, were fond of hosting their friends. When they did, it was Tom that was invariably prevailed upon to mow and mark the court, the gardener not being there on the weekends. He learnt quickly that it meant an opportunity to extract compensation from his siblings, and the amounts owing to him from his brother and sister were dutifully noted in his diary. Five shillings (the equivalent of 50 cents when decimal currency was introduced in 1966) was a standard payment for such a chore, and as his funds accumulated he found himself cast in the role of a lender, advancing sums as high as twenty-five shillings (twenty shillings made up a pound), usually to Charlie.[40] Tom also earned pocket money by working as a ball boy at the King's Park Tennis Club during summer. Putting the advances to his brother to one side, he tended to be prudent with his earnings. The future accountant can even be glimpsed when he noted, aged fifteen, he had just deposited his first £1 at the bank.[41]

His most enthusiastic pursuit, however, was fast becoming golf. By the age of twelve he had begun playing at the disused six-hole course on the reserve at Keane's Point, just down the street from the family home. Though neglected, it was still sufficient as a place to learn the basics of swinging a club.[42] His interest in the game was soon being readily cultivated at school. Before taking up his position at Scotch College, 'PC' Anderson had been among the best amateur golfers in the United Kingdom, winning the 1893 British Amateur Golf Championship at Prestwick Golf Club in Scotland.[43] Upon arriving in Western Australia, he had helped to establish the Cottesloe Golf Club and been responsible for laying out its nine-hole links course overlooking the ocean at Seaview.[44] Like many aspects of his personality, Anderson's enthusiasm for golf rubbed off on the boys under his charge. It was certainly the case with Tom. He abandoned Keane's Point and began sneaking onto the Seaview course to practise there, and before long he had roped a group of his friends into a well-organised, if informal competition on Saturday morning in the hours before the members played.

As he transitioned to upper school, Tom developed another new interest – girls. A young lady, Joan Clifton, had caught his eye, and he was taking every chance he could to meet up with her at the movies or one of the many dances held on the weekends around Perth. He was invited to meet her parents – 'I like Mrs C very much' – and they trusted him sufficiently to allow him to escort Joan home in the evenings.[45] His diary, once focused on cricket, now served as a notebook for the different steps to the dances in vogue at the time. A preoccupation with fashion also became apparent. He began wearing trousers, or 'long 'uns', and purchased his first sports coat.[46] Yet he would forsake all of this and spend the evening at home with his mother when Robert, Charlie or his sisters were not around. Between his father's commitments in the Southwest or interstate and his siblings' full social calendar, this occurred fairly often.[47] During school holidays, it was common to receive an invitation to visit the family farm of one or other of the boys enrolled at Scotch College as boarders. Don Stewart, a close friend and one of his golfing buddies, was among them. He went to their farm at Gnowangerup a number of times to spend a week riding motorcycles and helping out with lambing, ploughing, seeding and other tasks. Tom enjoyed these trips, describing them as 'bonza'; this was his most sincere complement ('School dance. Had bonza time with Joan') at the time.[48]

Robert had been eyeing more than bandsaws and tractors when he visited the United States, as he returned as the owner of a Buick automobile. He was still reluctant to drive himself and only had a chauffeur during working hours, so when the car duly arrived it was often necessary to find somebody who could drive it on behalf of himself and the wider family. Charlie was not an option as he had recently departed to study engineering at the University of Melbourne. Jane drove it for a while, but when she crashed into a bus in West Perth, damaging both vehicles extensively, the only option remaining was Tom.[49] Though still eighteen months away from the legal driving age, he was more than capable of working the pedals at the same time as looking out above the steering wheel. Accordingly, he began driving his father to the office each morning, before catching the train to school and returning after his afternoon sports to drive Robert and the Buick home again. It quickly caught on, and he was soon driving his sisters around town on the weekend to one engagement or another, or ferrying guests home from Innerhadden after one of the parties there. 'Our dance in the evening. Pretty good show I thought', he noted at the beginning of 1927. 'Drove some of the mob up to town after and bed at 3:30 am. Had a bonza time.'[50]

Tom (centre) as Captain of Scotch College's First XI, 1927 (Bunning Family Collection)

Later that summer, Robert and Helen embarked on a major renovation of Innerhadden.[51] With the work set to continue for some months and an extended interstate holiday planned to coincide with it, they decided to enrol Tom as a boarder for his final year at Scotch College. For the remainder of 1927, there would be no more morning trips to head office with his father, and much less running about in the car on the weekends. When school reassembled, PC Anderson pulled Tom aside for some words of advice. 'Had talk with the Boss after prep', he wrote at the beginning of February. 'Told to keep off the girls etc. Am going to cut out French.'[52] His classes would be English, mathematics, applied mathematics, physics and chemistry. He would also serve on committees for sports and for the *Reporter* (the school magazine), was made an officer in the cadets, and joined the shooting team and dramatic society.[53] On top of this he was made a prefect, which conferred the responsibility of policing the nightly 'raids' of one dormitory against another, and was appointed as manager of the tuck shop, a role the other boys coveted. When cricket resumed, he was elected captain of the First XI and started the season well with the bat, though his form in the warm-up games did not continue in the interschool competition. Later that year, when the football season began, he held down a place in the first team.[54]

Despite all of this, he still found time to ignore the headmaster's advice. A new girl, Betty Woods, was attracting his attention. He never missed a chance to call her in the evening nor to catch up on the weekend. There were nights out at White City, the fairground on the Esplanade with a colourful reputation, and no shortage of dances or tennis parties on the weekends.[55] From time to time, Tom even found himself at Colin Street. The extended Law and Bunning families mixed in the same social circles and, like Innerhadden, Lexbourne House had a tennis court that was frequently used on the weekends. Betty was a friend of Margot's sister Kathleen, and this gave Tom all the more reason for stopping in: 'Went up to town', he noted in his diary, only weeks into his sojourn as a college boarder, 'To Laws. Went in and saw Betty.'[56] Margot herself was not around at this time. She had spent a year at Kobeelya, a boarding school in Kojonup, before being sent to complete her education at Clyde School in Macedon, Victoria. She didn't mind the school so much but hated the three long, return, transcontinental trips she now made every year.[57]

∞

Lexbourne House, Colin Street, West Perth (Bunning Family Collection)

Away from home, Robert Law's career was continuing to flourish. Shortly before the war ended, he had helped to establish the West Australian Portland Cement Company. It was operational by 1920, manufacturing cement for a fraction of the price of imports. Two years later, he sold off his interests in pipe making to the Hume Pipe Company and moved to modernise his brickyard ventures by electrifying the Helena Vale works and upgrading its equipment. Shortly afterwards, he incorporated the Metropolitan Brick Company Ltd to consolidate his brickmaking interests. A major new works was soon under construction near the Swan River at Maylands. His bricks, stamped with the brand name 'Metro', were to become the most widely used in Western Australia. After some early difficulties securing a suitable supply of lime, the newly renamed Swan Portland Cement Company was restructured during 1927 and began using Swan River oyster shell to manufacture cement at its new works in Rivervale, on the opposite side of the river to Robert's new brickworks. The cement produced at

Rivervale was of a superior quality and rapidly gained market share. Robert Law would remain chairman of both companies for many years to come.[58]

Outside of school and his romantic interests, golf remained Tom's main preoccupation. This was something that Anderson was more prepared to condone, and a weekend rarely passed without Tom playing at least one round. 'Golf morning with Geoff', read one entry for a Saturday in June 1927. 'Got 42, 42 – 84. Geoff got 97. Geoff came back for dinner', while the members occupied the course. When they drove back later that day, Tom scored 35 across 8 holes – an impressive score for a young golfer – before bad light put an end to play.[59] Geoff was Geoff Hill, and with Tom's other friends Don Stewart, Harold Greenway and Raynor Cramond, they had formed the 'Cottesloe Honorary Junior Members Club', otherwise known after its ringleader as 'the Tom Bunning gang'.[60] They became the bane of Bert Meecham, the chairman of the greens, who could see them playing from his house, which overlooked the course. He knew who the boys were and thought a quick word with their headmaster would bring them into line, but Anderson was having none of it: 'I look after the little beggars for five days a week – someone else can worry about them on the weekend' was his reply.[61] But the trespassing soon ended anyway. When he graduated from Scotch College, one of Tom's first actions was to become a formal member of the Cottesloe Golf Club.

As a teenager, the days that Tom spent alone with Robert were rare enough to warrant recording in his diary. There was one such occasion not long before his fifteenth birthday. The prime minister, Stanley Bruce, was in Perth, so Tom rigged up his crystal set so that he and his father could listen to a speech being broadcast that afternoon.[62] There was discontent locally over tariff protections for secondary industries in the eastern states, which inflated the cost of imports to Western Australia. The *Sunday Times* had even been campaigning lately for secession.[63] Bruce attacked this head on: 'For anyone to-day to talk of disintegrating this great nation of ours is an absolute betrayal of the men who fought for us in the war. That war cemented us into a great nation', he exclaimed. Robert, of course, was a manufacturer himself. Bunning Bros turned out kit or 'ready-made' houses for the farming districts and wagons and framing for truck beds, alongside its more traditional building products. His principles, however, favoured free trade; he was also an exporter now too, and had long railed against Millars' stranglehold over outside markets. Bruce saw the answer to the state's

ALBANY GOLF CLUB.

MATCH PLAY ODDS.

In Singles, ¾ of difference between Handicap allowances.

In Foursomes, ⅜ of difference between Handicap allowances.

A half stroke or over counts as one, smaller fractions do not count.

Name of Player: G. M. Bunning   Handicap: _____

HOLE	Yards	BOGEY	Player	Won X Halved O Lost —	Opponent	HOLE	Yards	BOGEY	Player	Won X H'lv'd O Lost —	Opponent
1 9	176	5		5	5	10 8	176	5	2	4	3
2 13	347	6		8	3	11 12	347	6	4	5	6
3 3	184	4		4	5	12 6	184	4	4	3	4
4 11	270	5		5	4	13 14	270	5	5	4	4
5 7	242	5		4	2	14 4	242	5	5	5	4
6 17	85	3		4	3	15 18	85	3	2	4	4
7 15	186	4		6	6	16 16	186	4	5	3	5
8 1	342	6		5	5	17 2	342	6	5	6	5
9 5	302	5		8	4	18 10	302	5	3	4	5
1st	2134	43		39	37	2nd	2134	43	35	38	43
							2134	43	38		
						TOTAL	4268	86	73		

Signature of Scorer: W. A. Anderson

Date: _____ 19__

Handicap _____ Nett Strokes _____ Holes Up/Dn _____

NOTE— Black Figures shew where Strokes are taken.

Top and bottom: Tom's scorecard from a round at Albany with his future best man, Bill Anderson, 1928 (Bunning Family Collection) grievances lay in attracting migrants and capital to develop primary industry, or the 'Men, Money and Markets' that was his mantra. 'You have a State covering nearly one-third of the Commonwealth; you have a population of about 350,000 souls. It is a task that might appal any people, but you have gone forward, done what you could, and have shown great courage and gallantry in undertaking the work', he continued.[64] In this, Robert could hardly disagree. He had built up Bunning Bros from modest beginnings before riding out the war and shaking off the creditors that had crippled him. Now, the future was brighter than it had ever been.

Indeed, the company's books had never been in better shape. In the decade since moving to Charles Street, Bunning Bros had grown its capital by £58,879, with most of this coming since 1919. As Walter Collins reported in mid-1924, 'there are few businesses of such magnitude in Western Australia where the assets have such great value relative to the liabilities'.[65] It hadn't all gone Robert's way – his kiln at Lyall's Mill had been a rather conspicuous failure – but the strategy of holding on at all costs through the war years had been entirely vindicated. The company had consolidated its concessions, upgraded its mills and introduced lorries and other modern equipment to its metropolitan operations. And it was holding its own in the export trade. The next few years would witness levels of production in the timber industry that would not be exceeded for another thirty years – more than 20 million cubic feet in 1926, with an export record of 12.5 million cubic feet, worth well over £1.5 million, a year later.[66]

It was at this stage that Robert stood aside as President of the Timber Merchant's Association, only to be coaxed back a year later to serve on a committee on industrial safety, providing advice on what would become the *Timber Regulation Act* (1926).[67] In his late sixties, he still went each day for lunch to the West Australian Club on St George's Terrace. His tendency to take a glass-half-full view of business opportunities, a common factor in most of his missteps, had been curbed by the cautious Collins and Arthur Petherick's judgement and experience since returning to Bunning Bros. But neither was able to dissuade Robert from what would become the most entrepreneurial venture of his career. During 1929, he secured a lease over Garden Island, south of Fremantle, with the aim of developing it as a tourist resort. The idea was to use second-grade timber that was structurally fine but not readily marketable to build holiday shacks and a new jetty, and to renovate an old tearoom on the island. Before long, the tradesmen at Charles Street were also constructing a 70-foot boat, the *Carnac*, to ferry holidaymakers to the island. None of it made any sense financially, though Robert was rather attached to the project and certainly enjoyed the opportunity to visit his resort with Helen and his daughters.[68] Tom once commented to Gavin that Garden Island never made any money and was a pain in the neck, with friends frequently ringing to complain that they could not get a booking on their favoured dates.

It had been some time since Arthur had retired. He travelled frequently, and Tom hardly knew him at all. In February 1929, Arthur died whilst in England. He had remained childless, and it had been clear since Tom's childhood that the company's future would pass one day to Robert's sons alone, provided they were willing and able to take it on. Charlie certainly expected to, upon completing his studies in Melbourne, as Robert had encouraged him to take up engineering to address the need for this exact type of expertise within the company. With Tom, Robert had been more circumspect. There had been no pressure to make any decisions on his future, yet the trips to and from Charles Street in his Buick were not strictly because of the lack of a chauffeur. As Tom would one day understand, he was being gradually introduced to the family businesses alongside his father: 'without realising it', he wrote, many years later, 'he was throwing the door wide open for me and I had just sufficient common sense at least to snap up some of the opportunities that he held out to me'.[69] Before his final year at Scotch had concluded, he had decided to pursue accountancy as his occupation and seek a career within Bunning Bros.

3

The younger set

ROBERT HAD ISSUED Tom with a stern challenge for his final year at Scotch College. Times were becoming tough, so he would only be able to follow Charlie into university if he finished as Dux of Scotch College. He finished runner-up, missing out to a student repeating his senior year with the top prize in mind. There was no consolation from his father, and so, not yet eighteen years of age, Tom began working at Bunning Bros. Robert had a few words of advice for him. 'There are three principles in this company that we value and I ask you to uphold – first to survive, secondly to look after your people, and thirdly to always keep a sense of decency about you', he said.[1] Charlie, newly graduated from the University of Melbourne, joined the firm at the same time. Disappointed to have missed out on university himself, Tom enrolled instead in a correspondence course in accountancy with Hemmingway & Robinson, a Melbourne-based agency.[2] With the Great Depression around the corner, it was a singular time to be learning the ropes of financial management. Australia would never experience a more severe or protracted economic crisis, and not for the first time, Bunning Bros would be forced to fight for its very survival.

Economic problems started to appear during Tom's first year at work, although nobody yet appreciated the scale of the slump that would follow. During 1928, residential and commercial construction began falling away, as demand for sleepers and other timber exports diminished. Coming off the back of several years of sustained expansion, the industry was suddenly confronted with the problem of spiralling over-capacity and price cutting. By the end of the year, Robert had been forced to close down his mills at Yornup and Muja, reduce Lyall's Mill and Argyle to operating three days a week, and lay off men at Charles Street.[3] The challenging climate also shaped the options open to his sons. Charlie had initially been sent to learn sawmilling, but with the cutbacks at the mills he soon left Bunning Bros to form a partnership engaged in building bridges in the North West districts. Tom had started as a yard boy at Charles Street, before Robert arranged a stint as an apprentice carpenter with a contractor building boarding houses at Southern Cross. Before the end of the year, he was back in Perth and working on the company's stock sheets and accounts, with the accountancy course occupying his weekday evenings.[4]

Charles Street was a crowded affair, even as the pace of daily activity was diminishing. The total area of land was 8 acres. Head office and a store fronted the street, with the joinery works and glaziers' shop behind. The yard, with its stacks of timber and small sawmill, occupied the rear of the premises. Imported timber was brought in from Fremantle and native hardwoods were brought via the main line to the Southwest, before being carted the short distance from the railway. During 1929, there were about forty carpenters in the joinery works and around the same number of men working in the yard, with each group looked after by a foreman. The company also employed a storeman and his assistant, and a blacksmith, sadlier and stableman. Inside the office there was only a modest staff. Robert had his own room, with Petherick and Johnston sharing one next door. The rest of the office was occupied by a purchasing officer, a typist, telephonist and mail boy, and a clerk, Don Stewart, Tom's friend from Scotch College. Tom had been allocated the adjacent desk, and when Charlie came back from his bridge-building venture, he found himself sharing it with his brother. Whatever space had remained free was now fully occupied.[5]

As Robert knew only too well, the risk of fire was a constant threat to the operation of Bunning Bros. His luck would soon run out. One Sunday in February 1929 a fire took hold at Charles Street, after sparks from a drum used for burning rubbish ignited a wall of the joinery shop. It was soon a raging inferno, not dissimilar to that which destroyed the old yard at Wellington Street: 'To those who saw it from a distance it was a spectacle not soon to be forgotten, as the sky was brilliantly illuminated for many miles round', reported one newspaper, 'but to those – and there were many hundreds – whose curiosity led them near to the scene, it presented an awesome sight. The flames reached to a tremendous height and the heat was terrific.'[6] The city's firefighters did all they could to prevent the flames spreading into the timber yard, but nothing could be done to save the buildings already ablaze. By morning, 'countless sheets of corrugated iron twisted into fantastic shapes, charred heaps of timber, wrecked machinery, and here and there, burnt and blackened wooden supports still standing in a desolation of ruin, and like stark and silent sentinels, a reminder of the terrific damage wrought by the outbreak'.[7] After the 1914 fire, Robert had been careful to be well insured, with four policies covering the Charles Street property. Damages of £20,000 were covered in full and rebuilding was soon underway.[8]

It was just as well, as the Depression had begun to bite. In the eastern states, there was considerable unrest among timber workers in response to a reduction in the industry's award rates. By the middle of 1929, the troubles were spreading to Western Australia. Some 900 men had been thrown out of work locally, although the peak of 2,000 lost jobs was still some way off.[9] The export-orientated Millars was particularly hard hit by the cancellation of overseas orders.[10] As sleeper orders were cancelled and stock accumulated on the docks, Bunning Bros inevitably suffered from the diminishing trade. If it wasn't for its diversified operations, these losses would have been even greater. The relative prosperity of the state's goldfields, an outcome of a sharp rise in the price of gold, provided the company with a lifeline. A renewed focus on the development of underground mining and the advanced treatment of ore created demand for mining frames, housing and other timber products. Robert opened a new yard in Kalgoorlie to handle the goldfields trade.[11] Bunning Bros also won the contract to supply flooring and joinery to the new Commonwealth Bank building in Perth, one of few major construction projects taking place in the city. It was all vital to keeping Charles Street, Lyall's Mill and Argyle running through the difficult times that followed the stock market crash of October 1929. Nonetheless, the company recorded a deficit of £5,000 in 1930, its worst result since the war.[12]

Away from work, however, neither the Depression nor the demands of nightly study had done much to hamper Tom's social life. The round of tennis matches, dances and picnics that had occupied the weekends during his last year at school had carried on into his early twenties, with cocktail parties, coming-of-age parties and the Western Australian favourite of receptions for visitors from interstate or overseas all now added to the calendar. If there was a change, it was that Tom's whereabouts on the weekends were invariably noted in the social columns of Perth's newspapers, which dutifully followed 'the younger set' about town.[13] Robert's children figured prominently in the social pages at this time ('The name Bunning, my dears, seemed everywhere'),[14] except for Gena, who would never marry and preferred to remain at home. Joe had aged into a gentlemanly figure who was known for his support of the arts and his fondness for the urbane atmosphere of clubs such as the Alliance Française. Flora's interest was music. Like her mother, she was a talented pianist and had studied at the Conservatorium in Melbourne.[15] Jane was a true socialite and a dedicated golfer, one of the best female players of her generation. Angie was only a year older than Tom and their friends tended to overlap, so it was natural they would hold a joint New Year's Eve party at Innerhadden to usher in 1931.[16]

Later that year, Charlie married Betty Barber, an accomplished artist and the daughter of Major General George Barber, in Melbourne.[17] One gossip columnist predicted Tom would be following in his footsteps 'at any minute'.[18] But the prophecy was wide of the mark. Tom went to London that year for his first extended holiday since finishing school; it was a gift from Robert for

Tom in England with his MG Magna, 1931 (Bunning Family Collection)

his twenty-first birthday, if not a token of compensation for having missed out on university. He spent time there with his cousin, Will Bunning, a future Secretary to the Australian High Commissioner. He also purchased his first car: an MG Magna, the only six-cylinder model that MG ever manufactured. An attractive two-door sportscar with a long sloping bonnet, it was a step up from the cumbersome Buicks and Chevys he was used to driving.[19]

On this trip Tom also went to the Royal and Ancient Golf Club of St Andrews, the first of many visits during his life. His golf had not suffered from the demands of either work or his social circles; indeed, during the early 1930s he had emerged as one of the best amateur players in Western Australia. After joining Cottesloe Golf Club formally his game had improved markedly, as he refined his swing and developed a ruthless efficiency on the greens. Within two years his handicap was down to four and he was playing in the club's A-Grade

Charles and Betty's wedding, June 1931 (Courtesy Sarah Blunt)

Pennant team. Though not the longest hitter, he had developed the ability to keep the ball low in the air, something he had honed at the links course at Seaview. This ability and his reliable putting made him a dogged opponent at match play, the form of the game he enjoyed the most. As early as 1930 he had won his first Catlidge Cup, the most prestigious individual trophy at Cottesloe after the Club Championship.[20]

Tom went overseas again in 1932, visiting England and Canada for the latter part of the northern summer. He played regularly during his travels, and he had won a trophy in the Lucifer Society competition, which was open to golfers spread around the Empire. Back at home, Cottesloe had relocated to a new 18-hole course at Swanbourne, further north and back from the sea than its previous 9-hole links course. Most of his old gang who had so irritated the greenkeeper at Seaview had also become members and were playing in the pennant team, at a time when Cottesloe was the strongest club in local competition. Their old headmaster, PC Anderson, still played regularly himself. Charlie, having retired from football, also played in pennants golf at this time.[21]

At the end of 1931, Tom completed his course and became an associate of the Australian Society of Accountants. The hands-on training he was receiving at Bunning Bros was proving no less valuable as an education. The timber industry remained in a parlous position, beset by fierce competition, high royalties and freight costs, and the need to negotiate cuts to wages and working hours through the arbitration court.[22] The industry particularly resented the competition of the State Sawmills, which did not pay state taxes and could therefore undercut private enterprise on the open market. The premier, Sir James Mitchell, was prepared to sell it off, but nobody, least of all Robert, could contemplate borrowing the funds required. The Sawmillers Association did succeed in securing reductions to royalties, inspection fees and charges by the government railways, although this did nothing to raise the price of sawn timber. Bunning Bros even declined one order for 300 loads of hewn timber because there was not even a prospect of breaking even. That August, the mill at Argyle was shut down entirely. On top of this, a bushfire had destroyed the Yornup mill as it lay idle amid the financial crisis. When bad debts were factored in, the company was losing £4 for every £100 it turned over, contributing to another deficit of £2,800 for the year. Great care had to be taken to collect outstanding payments and deposit them into the bank before the company could issue its fortnightly pay cheques.[23]

Tom with Geoff Hill, a fellow Cottesloe pennant team member in the early 1930s (Bunning Family Collection)

Tom with Kelly Rogers, a fellow Cottesloe pennant team member in the 1940s and 1950s (Bunning Family Collection)

A sleeper order for India and the completion of works at the Commonwealth Bank came at just the right time.[24] But the company's problems were far from over. On a winter's morning in 1933, fire again broke out at Charles Street. It started near the milling shed before spreading quickly to the timber stack; although the specific point of origin was never identified, the carelessness of itinerant campers in the vacant block next door was a likely cause.[25] A passing policeman raised the alarm and the central fire station immediately dispatched an engine; others from North Perth, Leederville, Maylands and Victoria Park arrived shortly afterwards. With a one-acre stack of timber already ablaze, however, there was only so much they could do. 'Tongues of fire leaping high into the air could be seen from all parts of the city', reported the *West Australian*. Once again, 'thousands of onlookers – some clad only in their night attire and dressing gowns – came to witness the spectacle…In the lurid glow of the flames, which at times shot up to a height of well over 100 feet, the faces of the people, and the surrounding buildings for hundreds of yards were lit up'.[26] The stack, the milling shed and several motor trucks parked nearby were completely destroyed. Losses were later estimated to be at least £25,000.[27]

What followed next was almost as devastating as the fire itself. That same morning, with Charles Street in disarray, Robert received a message from BR Fitzhardinge, the Bank of New South Wales's state inspector. Fitzhardinge had lately been going over the company's balance sheets and determined that a careful investigation of its affairs and position was in order.[28] The smoke was still clearing when he met Robert to outline his concerns: that 'the family were taking too much out of the business and that he was dissatisfied with the account and proposed to take action', as Tom later recalled.[29] Bunning Bros had no choice but to agree to an audit by the well-known Perth accountant SJ McGibbon. Robert returned to head office badly rattled, one the few times in his life that Tom saw him this way. It was apparent immediately that they would need to find a new bank, yet the Depression was persisting and banks were reluctant, as a general principle, to take on new business. In a manner nobody could have foreseen, Bunning Bros was at risk of losing its financial lifeline.

Tom, no less suddenly, had been handed a grave responsibility. At twenty-two years old, as the recently appointed company accountant, the task of working with McGibbon on the audit would fall to him. He had had an apprenticeship of sorts, having worked closely with Walter Collins over the past few years.

Although he had left Bunning Bros after 1924 to start his own accountancy firm, Collins had continued on as the company's external auditor and remained a measured and cautious influence over its finances. Some of this influence had rubbed off on Tom. Collins was in ill health now, however, and unable to lend any assistance; he died only weeks later, with the audit underway.[30] Tom would therefore work with McGibbon unaided. They spent several weeks working side-by-side, going through the ledger books for head office, the mills, and the branches at Fremantle, Bunbury, Collie and Kalgoorlie. Meanwhile, Fitzhardinge had made no secret of his intentions, letting it be known around Perth that he intended to appoint a receiver and sell off the company's assets. Given his appointment to Western Australia had been made for the purpose of reducing the bank's liability to failing businesses, there was every reason to believe the rumours circulating around the city.

By the same token, however, both Robert and Tom could feel assured the business was sound. Their industry was vulnerable to slumps in building and construction, fiercely competitive, and reliant upon the extension of credit to customers and the variable cashflows that resulted.[31] Yet Bunning Bros held assets valued at over £195,000, and although debt owing to the Bank of New South Wales had blown out to exceed £36,000, the losses at Charles Street would be fully covered by insurance and the prospects for returning to profitability when the economy finally picked up were good. Just as importantly, the company had a good reputation in the marketplace. In the end, the audit found precisely this – that the business was fundamentally sound. McGibbon presented his report to Fitzhardinge, who was obliged to consider the case for maintaining the company's account. In the end, however, the decision was taken out of his hands. Equipped with McGibbon's report, Tom went himself to see the English, Scottish and Australian Bank (ES&A, the forerunner to ANZ). In an age that placed a premium on seniority, it was a bold step to take, although the long-term outlook for the industry and the company itself was inevitably a factor to consider. Before the end of 1933, the matter had been settled. Bunning Bros transferred its account, taking out a loan for £22,000 and using the payout for losses at Charles Street to meet the obligation that had so troubled Fitzhardinge.[32] The ruthless handling of his family's business was something Tom would never forget. For the rest of his career, he had a simple maxim at Bunning Bros: 'we do not deal with the Bank of New South Wales again'.[33]

These had been tense months indeed. But nothing at work seemed to affect Tom on the weekends, or at least not when it came to golf. After Cottesloe moved to its new course, his game had reached a new level, and he now played off scratch. He tied for the first monthly medal to be awarded there with a score of 77, and in 1934, he equalled the club record with a score of 72. Earlier, while he was working on the audit with McGibbon, he had been unlucky to lose the final of Western Australia's amateur championship. In a tight, seesawing match at Royal Fremantle, Tom's straight drives and reliable putting kept him right in the contest against the more aggressive play of his opponent, HG Godden, a past winner of both the amateur and open tournaments. At the sixteenth hole both players bunkered from the tee. Godden attempted a chip but failed and remained stuck. The *West Australian* described what happened next: 'Bunning played a strong explosive shot, and struck the flag stick, which his caddy was still holding in the hole, and lost by Rule 32, which made Godden the winner of the championship, by 3 and 2'. Both men had played 'with perseverance, courage and determination, and it was a great pity that such a fine match was won and lost on a technicality'.[34]

Tom won the Catlidge Cup again in 1934, was part of Cottesloe's winning A-Grade pennant teams in 1935, and won his first club championship the following year, when he also equalled the new course record of 70. Some memorable rounds were played in these years, as his standing as one of the state's best amateurs meant he was invariably invited to play in exhibition matches with visiting golfers. One such match was against the renowned trick-shot exponent and former Australian Open champion, Joe Kirkwood. In an era when there were still few professional players and hardly any professional tournaments, amateur competitions were often played before large public galleries and attracted widespread coverage in the press. In these years, Tom was among the most successful and best-known golfers in Western Australia.

In other ventures, he was not quite so successful. Perth had long suffered from a reputation for being a backwater, a standing invariably confirmed by travel interstate or abroad. An attempt to remedy this led to one of Tom's more adventurous undertakings, when he partnered with friends to develop one of the city's first nightclubs, the 'Cosmo Club'. Located inside the Hostel Manly, a ballroom and hotel along Marine Parade in Cottesloe popular among local sporting teams and visitors from the country, it was launched to instant acclaim:

'One of the many attractions of the club', reported the *Mirror*, 'is the engagement of the Collegians dance orchestra, who have quite a following.'[35] But there would be no sustained success. The Cosmo Club may have perhaps been ahead of its time, as nightclubs only became common in Perth a few years later. On the other hand, the Collegians dance orchestra had all the hallmarks of dilettantes. Tom played the clarinet and saxophone, though his repertoire hardly extended beyond *Bye Bye Blackbird*.[36] Either way, it was a short-lived enterprise, and one that ended with considerably less fanfare than it had opened to.

By 1934, Bunning Bros had turned the corner. The company was supplying sleepers to the Commonwealth railways, joinery and flooring for the new university buildings at Crawley and the Boans emporium in the city, and prefabricated housing for mining and railway towns. Men were again being put on at Charles Street, including several apprentices. Lyall's Mill and Argyle had reopened. With the export market also bouncing back, attention could be given to the state of sawmilling operations. The mills still relied on horse-drawn transport and the company's ageing fleet of locomotives. The first step towards an upgrade would involve introducing diesel tractors to the Southwest. A new permit had also been secured at Yornup and plans for a modern sawmill were in development. Charlie had been steadily building his standing within the industry and was soon to be selected to accompany Stephen Kessell, the Conservator of Forests, to an Empire Forestry Conference in South Africa.[37] Tom continued to look after the company's accounts, as the ledger moved back into the black.

Robert was about to head overseas again too. It would be his grandest trip yet, as he was taking Helen and his daughters on a round-the-world journey that combined business with plenty of sightseeing and leisure. Only Angie was missing the trip, as she had married the pastoralist Dan Mackinnon the previous summer and moved to Pinnacles Station, in the interior of Western Australia near the mining town of Leonora.[38] They went by train to Melbourne and from there to San Francisco, where Robert was able to inspect the latest trends in sawmilling and timber processing. After crossing the United States, they travelled on to Great Britain and spent a week with Helen's sister in Scotland.[39] In London, Robert met with his contacts to gather intelligence on his rivals, Millars and the Kauri Timber Company, and learn about new ventures being planned for Western Australia's goldfields. They decided they needed a car to get about, so Tom was instructed to send a telegram authorising the purchase of a Ford V8.⁴⁰ In the autumn they went across Europe, firstly to Scandinavia, then from Brussels through Germany and Austria as far as Vienna, and back via Prague and Cologne. It was a whistlestop tour, though they all enjoyed it greatly: 'we could not do much sightseeing at each place but it was all very interesting to see all the different towns and villages and the people in them', Robert told Tom, before his departure on the long voyage home. The girls, he continued, 'were thrilled with it all, and you won't hear much else when Jane gets back'.⁴¹

Robert Bunning, early 1930s (Bunning Family Collection)

Robert's letters home suggest he was content to leave much of the day-to-day running of Bunning Bros to Petherick and his two sons. They also reveal his health was no longer what it once had been. Rather than the smooth cursive of years gone by, his writing had become much shakier.[42] On top of this, he had been losing weight lately: 'I have got down to 12 stone with my clothes on, lost over two stone', he wrote in one letter to Tom. 'I suppose it is the rheumatism.'[43] At home, Tom had still been in the habit of driving his father about town, although not as often as he had in his last years at school. It was on a trip home one evening, not long after the company had moved its accounts to the ES&A Bank, that he had asked him 'when are you going to retire, Dad?'. Robert's reply was unequivocal: 'when I pay off the overdraft'.[44] It was a step closer now. Bunning Bros recorded a profit of £10,433 in 1935. The point at which the debts that had been carried for decades would be paid off in full was within sight.

The new year began just as well. In London, Robert had negotiated access to a 25,000-hectare area of wandoo forest adjacent to the Albany Road near Boddington, which would be used to cut sleepers for the export trade. There was plenty of work for the mills filling orders for heavy section timber for the goldfields. A fire at Lyall's Mill in March 1936 destroyed the mill buildings and plant, though insurance covered all but a few hundred pounds of the cost of a full rebuild.[45] In the end, it was only a minor setback, although nothing could prevent the joke about 'Burning Brothers' doing the rounds in Perth and the Southwest for years to come.

Robert therefore had every reason to feel satisfied as he contemplated the fiftieth anniversary of his arrival in Western Australia. The business he had built from scratch, initially with his brother and then increasingly on his own, was the largest in the local timber industry to be privately owned. It had outlasted the Great Depression and would be carried forward for decades to come by his two youngest sons, for the benefit of his family at large. Cheerful and gregarious, in good times as well as bad, he was widely respected and liked by everybody he knew. A dinner held to commemorate his milestone at the Palace Hotel in August 1936 was attended by the industry's leaders and some of the state's most senior business figures. Sir Talbot Hobbs, the Great War general and a prominent architect, was among them, as was Sydney Stubbs, a hardware merchant, past Mayor of Perth and former Speaker of the Legislative Assembly. So too was Norman Temperley, the local manager for Millars and a good friend of Robert despite their commercial rivalry, and Henry Downing, a King's Counsel who had represented Robert in his cases against the Abrahams brothers many years earlier. All the senior staff at Bunning Bros were in attendance. There were speeches in Robert's honour, before he rose himself to address those present:

> *It makes me a very proud man to receive the welcome you have given me tonight to celebrate the event of my completing fifty years of business in Western Australia. And to meet so many of my old friends who I have been associated with during this time. Of course, the Perth of that day was vastly different from the Perth of the present as there were not 50,000 in the whole of Western Australia at that time, the only railway was the line to York and a short line from Geraldton to Northampton. There was no parliament and WA was governed as a Crown Colony under Governor Broome...*[46]

Robert paused, then fell backwards. Those nearest to him rushed to his side and the family friend and physician, Bruce Hunt, immediately came to his aid.

Robert Bunning's Commemorative Dinner, Palace Hotel, Perth, 12 August 1936 (Bunning Family Collection)

There was nothing that could be done – he was dead. His friends and colleagues were stunned, and many left the hotel in tears. Hunt had told Tom only months earlier that he feared Robert may not have had much longer to live, but nobody could quite have imagined it would happen like this.[47] In time, his death would become something of a legend in Perth's business circles.

The next morning, Tom and Charlie sat down with Joe and Arthur Petherick at Charles Street to work out what to do. They determined that Petherick would take over as managing director and the three brothers would maintain their existing responsibilities: Charlie would manage the sawmilling operations; Tom would look after the company's financial administration; and Joe would remain in charge of Perth Jarrah Mills.[48] Tom lost little time in shutting down his father's venture at Garden Island. It had been a dead weight financially from the beginning, eating up something in the order of £5,000 and attracting a regular stream of requests from friends and acquaintances for favours in booking accommodation. But with Australia's economic recovery underway, it would otherwise be business as usual. Within two years, the last of the money owing to the bank had been repaid.[49]

Robert's death marked a more profound turning point for Tom in other ways. He had never lacked partners for social engagements and for a time had been involved with Temperley's daughter, Dorothy. Within months of his father's death, however, his relationship with Margot had commenced. The pair had mixed in the same circles for years and knew each other well. Her Colin Street home was in its heyday as a venue for entertaining, and Charlie had been engaged briefly to her elder sister.[50] Tall, slender and fair, Margot herself had been a mainstay of the social columns in her early twenties. In fact, there was barely a weekend when her whereabouts (or what she was wearing) were not reported in the newspapers. On any weekend, this meant the pair would likely cross paths. It might be at a cocktail party, a dance or another formal occasion like the annual ball at Lake Karrinyup Country Club (where the younger men, 'instead of wearing black dinner jackets or tailed coats', opted instead for 'the white mess jackets which are so suitable for summer dancing'), or at something more casual, such as a crabbing party on the river (where 'all the girls wore slacks and most of the men shorts').[51] She had even created a stir by debuting one of the first two-piece swimsuits to appear on Perth's beaches: 'a backless deep blue and white top with blue trunks', it was reported the next day.[52] During 1936 she

Margot Law, early 1930s (Bunning Family Collection)

had travelled with her parents to Europe before continuing on to Chicago for the World Expo, calling at Japan on the voyage home.[53] That summer, back in Perth, she and Tom became something more than just friends.

Tom knew he had found the woman he wanted to marry.[54] Many of his friends were doing exactly the same. He had been a best man twice that year already, and Margot had been a bridesmaid at the wedding of her elder brother Gordon.[55] They were spending much of their spare time together. On one weekend, it might be a cocktail party at Minnewarra, the Cottesloe residence of the Vincent family (one of whom, Oliver, would shortly marry Jane), or 'Pink tea' at the Hotel Adelphi, followed by the opening night of the Miami Club, a more successful successor to Tom's Cosmo Club. At the end of that summer, the pair hosted a 'chain dinner' for their friends, with cocktails at Colin Street followed by dinner and dancing at Innerhadden. Their engagement was announced in May.[56]

Margot travelling with Robert and Bertha Law, 1936 (Courtesy Elizabeth Green)

Tom's form on the golf course had never been better. He had been elected Captain of Cottesloe and won his second club championship in a row after acing the third hole in a match against his old friend and rival Geoff Hill. It was the first time a hole in one had been recorded at the Swanbourne course, though he nearly threw away the title when the match referee retrieved the ball out of the cup and asked him the number of it, only for Tom to momentarily forget it in his excitement of his hole in one.[57] He went on that season to win the Champion of Champions trophy against the best player from each of the Perth clubs, the first year this competition was held, when he was the most consistent player across two rounds in wet and windy conditions at Lake Karrinyup.[58] He also won the Commemoration Cup at Royal Perth and the Punchbowl Cup in the South West titles at Bunbury.[59] The 1938 season was not quite so successful, as he lost the club championship to Reg Forbes. His consolation was to lead Cottesloe to another pennant championship against Royal Fremantle at Lake Karrinyup. It was a tight

Tom on his way to equalling the course
record of 72 at Cottesloe Golf Club, 1936
(Bunning Family Collection)

affair against Keith Pix, also among the state's best amateurs, with Tom two down after the 27th hole: 'Then Bunning, great match player that he is, revealed his best golf, and Pix despite his skill and admirable calmness could not stop Bunning winning hole after hole.' The end, it was reported, 'came with great suddenness', with Tom's victory handing Cottesloe the title by four matches to three.[60]

Tom's and Margot's wedding was held a few weeks later, on 4 November 1938, at St George's Cathedral in the city. 'The bride, who was given away by her father, was a tall, graceful figure in a beautiful frock of magnolia satin fashioned on long elegant lines'. She was accompanied by sister Mary, Jane Bunning and her friend Mollie Noble (who was about to marry one of Tom's groomsmen, Peter Stuart Smith) as bridesmaids. Tom's best man was his childhood friend Bill Anderson, with Bob Holmes as his second groomsman and Oliver Vincent as his usher. A reception for about 200 guests followed at Colin Street. The newlyweds then departed for a honeymoon in Colombo and Singapore.[61]

Margot on her wedding day, November 1938
(Bunning Family Collection)

Back in Perth, Bunning Bros was at its busiest in more than a decade. The company had won contracts to build aircraft hangars at the airfield at Pearce, to supply housing to the new iron-ore mine at Yampi Sound in the state's far north, and, even further afield, for a major Commonwealth construction project in New Guinea. The work for Pearce was quickly followed by a second contract for hangars and housing at an airfield near Darwin. The sleeper trade was continuing to prosper, with orders from China, Ceylon, Iraq, Persia, South Africa and Egypt, along with other timber orders from the United Kingdom, Mauritius and India. The company continued to upgrade its equipment and now relied almost solely on tractors and trucks for moving logs and sawn timber. The mill at Yornup had been rebuilt and reopened, and another, smaller mill, Tullis, had been constructed to handle wandoo and jarrah from the land near Boddington. With an eye to the future, the company also bid for a permit covering some 55,000 acres at Nyamup, east of Manjimup. It was to be the largest concession Bunning Bros had ever held and would guarantee hardwood supplies for many years to come. By early 1939, construction of another large sawmill had commenced.[62]

Tom's career was beginning to take off. He had been elected to the Weld Club, Perth's most exclusive private club. This was something that had eluded his father, who, as a carpenter by training, was the practitioner of a 'trade' and therefore outside the criteria for membership, despite having built the club's building on Barrack Street. As a professional accountant, Tom was eligible.[63] It helped that he was also well-connected, and not only on the Bunning side. His new father-in-law, Robert Law, was now among Western Australia's most senior businessmen. Similar to Bunning Bros, both his family-owned Metro Brick and his joint venture, Swan Portland Cement, had come through the Depression and were prospering again from the recovery in the residential building and construction sectors.[64] He got on well with Tom, who could now benefit regularly from his counsel. Law's advice helped to sway Tom in favour of taking Bunning Bros back into brickmaking, when the company became the major shareholder in the local subsidiary of Dunbrick, a manufacturer of concrete bricks. Through Perth Jarrah Mills, the Bunning family then purchased forty acres of land at Canning, at the edge of Perth's suburbs, to supply sand to its new undertaking.[65] In early 1939, Tom also took on his first external board appointment, when he was invited onto the Perth board of the Commonwealth Insurance Company.[66]

Robert Law (Bunning Family Collection)

Tom and Margot had returned from their honeymoon to a new home of their own at 6 Osborne Parade, near the boundary between Cottesloe and Claremont. 'Cotswold' was a modern two-storey brick residence, named because of its likeness to the English Cotswolds architecture. It had been built during the early 1930s for a local doctor and had a generous lounge that was suitable for entertaining.[67] They were soon hosting parties for as many as one hundred guests at a time.[68] The house was on a large block, and Tom had begun to contemplate renovations to better cater for a future family. He was also beginning to think about building a second residence in the country, where he could spend quiet weekends with Margot and, down the track, their children. He wanted at least 1,000 acres, with a good supply of water, although he had not yet decided whether they would plant fruit trees, raise cattle or find some other use for the land.[69]

Their days as members of Perth's younger crowd were coming to an end. But it was more than the transition to married life that was shaping their future. By the early part of 1939, the prospect of war breaking out in Europe seemed increasingly certain. Great Britain and the Empire would almost certainly be dragged into it. For Tom, it was not a matter of jingoism but rather a question to be assessed rationally and according to his own values and beliefs. He recognised he had enjoyed good fortune in his upbringing and position in Western Australian society and accepted that it came with a responsibility to give back when it was required.[70] It seemed like that time had arrived. On 28 April 1939, he enlisted in the 25th Light Horse (Machine Gun) Regiment, a newly created militia unit and the last Light Horse regiment to be raised in Australia.[71] Many of his friends were doing the same. His earlier training in the cadet corps at Scotch College was immediately recognised, and he was assigned the rank of Lieutenant in the Commonwealth Military Force. The 25th was headquartered initially at Swan Barracks in the city, with troops also formed in some of the country towns.[72] In August, the regiment came together for the first time for a training course at Guildford.[73] A few weeks later, when Germany invaded Poland, World War II began. Tom was sent away immediately for training at Rockingham. Margot would be left at home alone for the first time since they married. It would be a long time indeed before their normal lives resumed.

4

Officer, husband, father

Tom's early months as a military officer involved a series of training camps around Western Australia. The first, at Rockingham, was followed in the new year by camps at Melville and then Canning Dam, at which point he came to regard himself as full-time soldier. The war was going badly for the Allies, with the retreat at Normandy and France's capitulation followed by the Battle of Britain. He remained at Cotswold during 1940, managing his training commitments with his job at Bunning Bros, though as it became clearer that Australia would be called upon for assistance, he made the decision to transfer from the militia to the Second Australian Imperial Force (AIF). This meant he was eligible for service overseas, and to prepare for it, he would be leaving the comforts of home indefinitely for the main army camp at Northam, where units already on active service in Egypt and Palestine had previously been trained.[1] He was promoted to captain at this time and posted to a new unit, the 2/4th Machine Gun Battalion. There would soon be something else to occupy his mind as well. Within weeks of his enlistment, Margot discovered she was pregnant. As the news coming out of the battlefields in Europe, North Africa and the Middle East was growing more complex by the day, they had to also contend with the reality that their first child was now on its way.

The new unit he was joining at Northam was a specialised battalion of motorised infantry designed to provide mobile firepower, the need for which had been among the main tactical lessons that had been learnt during the First World War.[2] Its personnel were drawn entirely from those who had enlisted in Western Australia. There was a core of thirteen officers in the 2/4th under the command of Lieutenant-Colonel Michael Anketell, a veteran of the Western Front and longstanding militia officer.[3] These included five captains, each responsible for a company that would, at full strength, comprise around 150 men. Albert Saggers and Archibald Thomas had been with Tom in the 25th Light Horse; Saggers was a footwear merchant and Thomas a bank officer. They were joined by Alfred Cough, a building contractor from Busselton, and Oswald McEwin, a sales manager. Though McEwin was Tom's age, the others were older men. The recruits, by contrast, were mostly aged in their twenties and hailed from the goldfields, the country districts and the suburbs of Perth. It was a rush to settle in and prepare for their arrival. 'It is a terrible scramble for a start', Tom wrote home, 'but we have got the mess going at least sufficiently well to serve a reasonably cold beer and to dish up not a bad meal'. Stores were being issued and an initial contingent of some 400 men were arriving by rail within days.[4] 'Margot you are the grandest person in the whole world and if ever anyone had something to fight for and some incentive to do a good job, well that person is me'.[5]

For any soldier, the post was the main and often the only lifeline to home and those that had been left behind. Letter writing was part of Tom's daily routine, although it wasn't always easy to find the time. 'B Company' was now being formed, and with raw troops needing to be kitted out and trained from scratch, there was a full schedule six days a week, with reveille at 6 am. The officers had their own mess to retire to in the evenings, but often there were visitors to host from other units under training at Northam, or visits to reciprocate to the officers' mess attached to the air-force training camp further inland at Cunderdin. On Saturday evenings, Northam's hotels and billiard rooms were the main attraction.[6] With church service on Sunday morning, there was really only a single afternoon when he was able to catch up on the mail. Margot naturally took precedence, although Tom also wrote regularly to his mother and to Robert and Pauline Law, and, when he could, to his siblings and friends.[7] After a month in camp the first leave was granted, with preference to married men. Tom was given a week off, just in time to catch the train down for Christmas.[8] Before he was dismissed, the 2/4th received its unique colour patch, which the

Tom, mid-1930s (Bunning Family Collection)

troops wore to identify their battalion. This was a black and gold triangle, an acknowledgement of their unit's Western Australian origins.⁹

Perth was the same hive of activity it always had been, with the main difference being that so many men were now in uniform. There was certainly no shortage of social engagements, nor of news to catch up on from friends who had also accepted commissions or otherwise signed on with the AIF or another branch of the armed services. When the war began, Charlie had volunteered for the Royal Australian Engineers. During 1940 he was seconded or 'manpowered' to the Commonwealth Timber Control Organisation within the newly formed Ministry of Munitions, where he would work to ensure the nation's supplies of timber products would be maintained despite looming labour shortages and new constraints on the import of softwoods. It meant travelling even more frequently than before, not only in the southwest but as far afield as the east coast and

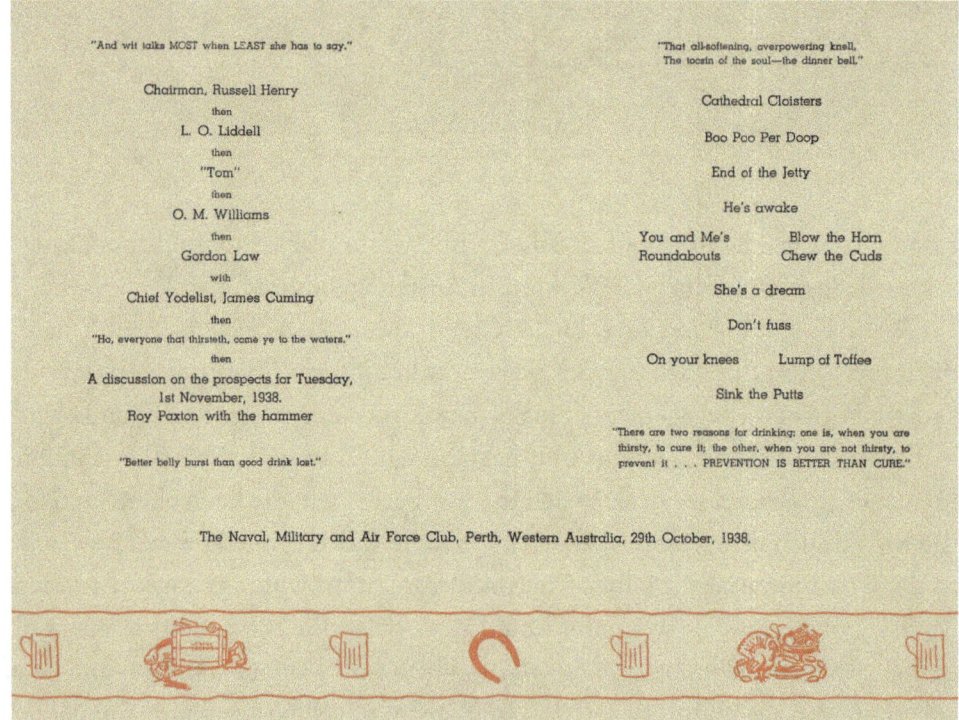

Top and bottom: Tom's Buck's Night Program, October 1938 (Bunning Family Collection)

Northern Territory, although he, too, was able to visit home at this time.[10] Flora was involved in organising and performing at concerts being held to benefit the troops by raising funds for the Red Cross and Camp Comfort Fund. This was a role she kept up for the duration of the war.[11] With Jane and Oliver Vincent in residence at Cotswold, it was a lively week indeed. Tom and Margot brought in the new year together, and a few days later they attended the wedding of a mutual acquaintance. Then it was time to part again, as she joined the Laws on their annual holiday in Albany, and he returned to camp.[12] The full heat of summer had set in at Northam, as the serious business of training resumed.

The focus now was to initiate the battalion to its main weapon, the Vickers machine gun. This was a heavy, water-cooled gun with a reputation for reliability that had been forged in the mud and dust of the Western Front. Several veterans of the First World War were attached to the 2/4th as instructors on its deployment and operation. There were also basic rifle drills and additional lessons on other infantry weapons, field-craft lectures, map-reading exercises and, for each platoon, tactics for defensive and attacking operations to rehearse. A stickler for physical fitness, Anketell also arranged route marches through the countryside, despite the hot weather. The men soon graduated to more-complex firing exercises, night manoeuvres and instruction in the handling of military vehicles.[13] Films were put on in the evenings and concerts held for the camp as a whole. Cricket was played on Sundays, although Tom could not force his way into the battalion's first eleven. He was aware of the need to build discipline in his troops. Australians, he had found, held peculiar attitudes in relation to soldiering. 'Not only have we been bred on the idea that it was one of our favourable characteristics that we would not be disciplined, but also we have been brought up in the idea that having put on uniform our real duty was to take every possible opportunity for drinking as much beer as we could cram into our stomachs and also to take advantage of anything that any girl had to offer'. He considered himself broad-minded but, 'I did not think it possible that man would devote so much time and thought to beer and women and be as thorough in their exploitation of opportunities'.[14] Cultivating good conduct across the company at large was as tough a task as any.

There was good spirit and enthusiasm all the same, and this acted to build pride in the battalion. In early March, the 2/4th set off on foot to Perth via Clackline, Lake Leschenaultia and Bassendean. With supporting vehicles in tow,

The 2/4th Battalion on the march from Northam to Perth, March 1941 (Bunning Family Collection)

the battalion made up a column over a mile long. The march was covered in all the newspapers and even filmed for the newsreels that played in cinemas around the country. On the third day, it concluded with a parade through the city and a salute to the Army's Western Command, the Western Australian Premier and the Mayor of Perth along St George's Terrace. A crowd numbering in the hundreds had gathered to welcome them, and after lunch was served to the battalion's full complement of 800 men, they were dismissed on weekend leave. Margot's pregnancy was noticeable now, and Tom was obliged to drink to the health of their child more than once during his brief stay at home. When training resumed there was renewed focus on live firing exercises, with dedicated coastal defence drills taking place at Mullaloo and Lancelin over the weeks that followed.[15]

The 2/4th Battalion's march through Perth, March 1941, Tom front left (Bunning Family Collection)

The question of what exactly they were training for dominated conversation in the mess. The AIF now had three divisions or some 60,000 men overseas, in addition to those serving in the navy and air force. During May a fourth division, the 8th Division, was officially designated. The 2/4th was duly allotted to it.[16] Although the Australian forces had won a string of victories against the Italian army in North Africa and Vichy French forces in Syria, the Germans were now entering the Mediterranean theatre in force, and, in Europe, France had fallen and the German invasion of Russia was underway. There were worrying signs in the Pacific, with Japan now aligned to the Axis powers that were at war with the British Commonwealth and its allies.[17] In the context of this uncertainty, the Australian government decided on a home defence role for the new division. For the 2/4th battalion, this meant a transfer to Adelaide, where they would be ready for quick deployment and continue training in the meantime.[18] When the order was received in July, Margot decided on a move of her own. Rather than remain at Cotswold, the house would be let instead to Jane and Oliver Vincent, who were now expecting a child of their own. She would return home to stay with her parents at Colin Street.

Of course, departing for South Australia meant being away for the birth. Margot went to see Tom off at Fremantle ('you just don't know how much I would have loved to hop that ruddy fence', he wrote on the voyage over) as the battalion boarded MS *Duntroon* for Port Adelaide.[19] From there it was a short trip by train to the camp at Woodside in the Adelaide Hills. The picturesque surrounds helped to alleviate the anxiety of leaving home at such a time. Soon after arriving, he wrote:

> The country here is absolutely lovely. We are 1400 feet up and naturally it is bitterly cold at night. Where we are the country is undulating but is surrounded by hills and ranges and there are lots of beautiful little valleys…Around about us are all farms but in the ranges proper within 3 or 4 miles of the camp it is mainly orchard country. The ground is nearly all very clayey and looks absolutely beautiful ploughed up. I went for a drive about this afternoon and my only wish was that you could be with me…It is all wonderfully green and really just like the English countryside.[20]

It was a good location for training, apart from all the fences. There were route marches to distances of up to eight miles each afternoon and, for the evenings, similar facilities for recreation as at Northam. The battalion would also be permitted on weekend leave to Adelaide.[21] A local grazier stationed at Woodside as the commander of an artillery unit arranged for Tom to be made an honorary member of the Adelaide Club, which he found to be a welcome change from the barracks: 'terribly old and quiet and just like the Weld Club', he thought.[22] Better still, he could use the telephone to place calls through to Colin Street. Margot was becoming anxious as her pregnancy approached full term, so that regular contact was a comfort to them both. 'Darling, I am not the slightest bit worried about the show', he wrote at the start of August. 'I feel completely confident that everything will turn out just as you would wish it', even if he couldn't be present himself.[23]

At Woodside, the endless gun drills and firing exercises were broken up by a 30-mile march to the peak of Mt Lofty, 'the most strenuous day of our career', in

Margot Bunning, c. late 1930s (Bunning Family Collection)

Tom's view.[24] It remained bitterly cold, and it became all the more uncomfortable after flu swept through the camp.[25] Down in Adelaide the residents were proving to be remarkably hospitable, such that his weekends were fully occupied by cocktail parties, dinners, dances and other engagements. It was so much like home that he was continually being introduced to people who had met Margot before the war.[26] In mid-August, a telegram arrived at the Adelaide Club: 'I opened it with a breathtaking rip only to read from the contents that Charlie would be arriving here on Monday'.[27] Two days after meeting his brother for breakfast at the railway station, he was notified that Margot had given birth to a son, Gavin Law, at Kensington Hospital in Subiaco. 'Darling you are marvellous', he telegrammed her, adding that he was 'absolutely thrilled to the core'.[28] With the permission of his commanding officer, Anketell, he was able to fly home to spend a week with his wife and child. 'Darling, it was absolutely grand to be able to get over and see you and Gavin and I simply loved every minute of it', he wrote upon returning to the camp.[29] It had come just in time. Leave was cancelled at short notice for the entire battalion and another march arranged instead, this time to Mt Barker. Although only 18 miles long, it involved a steep climb to the summit, 'quite the toughest we have had'.[30]

The sudden restriction of weekend leave pointed to a shift in military planning that would soon be laid bare to the battalion. Japan's aggressive posture in the Pacific was of increasing concern to the Allied powers, especially after the Vichy French government yielded military bases in Indochina to the Japanese air force and navy. One brigade of the 8th Division had been dispatched to Singapore in October 1940, and now another was on the way to reinforce Commonwealth forces there and in Malaya. This left the 2/4th as one of the few trained AIF units remaining in Australia. Leave was reinstated after a month, allowing Tom to spend a few days as a guest at a sheep station near Peterborough, halfway between Adelaide and Broken Hill.[31] He and Margot must have both sensed the next move was close by, because in late September, barely a month after giving birth, she and Gavin boarded an aircraft at Maylands aerodrome for an all-day, two-stop flight to Adelaide. As with his flight home, it came just in time. They had a few precious hours together, all that could be allowed. Back at Woodside, orders were received to proceed to Darwin for garrison duty in the Northern Territory. A final gruelling march was made to Waterfall Gully in the foothills above Adelaide, before the 2/4th packed up and began the long journey north.[32]

After a first stage by rail as far as Alice Springs, the battalion journeyed on to Darwin aboard a convoy of motor trucks. The route took them through parts of Australia Tom had not seen before, and the journey proved to be an interesting one. They were now in an operational zone. All outgoing mail would be censored by the officers.[33] Outside of their daily rations, the two staples of a soldier's life remained cigarettes and beer, but whereas the former were given away freely at each canteen they stopped at, the latter was becoming harder and harder to locate and more expensive when it was available.[34] Tom had been assigned a batman, Private Albert Brooksbank, to run messages and other errands.[35] The men slept under mosquito nets at night and were now kitted out in shorts and shirts, a welcome change after so many frosty mornings in South Australia. 'Goodness knows when I will see a sweater again', he wrote. 'It is really a treat to get some hot sun again.'[36] The monsoon was approaching, and the men were busily preparing their camp for the rain. 'You should see the troops now. They never wear shirts except for meals and special parades. By golly they look fit.'[37]

It was not only the climate that was different. There were military personnel stationed all around Darwin, naval vessels in the harbour, and plenty of aircraft flying overhead. This lifted the mood in the battalion, dissipating the sense of disappointment that had developed from being long overlooked for a posting overseas. Now they were surrounded by their comrades in the AIF, rather than the militia units that had also been stationed at Woodside. A new sense of pride took hold: 'even in this short time I can see that the chaps are becoming just a little smarter and more regimental', Tom observed.[38] Soon they had their first real assignment. During November, orders arrived to head south to Adelaide River to undertake guard duty over vital petrol and ammunition supplies and the military jail located there. 'Have you heard of this place before?' he asked Margot. 'I must admit that up until three weeks ago, I hadn't, but henceforth it will stand in history as the first place to which Gavin MacRae Bunning took his troops and had them as an independent command.'[39]

Detached from the other company commanders and battalion HQ, and together with his men in a compact camp of canvas tents, Tom saw a side to them not as readily apparent in a larger barracks. They were constantly complaining: 'I realise afresh that they probably started grumbling on the first day they joined the army and as long as they draw breath in uniform they will continue to do so'. Their conversations were clearly audible in his tent: 'the language of course is absolutely shocking'. They were paid each Friday, 'and with nothing to spend their money on are either gambling or drinking it away'.[40] Guard duty in such a remote place tended to be approached rather casually, and he found it necessary to keep a close eye on the night shift and rebuke men for carelessness on more than one occasion.[41] And yet these were among the happiest days the 143 men of B Company spent together. The wet season had arrived, and with it came spectacular lightning displays in the evening sky. The camp was surrounded by wetlands with prolific wildlife, and Tom readily issued ammunition to off-duty men, who obligingly furnished ducks, bush turkeys and wild pigs for the evening meal: 'I am sure it is dashed good training for the troops and am going to give them as much of it as possible'.[42] He had leaned on Petherick to use his shipping contacts to send up beer as well, so that they had one of the best supplies anywhere in the Northern Territory.[43] Route marches were reduced to a leisurely

15-mile round trip to a waterfall he had found that was shaded by tall palms and with crystal clear water, 'as pretty a tropical scene as you would see anywhere'.[44] When they weren't out marching they swam instead in the Adelaide River, 'with an occasional stick of gelignite thrown in to keep the crocodiles away'.[45]

A senior officer came down from Darwin towards the end of November to distribute *The Handbook of Pidgin English*. It kept them all laughing for days, even if the implication was that a posting in New Guinea or the South Pacific lay ahead.[46] When the attack on Pearl Harbour came a fortnight later, it created a degree of excitement but no real surprise, as Japan's entry into the war had long been expected. The news, a few days later, that the Royal Navy's battleships *Prince of Wales* and *Repulse* had been lost was a more worrying development. Tom told Margot that although he feared the Japanese might secure some early victories, he doubted they would prevail in a protracted struggle against the Allies, and he didn't think the fighting would ever reach Australia.[47] Nonetheless, he encouraged her to speak to her father about the possibility of evacuating to a safe place inland in the event that she and Gavin were ever in danger themselves.[48]

As Christmas approached, Tom found himself growing busier by the day. He still had the company to run at Adelaide River but was being called more often into HQ at Darwin. The place was awash with rumours and reports from Pearl Harbour and elsewhere being brought in by American pilots and other military units who were rapidly relocating to new bases around the town.[49] On Boxing Day, B Company packed up and moved back to rejoin the battalion. The 2/4th had received orders to prepare for embarkation. Tom set out to catch up on his correspondence. There was a letter from Petherick and a card signed by 'all the old hands' at Charles Street that awaited replies, old friends such as Geoff Hill and Frank Downing to respond to, and all the family to write to as well.[50] It was just in time for the mail in Darwin. By 1 January 1942 he was on the high seas, to a destination as yet unknown.[51]

The battalion had shipped out the previous evening. In the harbour they passed the USS *Houston*, which would be lost barely two months later alongside HMAS *Perth* in the Battle of Sunda Straits. That evening, the men welcomed the new year with a midnight toast on deck.[52] At Port Moresby they transhipped to HMT *Aquitania*, a cruise liner pressed into military service as a troopship. The *Aquitania* then went to Sydney, where some 2,500 AIF reinforcements were taken on board. They were given shore leave, giving Tom the chance to call home from

Tom, c. 1941 (Bunning Family Collection)

the Australia Club, followed by a long lunch with friends, then an afternoon of snooker at the University Club. When his troops came back, he found several of them 'covered with black eyes and thick lips', with more fisticuffs on board before all their grudges were settled. The next destination was Fremantle and he, like everyone else, was looking forward to shore leave there.[53] This time, however, shore leave was not allowed. As the *Aquitania* lay in Gage Roads off Fremantle, groups of men began to slip away without authority on the vessels delivering supplies. Tom effectively turned a blind eye, even at the risk of an official rebuke, because he felt the army was not being fair.[54] But as an officer there was no question of going ashore himself, however difficult it must have been to be anchored off Cottesloe with his wife and son only a few miles away. They were soon underway again, escorted by HMAS *Canberra* to the Sunda Strait, where the battalion disembarked into two small Dutch vessels. They were now in an active war zone and the destination was clear. On 25 January they arrived in Singapore and were sent immediately to prepare defences in the island's north.

The situation at this time was nothing short of desperate. Just as the 2/4th was taking up positions along the narrow Johore Strait, which separates Singapore island from the mainland, all British, Indian and Australian forces were being evacuated from the Malayan peninsula. The city, the naval base and the airfields were subject to daily air raids, and when Johore itself was abandoned, most of the island fell within range of Japanese artillery as well. The RAF and RAAF had a chronic shortage of aircraft, and artillery units were under strict orders to conserve ammunition, even as the enemy began massing across the Strait. The civilian population, swelled by refugees from the mainland, were traumatised from the constant bombing, and the Indian troops in particular were poorly trained and low on morale following bad defeats on the peninsula. The Royal Navy was powerless to offer any resistance to the land-based assault now imminent. Yet Singapore's commander, Lieutenant-General Arthur Percival, intended to hold the island in order to exhaust Japanese forces and enable the Allies to build up strength for counter-offensives in Burma, Malaya and the Philippines.[55] The battalion had a key role in his plan. B Company was tasked initially with constructing weapons pits in the vicinity of the naval base before joining the 8th Division's 27th Brigade in the causeway sector, which defended the coast between the causeway to Johore and the mouth of the Kranji River. D Company was on the opposite side of the river with the 22nd Brigade, also part of 8th Division. C Company went to join the 44th Indian Brigade in the island's southwest corner, with A Company held in reserve.[56] When the causeway was blown up on 31 January, the siege of Singapore had begun.

B Company had been positioned to cover the last withdrawals across the causeway before attaching platoons to each of the 27th Brigade's three regular infantry battalions. These had all been in Malaya since mid-1941 and had taken part in the fighting there. The 2/26th Battalion, originating from Queensland and northern New South Wales, had participated in defensive operations at Johore. The 2/29th, from Victoria, and the 2/30th, from Sydney and the Riverina, had fought successful actions at the Battle of Muar, only to withdraw when the Indian brigades either side of them were routed.[57] Each was now topped up with reinforcements that had arrived alongside the 2/4th. Tom set out to reconnoitre his sector, and with his officers, attended briefings on enemy tactics.[58] The arrival in

Singapore of Britain's 18th Division, together with a second battalion of machine gunners, completed the forces at Percival's disposal. He had some 85,000 men under his command, but of those only thirteen battalions were from the United Kingdom and six were from Australia. More than half of the defenders comprised Indian or Malay units and most of these were considered to be second-rate units, although some, like the Gurkha battalion positioned on the 27th Brigade's right flank, were formidable soldiers. The Japanese could marshal as many as twenty-seven battalions for an invasion, supported by complete dominance of the air, and with reserves available elsewhere in Malaya and Indochina.[59]

The attack fell on the evening of 8 February. Its main thrust came across the Kranji in 22nd Brigade's sector, where mangroves and thick jungle best suited the strategy of infiltration and outflanking that the Japanese had used to such effect in Malaya. In darkness, and covered by intense artillery and mortar fire, some sixteen battalions attacked a front defended by only two AIF battalions reinforced by the machine gunners of D Company. The Japanese were met by intense fire from the Vickers machine guns, yet they came in such numbers that groups of them were soon established ashore. Following vicious hand-to-hand combat, and with their ammunition nearly exhausted, the Australians were forced into fighting withdrawals, as the attackers constantly sought to outflank and isolate pockets of resistance.[60] Heavy casualties had been sustained. With the situation becoming untenable, a new perimeter was formed a couple of miles inland around the major airfield at Tengah. The reserve company of the 2/4th Battalion was being rushed to the area, along with the 2/29th Battalion and their supporting platoon from Tom's B Company. They had orders to counterattack, but these were soon abandoned as the Japanese concentrated their assault against the airfield, one of their major targets.[61] The first B Company man to be killed in action was lost in this engagement.[62] The rest of the company were still positioned around the causeway, where they sat out the night under constant shellfire from the mainland.[63]

Increasing air and artillery bombardment during 9 February signalled the next assault was imminent. It came at dusk, spearheaded by the elite Guards Division. Both the 2/26th and 2/30th were soon engaged, supported by the machine gunners, who laid down a withering fire that pinned the Japanese down before the relentless waves attempting to cross the Strait enabled the attackers to regain the initiative. Conscious of the gap in his line brought about by the departure of the 2/29th, and fearing for the flank exposed because of the ground captured the previous day, the 27th Brigade's commanding officer, Brigadier Duncan Maxwell, ordered a withdrawal to new defensive lines back from the shoreline at Mandai.[64] Before moving, the Australians demolished the fuel tanks near the naval base. Some 2,000,000 gallons were set alight, causing burning oil to flow down across the Japanese positions and flames to seep out across the Strait. With the enemy suddenly vividly illuminated, the machine gunners poured fire into their positions. Then, with dawn approaching, they fell back to their new lines.[65]

It had been a trying baptism of fire. B Company remained cut off from the rest of the 2/4th, and the constant artillery and mortar fire broke lines of communication by cutting telephone cables and hindering movement across open ground. On more than one occasion, Tom had to venture out to make contact with adjoining units.[66] As the Japanese hurried in reinforcements, including tanks, the defenders found themselves heavily outnumbered. Tengah airfield had been lost, and the thrust of the attack was continuing against 22nd Brigade forces and the reinforcements sent to their aid. B Company's 7 Platoon, cut off from the 2/29th Battalion when Tengah fell, had withdrawn under heavy fire to the new Australian line.[67] On 11 February, a counterattack ordered by Percival failed miserably when the Indian troops committed to it quickly disintegrated, leaving the depleted and exhausted Australian battalions dangerously exposed. In the 27th Brigade's sector, a period of confusion followed the relocation to Mandai. after the Brigade was first placed under an Indian division before reverting to 8th Division command, and orders for a counterattack were abandoned when they arrived at the frontline just as the Japanese launched a fresh assault. B Company's 8 Platoon was thrust into the thick of the fighting as wave after wave of attackers were repelled at point-blank range.[68] They held out for several hours but, low on ammunition, with several wounded, four dead and the infantry falling back, they packed their guns into a truck and prepared to withdraw. Finding the road blocked, the truck was abandoned and the wounded carried to safety through the jungle. Amid widespread chaos, Tom set about reorganising his platoons. New guns were located to replace those lost at Mandai, and the company distributed to a new defensive perimeter surrounding the city of Singapore itself.[69]

The rest of the 2/4th Battalion remained to the south-west, where the fiercest fighting was taking place. They were in their fourth day of combat and facing overwhelming odds. The casualty list continued to grow. Oswald McEwin and a number of men from HQ Company were lost on 12 February in a bayonet charge to retake a hill that overlooked defensive positions. Lieutenant-Colonel Anketell was badly wounded a short time later as he rallied his men against the latest assault.[70] They were pushed back again to the outskirts of the city. With the general retreat the 27th Brigade no longer had a sector of its own, but what remained of the 2/26th and 2/30th battalions continued to fight on, providing cover to units withdrawn from the northern sectors of Singapore island. By 13 February most of B Company was dug in along a ridge at Pasir Panjang, alongside a mixed force of Australian, British and Indian troops. They were under constant bombardment. Another attack was fought off the next day, but the cost to the company was again high.[71] Percival had long since recognised his situation was hopeless: he had no reserves left, too many of his troops had been utterly routed, the Japanese had captured the reservoirs that supplied Singapore with water, and their air force was steadily reducing the city to rubble. He had orders to fight on, but when Churchill himself signalled that further resistance was now futile, a deputation was sent out to the Japanese lines. Percival accepted terms of surrender on the evening of Sunday 15 February.[72] At 8.30 pm, the order to lay down arms was received at B Company HQ.[73]

Tom went out immediately to alert his platoons of the ceasefire. They were 'abjectly miserable' at the order to stand down.[74] The company had 136 men still in the line, and not only were all of its twelve Vickers machine guns operational, they had acquired and deployed an additional two from other units in retreat. At least 400 enemy soldiers had been killed during the six days of combat they had engaged in. Now came the shock, disappointment and uncertainty of surrender. Tom arranged for a case of whisky to be opened and issued among the troops, then headed to battalion HQ for orders. When he returned at 2 am, 'we proceeded to open a tin of every variety of food in sight and ate the best meal that we had experienced since arriving on this Godforsaken island'. There had been little else but tinned beef, bread, cigarettes and tea since they disembarked. It was, he recalled, 'the one and only time that I have permitted myself any license with army food and is the last decent meal we had'.[75]

The news of Singapore's capitulation broke in Perth the next day. There had been no greater military setback in the history of the British Empire. About 80,000 Allied troops, including 15,000 AIF soldiers, were now prisoners of war. Bali and Lombok were captured within days, isolating Java and exposing Australia's north to attack. Darwin was bombed for the first time on 19 February. For an anxious Australian public, it seemed as though their worst fears were unfolding by the day. Just after Christmas, the new Prime Minister of Australia, John Curtin, had appealed to the United States to defend Australia from invasion. Yet America had only just entered the war itself, and its manpower and resources, though vast, still lay on the other side of the Pacific Ocean. The Japanese, by contrast, were now on the nation's doorstep.

Right up until the order to sail from Darwin came through, Tom had held on to the hope that he would have a final opportunity to visit home. Margot had been holding off on Gavin's christening in the hope he could be present for it. Now, however, she went ahead with the ceremony in his absence. When the news of Singapore's fall came through, she made the decision to relocate with Gavin to Pinnacles Station at Leinster, near Leonora, deep in the Western Australian interior. Jane relocated with her new child at the same time.[76] They would remain there with Angie and Don McKinnon indefinitely, safe for the time being but without any further information from the 8th Division, and hence, no knowledge of Tom's whereabouts or fate.

What followed was the single hardest day of Tom's military career. After Japanese patrols reached the 2/4th positions, several of the officers were escorted away, leaving him as the senior officer remaining within the battalion. Lines of communication were still open to Brigade and Divisional HQs, and orders duly came through to depart for the British military barracks at Changi, at the eastern end of the island. Tom was obliged to take incoming telephone calls in the presence of passing enemy soldiers, one of whom brandished a pistol in his face, before the lines were cut and the Australians were herded towards the nearest road. As their trucks were being driven away, Tom leapt aboard one and rode it to the nearest Japanese base, where he was able to persuade a commander to release the vehicles and basic supplies they carried.[77] He then joined the march across Singapore. Although the trucks had been recovered, he would not allow his men to ride in them, as his orders were clear on this point; and in any case, 'we were marching between units who had been fighting, not for ten days, but for six weeks solidly, and what they could do I was determined we could do'.[78] It contributed to a painful journey. Their destination was approximately 16 miles away, and it took nearly eight hours to cover the distance. Each company was then allocated a bivouac, before Tom lay down to rest at 4 am, thus ending 'the most trying day I have ever experienced'.[79]

The 2/4th had lost 136 men in the defence of Singapore. At least 100 more had been wounded. B Company had maintained good order throughout, despite being cut off from battalion HQ from the first day of battle, and as other Commonwealth forces crumbled around them. Tom's conduct was praised by Brigadier Maxwell, who recommended him for a Mention in Despatches:

> It is desired to bring to your notice the excellent work done by Capt. Bunning when his Coy was under command 27 Aust. Inf. Bde during the operations on Singapore Island. He was absolutely tireless and personally supervised the siting and preparation of all machine gun posts. At all times he showed a complete disregard for personal safety. His platoons were of necessity widely dispersed and a report of an enemy attack on any section of the front invariably called for an immediate reaction on his part. "I would like to go forward at once and see what I can do", and he went. His cheerful disposition and leadership were far above the average and did much to maintain the high morale of his troops under fire and frequent low air attacks. It is considered fitting that he should be mentioned in despatches.[80]

Nothing ever came of this recommendation. Maxwell was among the senior Australian officers taken from Changi to Taiwan for the term of his imprisonment. His commander, the 8th Division's General Gordon Bennett, had fled Singapore just as Percival was initiating negotiations with the Japanese.[81] Anketell had died of his wounds in hospital shortly before it had been overrun and the wounded finished off with bayonets.[82] It hardly mattered to Tom anyway. 'For myself I am no hero, but it was one of my greatest disappointments that after one week of fighting, during which every man in the company had become initiated and all sections of it had shown that they could do their job, we had to partake of surrender'.[83] As the reality of his captivity set in, his thoughts turned instead to his family at home.

H/d M.G. Bn.
Changi.
11. May 1942.

The following is a copy of communication received from Brig. D.S. Maxwell, Brig. Comd 27 Aust. Inf. Bde.

Breen Major
Comd. H/d M.G. Bn.

H.Q. 27 Aust. Inf. Bde
A.I.F. Malaya.
2. Mar 1942.

Confidential

H/d M.G. Bn.

RECOMMENDATIONS FOR HONOURS AND AWARDS.

It is desired to bring to your notice the excellent work done by Capt. BUNNING when his Coy was under command 27 Aust Inf Bde during the operations on SINGAPORE ISLAND.

He was absolutely tireless and personally supervised the siting and preparation of all machine gun posts. At all times he showed a complete disregard for personal safety. His platoons were of necessity widely dispersed and a report of an enemy attack on any sector of the front, invariably called for an immediate reaction on his part. "I would like to go forward at once and see what I can do". And he went.

His cheerful disposition and leadership were far above the average and did much to maintain the high morale of his troops under fire and frequent low air attack.

It is considered fitting that he should be mentioned in despatches

D.S. Maxwell. Brig
Comd. 27 Aust. Inf. Bde.

Copy of Brigadier Maxwell's letter recommending Tom for a Mention in Despatches, May 1942
(Bunning Family Collection)

5

Prisoner of war

NEARLY 15,000 AUSTRALIANS were captured at Singapore, and in the months that followed their numbers were swelled by thousands more taken at Java, Timor and other battlefields in the Dutch East Indies. Yet for every AIF prisoner there were two from the British Army and three from Indian units. They would all be sent initially to Changi, the barracks and headquarters of the island's peacetime garrison. The column that set off after the surrender was miles in length, Tom recalled, 'and consequently very slow and cumbersome and every man was carrying on his person the whole of his worldly possessions'. The 2/4th had lost almost all of its gear, although the battalion remained together for the time being. Almost to a man, they were distressed by their defeat and embarrassed, if not ashamed, at the speed and scale of their capitulation.[1] The Japanese had not anticipated so many POWs when their invasion began and were content to allow their orders to pass down through the existing organisational structure of the captured forces. Maintaining discipline was as important as it had always been, but it was more difficult than ever when so many soldiers were exhausted and disillusioned.[2]

As they entered Changi, then, Tom's rank and the responsibilities attached to it were intact. The battalion was quartered initially at Selarang Barracks, a complex of three-storey buildings south of Changi village that was given over to the AIF. Sanitation and hygiene were immediate concerns. Dysentery was already present within the crowded camp, so men were dispatched at once to dig latrines, sink wells and clear out antimalarial drains.[3] Many were also soon engaged in scrounging for whatever could be found within the camp's perimeter. Some useful furniture and clothing was brought in, but when B Company men returned from one trip with a piano, 8th Division stepped in with orders to reign in the foraging; 'back went our piano and some of the more obvious articles that had been taken', Tom noted. Under the circumstances, he was not dissatisfied with his own kit – three pairs of shorts, three shirts, four singlets, four pairs of socks, his army boots, a second pair of shoes and some sandals, a pair of pyjamas and some bedding, plus a decent supply of soap, razors, shaving cream and toothpaste, and plenty of cigarettes.[4] Brookie remained with him as his batman. The 2/4th was allocated a group of bungalows designed in peacetime for married officers. Some 255 went into a single house under Tom's command. His own quarters were in a large room shared with six other officers.[5]

It was necessary to adjust immediately to a rice-based diet and rations that provided about half the sustenance they were accustomed to. As the army cooks had no practice in preparing rice, constipation and other digestive complaints were soon widespread. The meagreness of these meals was depressing. 'It is quite the hobby now to talk about food and "meals I have eaten" and "meals that we should eat". When I run through what I used to consider a normal meal I am absolutely staggered with its horrible richness and the extravagant standard to which we ate', he observed, only weeks after his arrival at Changi.[6] Another sobering realisation was that contact with the outside world was cut off entirely. 'When we became Prisoners of War it was obvious that we would not be sending or receiving many letters and this prompted me to start this diary', he wrote.[7] Each entry would be addressed to Margot. He started writing it 'in the hope that, firstly I may be able to send it on to you perhaps a month or two before I get home myself and, secondly, that when I do get home this will be a good medium to assist me to go through the whole story in a more or less chronological order and systematically. If I tackle it in this way, then I know that I have told you all that there is to tell so that subject need never be mentioned again.'[8]

For weeks, the Battle of Singapore dominated conversation. Tom recognised that a lack of air power and naval support and too many inexperienced ground forces had been critical factors, although an underlying failure to adequately

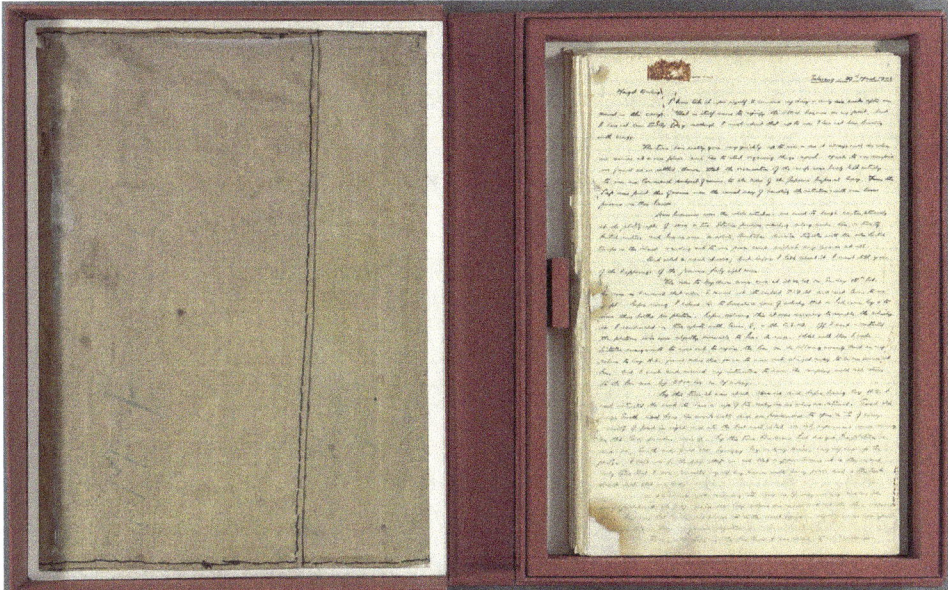

Tom's POW diary (Bunning Family Collection)

prepare for and lead the campaign was undeniable too.[9] The men certainly felt their leaders were at fault for the defeat. 'One can't blame them for being rather embittered against the powers that be for being landed into this situation. The whole campaign absolutely stinks of bad leadership, lack of imagination and lack of any intelligent thought or appreciation', he recorded, 'and as far as the troops now in this camp and especially this unit, which was simply sacrificed on the altar of God knows what, they feel very definitely that they have been sold.'[10] Most of them had decided that POWs should not be bound to the authority of their officers. The Japanese, however, had made it clear that they expected their orders to be enforced through the pre-existing chains of command. Their own soldiers were sighted infrequently, with guard duty assumed by Koreans and by renegade Sikhs who had sided with the enemy.[11]

In mid-March, two B Company men slipped the perimeter and swam to the mainland, only to be recaptured days later. They went straight into solitary confinement and there was nothing that Tom or anybody else in AIF command could do to assist them. It was a terrible situation, and yet the pair had been fortunate to escape execution, which had occurred hundreds of times during the surrender itself and was the standard penalty for any apprehended escapee.[12] The incident may have nevertheless helped to restore discipline among the men. They were disheartened and frustrated with their predicament or, as Tom described it, 'so disgusted with the exhibition of fighting that had been put up and with the thought of having capitulated that they did not feel like responding to anyone's authority'.[13] After a few weeks, however, the situation began to improve, as they all became resigned to their situation and easier to deal with for their officers.[14]

It was imperative to keep the men healthy and in the best spirits possible. AIF command understood this and rolled out a comprehensive program of education and entertainment. Tom was called upon to devise and teach a course in 'Business principles and accountancy' for the battalion, and he soon had 120 men enrolled in it.[15] He also helped to organise sports, and before long a regular fixture of cricket, football and rugby matches was underway. Beyond teaching his own course, he enrolled to study social sciences and regularly attended the weekly lectures, which ran on Fridays and covered an eclectic mix of topics that reflected the civilian expertise of the speaker in question. He soon delivered one himself, on the 'Milling and Marketing of Jarrah', which lasted an hour and a quarter; 'rather too long for an audience that in the main is sitting on its tail on a hard tiled floor', he decided, splitting it into two separate lectures for the future.[16] An education centre and library had been set up and he visited it frequently to borrow books that interested him – textbooks in accountancy and economics were the most prized, followed by works on history and military history, biographies and literature. He played in the Bungalow's cricket side on Saturdays, and in his spare time he helped out in the vegetable gardens being set up around the camp.[17]

Inevitably, the prisoners discussed the war and its progress. In the absence of reliable information, rumours flew about wildly. The rapidity of Japan's advance may have encouraged some to anticipate an imminent end to hostilities, while for others good news might have aided morale, but either way the prison grapevine was way off the mark, because the first week of April 1942 furnished reports of paratroops landing in France, Hitler calling for an armistice after heavy bombing of Berlin, America's recapture of Luzon, a Japanese evacuation of Java and Sumatra, and Russia's advance into East Prussia.[18] Tom had enough sense to be sceptical: 'the rumours that we have been hearing lately have been so trashy that it has led me to wonder just how much of the news that we get is true…Then some one comes in with another silly rumour and then one goes down to eat a meal of plain rice tempered with black tea and so on until a little bit of misery sets in temporarily'. Despondency came and went often during these early months at Changi. 'During these last few days I have been feeling pretty fed up', he confided. 'I am afraid too, Darling that as I write this diary, I am constantly thinking of you and Gavin and thinking of all the things that we could be doing together'.[19]

Margot had no option but to be stoic herself. She waited patiently for further news of the 8th Division's fate and remained hopeful that Tom was alive. It probably helped that life at Pinnacles Station was keeping her busy. She had Gavin to nurse, of course, and much work in the kitchen and around the homestead to help out with. It was only in late June that she learnt that mail could be addressed to POWs via the Red Cross in Geneva. Their son was a picture of health, she wrote proudly, on the verge of crawling and with his first teeth pushing through. 'I have done everything possible to get some news of you but all to no avail so I just must be patient. I pray that you are well and fit'. There was much to report on the movements of their friends, yet little could be said on account of censorship and because only a single small page was permitted to be sent. 'Keep going my darling things must come all right in the end. Don't worry about us…I love you more than ever'.[20]

When an officer's school was established, Tom was seconded to it to further his training. He was there when it was announced that 3,000 Australians would be departing to labour camps in Borneo and Indochina. Some fifty B Company men were included in this draft. He had graduated to the senior officer's school a month later when another 1,600 were dispatched.[21] It was widely conjectured that the remainder of the AIF would also soon be on the move, although the destination was the subject of much debate among the prisoners. Tom naturally took an interest in the matter, but his view was simply that he would follow the orders he received: 'if we have to move I have no objections to going'.[22]

In the meantime, he made the most of the courses he was attending. 'If I can get some good training while I am here then I may be worth something as a weekend soldier on my return and there is always the chance, remote perhaps, that we may fight again in this war'.[23] A pay system and canteen had been set up, where extra food, tobacco and toiletries were available. Most of those left at Changi were in reasonable health, although some still carried wounds from combat, others were suffering from skin complaints, and some had gone down with beri-beri as a result of vitamin deficiency. Visits to ill men in the camp's hospital became a fixed part of his week. His physician and friend from Perth, Bruce Hunt, also a POW, was a senior doctor at the hospital. 'He is doing a grand job and is quite the most outstanding quack…Everybody who becomes an inmate seems to strike him and I have not heard one man who has not had a good word to say for him'.[24] In the evenings, Tom worked on plans to overhaul the accounting system at Bunning Bros. His other preoccupation was developing a scheme for the farm he hoped to acquire upon his return:

> For some time past I have been thinking about the possibility of starting a farm…I can think of nothing more desirable that taking you and Gavin up there and pottering around…Then I visualise returning to Cotswold with the car loaded with eggs and cream and new potatoes and vegetables and fruit and perhaps a side of lamb or leg of pork – oh what happy thoughts these are.[25]

In August, they received their first reports from the outside, when two naval officers captured in the Indian Ocean arrived with information from Australia barely a month old. A large build-up of American forces was underway, and the front line was holding in New Guinea, but the news from Europe was far from promising. Tom confided that his hopes of returning home by Christmas were fading, yet outwardly he was optimistic, laying bets on the end date of the war that he didn't expect to win.[26] Japanese officers had recently interviewed prisoners with first-hand knowledge of Darwin, Perth, Derby, Broome and Geraldton, hardly a positive sign, so keeping spirits up was important. Dengue fever had been reported in the camp and the rice ration cut to 2 oz. per man daily, though the canteen remained well stocked, and Red Cross supplies had arrived from South Africa.[27] Tom weighed himself and found he was 164 lbs, 2 lbs heavier than normal, which he attributed to the lack of physical activity inside the camp.[28]

At the end of August, the Japanese reformed their administration of Changi. Security was tightened and the POWs were asked to sign a form stating they would not attempt escape. They refused, and in retaliation, some

15,000 prisoners were herded into an area of Selarang Barracks barely 9 acres in extent. Rations were cut by two-thirds, and four men who had recently attempted escape were executed in front of senior officers. It forced the hand of the British and Australian commanders, who reached a compromise with their captors, lest their men be left to wither from dysentery or diphtheria in the overcrowded conditions. The Japanese issued an order for the declaration to be signed, which was obeyed under duress.[29] The incident struck Tom as a turning point. Although command had taken the only sensible option and morale had remained high in the barracks the whole time, harsher treatment of the prisoners had been signalled: 'whether we like it or not we may well have our hardest time ahead of us', he wrote in his diary.[30] Conscious of the event's broader significance in terms of the AIF's conduct and his own experiences as a POW, he also penned a separate, detailed account of the Selarang Barracks incident, which is reproduced as an appendix to this biography.

Selarang Barracks, Changi, during the incident of 30 August – 5 September 1942 (Courtesy Australian War Memorial)

Returning to their old quarters was a welcome move, nonetheless. Tom was happy to be back among the battalion, and he continued to get on well with the officers he lived with. The men were busy organising cricket and other sports facilities, and the AIF had arranged for the building of a concert hall for use in the evenings. Their diet remained poor, although palm oil, rice polishings, coconut, peanuts, eggs and 'whitebait' (dried fish) lent some variety, as well as adding essential protein and vitamins.[31] Boredom, and what Tom described as 'laziness', by which he meant both physical inactivity and a lack of intellectual stimulation, were the main problems that needed to be managed. 'I feel there are three aspects in this place we must watch', he reflected. These were physical and mental fitness, and 'self-respect', which in essence was that 'if in every action taken which first calls for thought, a quick check up is made to see whether the course decided upon might damage one's self respect, the correct answer becomes reasonably obvious'.[32] He resolved to start a daily period of education for the men under his command. All of them, he reasoned, should keep an eye on the future: 'everyone has his own future to consider and unless he has something in mind and some keenness to develop his own mental powers, then he will be far worse equipped to earn his own living and to better his position than before he enlisted'.[33]

These thoughts reveal a determination that time spent as a POW would not be altogether wasted. Many of the senior AIF commanders had by now been sent away to Japan, and Tom recognised that as one of the remaining officers he needed to set an example and stay strong of mind, even if in private there were bouts of despondency and homesickness. 'I am afraid I have been feeling rather disgruntled lately', he wrote at this time, 'but am not quite sure what is upsetting me. I miss you in a hundred different ways, Darling and not the least in that I would love to talk to you, to get your ideas on my thoughts which would help so much to check up on my perspective'.[34] When their anniversary arrived, he perceived that a new role for him was beckoning. A body called the 'Garden Control Group' had been formed to better manage the supply of vegetables, and a friend in 27th Brigade HQ, Pat Garde, had asked him to join it. Seventy acres had been allocated for farming, and 700 men would be allocated to work it. 'Subject to suitable arrangements being made [for] our own troops, I am definitely a starter'.[35]

What he didn't yet realise was that this decision would come to define his experience as a POW. On the same day he joined Garden Control, he had written of his hope that he would be home for his next anniversary. His fate was instead to spend the next two and a half years at gardening. At the end of his first day, he had settled into a routine that would change little thereafter:

> We rise at 0745, breakfast at 0830 and this morning I was over at 18/26 Bn. at 0910 to pick up their party. Work starts at 0930 and we work through until 12.30. One hour for lunch which is brought out to us, work starts again at 1330 and we go through until 1700. We have 10 minutes off every hour and tea morning and afternoon. I wandered around without a shirt until after lunch when the sun started to hot up and tonight I am as red as a beetroot. The day is very long but it is a very good one.[36]

What did change were the men assigned to him. The Australians he started out with were soon replaced with a cosmopolitan party of prisoners from the Dutch East Indies, 'Arab, Mongol, European, Malay, Javanese [and] Chinese', which 'when properly organised are solid workers', followed by Scotsmen and then Americans, who were ill-disciplined and poor workers: 'I must say I was not at all impressed with them'.[37] They grew spinach, sweet corn and other Asian vegetables, which went into stews and soups that gave vital nutrition to the POWs.

When the monsoon arrived, it made gardening difficult and left everything musky and damp; 'by holey, how it has rained', he recorded in mid-December.[38] There was a sameness to each day that lent added significance to milestones in the life he had left behind. He carefully managed his supplies so that a special dinner could be put on for Margot's birthday. 'We opened a tin of sweet milk, a tin of fish and a tin of butter and really ate until we could eat no more…of course after I had been in bed for a few minutes I developed a beautiful tummy ache and couldn't get to sleep for an hour or two'.[39] On Christmas Day they had carols in the morning, then a lunch of soup, roast chicken and pudding, before presents were distributed by Brookie; 'these transpired to be odd items looted from our own personal gear'. In the afternoon there was a game of Australian Rules football, followed by more singing in the evening.[40] These were rare indulgences indeed. As their term as prisoners slipped past twelve months, Tom noted they 'have had no meat for two and a half months, no bread for four months, no milk for two and a half months, no jam for three months…Breakfast consists of ground rice porridge, with quala malacca and coconut and tea. Lunch is vegetable stew with rice and [dinner] whitebait rissoles and vegetables with some sort of sweet that is always the tastiest dish of the day'.[41] And so the days passed by. 'Life is singularly dull and uninteresting lately', he remarked.[42]

In all this time, the prisoners had only twice been issued with cards upon which short messages could be sent home. Tom's first took a year to reach Perth.

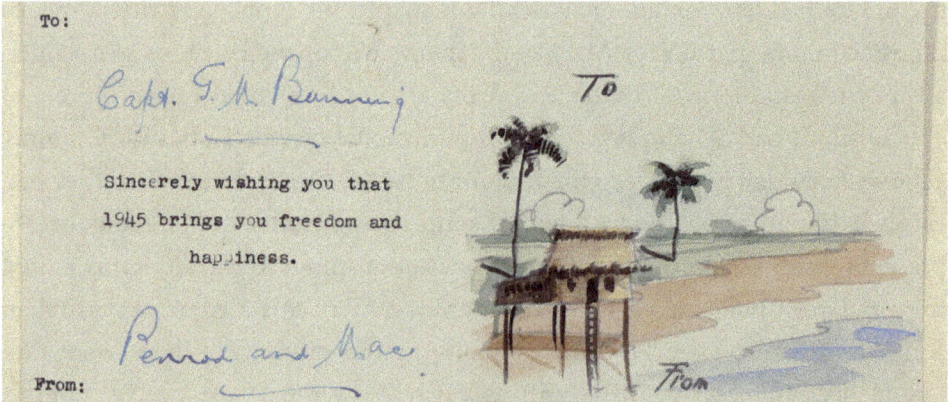

Top and bottom: Christmas Cards addressed to Tom, December 1943 (Bunning Family Collection)

News of his whereabouts had at last been confirmed in January 1943, when a telegram arrived from the army. 'I can't tell you what it felt like. I was quite light headed for days. I always knew you would be alright but I must admit it was good to know', Margot wrote.[43] She had returned to Perth mid-year, when the danger of a Japanese invasion had passed. Much had changed at home. Domestic help was impossible to obtain, making it difficult for a large household like Colin Street. Rationing was in place, and the shortage of petrol meant that private vehicles were rarely used, although when Robert Law obtained a gas producer for his car, Margot was called upon to chauffeur him around town. So many of their friends had moved on, taking posts in the military or marrying and moving interstate. The city was full of Americans. 'I have been into town and to the pictures several times and have felt most peculiar. The place is full and I don't know a soul'.[44] She kept in touch with the B Company wives despite there being no news to share, and she called regularly on Helen at Innerhadden.[45] Gavin's first birthday had come and gone. Only one letter per month was permitted, and she always filled them with reports on his growth. 'Our son is a little boy now', she wrote in March, 'walking all over the place and getting into all sorts of mischief'.[46]

Their son's future was a question Tom pondered often. He declared to her in his diary:

> He must learn to box and to fight, he must go down to the mills during holidays and also on to farms, he must take an interest in Cadets and in the Militia, learn to fly and be used to living and camping out. He must develop some sort of talent to entertain other people, he must spend up to twelve months or more at manual work and naturally must be well qualified in all sporting activities. No doubt you also have very definite ideas as to his training.[47]

He continued to attend lectures whenever possible and to read as much as he could in the evenings. It all helped to keep his mind strong.

> The year has really gone very quickly and somehow little happenings from time to time have relieved the monotony. I have met hundreds of good fellows, have made some firm friends, have seen enough sides of human nature sometimes to be proud to be an Australian and at other

times to be disgusted and really the existence here has had an element of interest in it.[48]

Finally, after thirteen months as a prisoner, he received his first mail. It was something of a deluge: three letters from Margot enclosing photographs of Gavin, and one each from Helen, Flora, Jane and Charlie:

> Darling I can't describe to you everything that went on within me as I read and re-read your letters. But they told me just what I wanted to know and said the things that I have been longing day after day to hear you say.[49]

This was a difficult period for him. Another 2,500 Australians were being organised for departure to Thailand, and what was left of B Company was going with them. Tom was lobbying to go along too, although he knew this was unlikely, owing to his role within the camp. He had always done what he could to keep the 2/4th together, attracting the ire of 8th Division HQ in late-1942, when he intervened to stop the battalion being split between barracks.[50] But now it was inevitable that their paths would diverge. They marched out in mid-March: 'it tore my heart to see them go and just at the moment I feel that I would give a lot to be with them'.[51]

When another draft of 3,300 AIF prisoners was called for a month later, Tom was told by HQ that he was in it. 'I am rather looking forward to it', he wrote, because he knew a lot of the men going away and didn't want to be among the few Australians left at Changi.[52] The next day, however, he was advised the Japanese would not release Garden Control officers. When he was at the hospital to have some blisters treated, Bruce Hunt told him that he was going with the party. 'There is no doubt that Bruce has done a wonderful job in this camp and has left a wonderful impression with every man', he wrote, after farewelling his friend.[53] Labour was becoming scarce, and Tom was now doing much of the digging and raking in the gardens that previously he had only supervised. As well as blisters he had developed rashes, including a dermatitis the prisoners called 'rice balls' – an uncomfortable complaint that was widespread in the camp. The Red Cross rations had long run out and their daily fare comprised rice, vegetables and a tiny portion of fish, augmented by fruit purchased from the canteen. Despite this, when he weighed himself in mid-1943 he found he remained at his normal weight.[54]

There were now fewer than 2,500 Australians left at Changi. Tom's quarters were shared with English officers, whom he found to be more worldly and interesting than the countrymen he had long been surrounded by. He read as often as he could and chatted about the farm with Brookie, whom he hoped would be its caretaker. A few golf clubs and some balls had been found, and Tom enjoyed hitting these about the padang (the barracks' playing fields) in the afternoons. After a string of good performances on the cricket field, he earnt selection to the main Australian side. The days were otherwise unchanged. 'We are down in the Garden until 5 o'clock each day, arrive home at 5.30, have a cup of tea and then a very welcome shower and by then it is nearly dinner time. We amble through dinner and then hang around for the Roll Call at 7.15.' One of the peculiarities of Changi was that the camp ran according to Japanese standard time, making for long hours of sunlight in the evening. 'By the time this is over it is 7.30 and still broad daylight so one stays about on the grass talking about this and that. After that the odd visitor is to be contended with before one fights one's way up to one's room and as there are now five of us together to a room, solitude is not so easy.'[55]

As 1943 slipped by, Tom's morale began to falter. English officers were too narrow-minded and too prolix in their mess conversations for his liking: 'they do talk absolute rot for quite a long time', he had decided.[56] Even Brookie was starting to get on his nerves. Homesickness was the root of it. Musical performances often pushed him into melancholy.[57] Reports that allied forces were building up in Australia had filtered into Singapore, but it was a mixed consolation for the prisoners. 'Poor Margot, how grim it must be for you to be receiving absolutely no news at all. I wonder that you don't write me off altogether and go off with some dashing Squadron Leader', he wrote. It had been almost two years since their fleeting encounter in Adelaide. 'Recently it has been taking me a long time to get to sleep at night. This is natural to a degree...Last night I thought about you so much that I developed the most terrific yearning for you and had to get up and walk up and down outside for some time to bring me down to earth again.'[58]

His diary entries were becoming less frequent, but he took steps to store the diary with medical staff at the hospital in the event he was also sent away to a labour camp. Increasingly, what he did write was a receptacle for his reflections

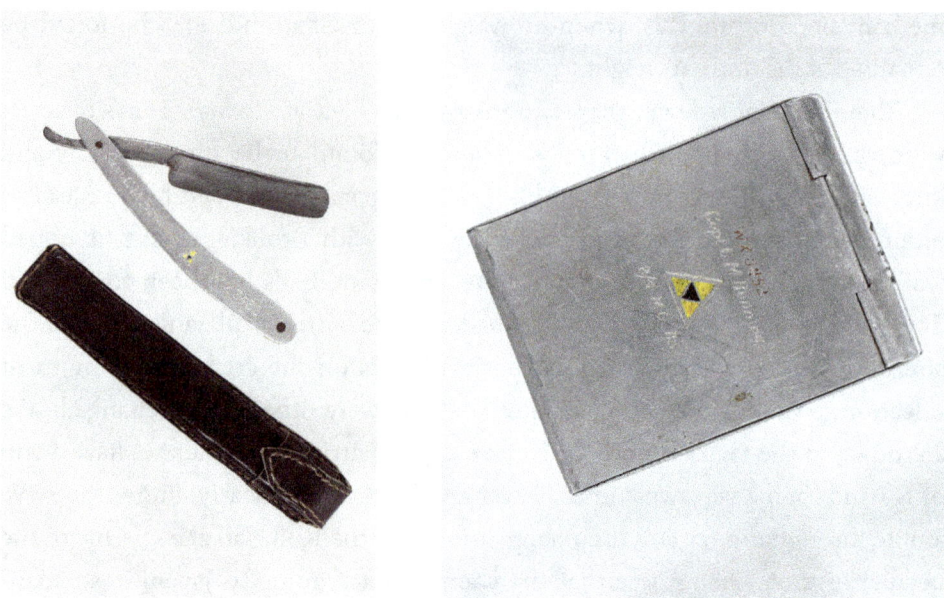

Top left, top right and bottom: Articles made for Tom inside Changi POW Camp (Bunning Family Collection)

on life as a prisoner. On his mess companions he admitted 'a certain jealousy for the aptitude of Englishmen...I like them. I like them for many reasons and admire many of their characteristics and as sociable companions their attributes more than outweigh the faults that I have mentioned'.[59] He reflected on his captors as well. They could be wantonly cruel in their punishments, and it was necessary to stand up to them to prevent abuses, yet he admired the efficiency of their organisation and recognised that most were sincere in their efforts to abide by an honourable code of ethics at Changi.[60] To his mind, the question of Japan's importance to the postwar world was also undeniable. With an eye on this, and another on day-to-day imperatives, Tom took up Japanese lessons within the camp to acquire a basic vocabulary.[61]

Finally, a new batch of letters arrived, which enclosed photographs of Gavin at his first birthday and news from Margot to the end of August 1942. Her letters described their son's growth and what a comfort he was to her in Tom's absence, how different Perth had become, and how those who remained at home were keeping up the vestiges of their former lives through the odd vacation and social engagements of one kind or another. The anxiety of uncertainty had eaten at her as well. She wrote in May:

> Another month and still no letter from you...It's my birthday today – remember? As it is a Sunday today I can't celebrate much. I almost forgot it till Molly produced a bottle of gin, a great luxury these days. How are you Darling? I just spend my life wondering.[62]

He had marked the occasion with another lavish meal in the mess:

> I provided a tin of bully [beef], Chappie a tin of pineapple, Pat some eggs and Michael some bananas, together with two beautiful papayas... Then to cap it all off I had a beautiful dream about you in which we were both sitting up having breakfast in bed.[63]

She had continued to write regularly, but that mail was still more than a year away.

These letters were certainly a tonic. After receiving them, he returned to his plans for Bunning Bros with renewed enthusiasm, laying down a detailed costing system and organisational restructure to be implemented upon his return. When this was completed, he turned to the design of a new office block and arranged for a fellow officer, an architect, to help out with the sketches. There were many things he had heard spoken about by his comrades that he wanted to try for himself. He wrote, 'If you are agreeable, Darling, I am resolved that in future we will try something new every year from fishing on the Barrier Reef to Canoeing down the Blackwood and from skiing at Kosciusko to mountaineering in New Zealand'.[64] It all helped to alleviate the dreariness of his routine. He described it again on the occasion of their fifth anniversary. 'Arose at 8.15, breakfast of browned rice, coconut and sugar with two pieces of fried bread.' He was at the garden by 9.15 am and spent the morning raking around a crop of beans. 'Lunch at 12.30 consisting of vegetable and rice stew together with terrible fish cake and slab of bread with banana spread on it (very thin).' Work among the coconut trees occupied the afternoon. At 5 pm he returned to his quarters and read for an hour. 'Dinner at 6.15 - little fish (2), sweet potato between flap jacks, fried rice, towagay amaranth and a very nice fried doover with papaya and mango spread on the top. After dinner I write in my diary'.

Design for new Bunning Bros head office, drawn for Tom inside Changi POW Camp, 1943 (Bunning Family Collection)

In September 1943 the initiation of air-raid training signalled that the war was turning against the Japanese. So too was a reduction in the official ration scale shortly afterwards.[65] The momentum had shifted in the Pacific theatre, as Japan was forced onto the defensive in the Solomon Islands and New Guinea, and British forces began guerrilla operations in Burma. But as Christmas approached, the most distressing news yet to reach Changi came to hand. Some survivors of the Thai–Burma Railway had returned to Singapore, and at once it became apparent that they had experienced the most appalling brutality and deprivation. As shock and anger rippled through the camp, Tom did his best to account for 2/4th casualties. At least ninety-two had perished, twelve from B Company. Malaria, beri-beri and tropical ulcers were rife among returning men, and all of them were emaciated and weak. Not all of these would survive. As many as a third of the Australians sent away were now feared to be lost.[66]

Tom's diary was not kept surreptitiously, but this meant he had to be guarded in it. For instance, whereas he didn't hold back in his musings on allied leaders, remarks specific to Japanese conduct were rare. Similarly, when the two B Company men escaped in March 1942, he wrote they had been 'transferred'.[67] He was careful now with what he wrote about the Thai–Burma Railway. 'I could fill a book with the things I want to say but it is possibly wiser to keep most of it in my head. After all we are still POWs.'[68] The effect it was having on him was clearly palpable all the same. In the new year he composed an entry that he intended for Margot in the event of his death:

> Firstly, Darling, I wish to tell you in deepest sincerity that my love for you and my feelings towards you have never been stronger than they are now...Now that our lives are bound together, thoughts of you seem to inspire my every effort and were this not so, life for me would seem to be very empty...Bearing in mind Darling that you won't read this if I am present to read my diary to you, if in the future you meet anyone who wants to marry you and you feel that you could love and with whom you could live happily, then know that you have my blessing. Know that there is nothing that I would wish more than a full happiness that I am sure is only possible in married state with someone in whom you have complete trust and confidence.[69]

There was a long passage of instruction for Gavin's upbringing:

> I want him to go to prep school at the age of about 7, to start in early on physical training and to be brought up to become self dependent and responsible…Make him do some boy-scouting and try to develop his interest in nature (that is half the reason for the farm). Let him learn to use his hands in carpentry and so on and also in the art of fisticuffs…I intend to put him to work down at the mills in school holidays when he becomes 15 or 16…I am convinced that a university education is desirable. I want him to go in for debating and also some militia service – Air Force or Army…I would like him to have a year or so in England, possibly finishing his university career there, as long as this is not likely to unbalance him. Finally, I would like to see him in politics, but only as an honest to God, responsible, sincere, virile Australian.[70]

He had a message for his mother, a note for his sisters and a word of encouragement and advice for Charlie on the future of Bunning Bros. His experience had not been without some benefit:

> Perhaps I am a little more capable of independent thinking, perhaps I have a little more consideration for others before self, I hope that I will be a stronger driving force and will display more tenacity than I have shown in the past. I am a stronger personality than I was.

It remained only to say that he hoped she was proud of him. 'Above all Darling I want you to know that since leaving you I have not dodged or shirked any order or any duty that was rightly mine.'[71]

There could be little doubt that their existence was becoming more precarious. Malaria was spreading through the camp and prices at the canteen were rapidly inflating, even for the most basic items like maize, palm oil and bananas. Tobacco, their one luxury, was almost impossible to obtain. He noted ruefully at the end of February 1944 that 'today was my first day in the garden without any'.[72] Their daily rations were further reduced, and the allocated quantity of rice was rarely delivered in full. Men had taken to wearing footwear fashioned from rubber tires, and much of their clothing was little better than rags. Tom's standard outfit comprised a pair of patched trousers and a straw hat kept together with a canvas lining.[73] He was losing weight, becoming thinner about the shoulders and in his arms and thighs. The decision was made to forgo the afternoon stew served to his labourers to save vegetables for the camp as a whole. When it rained in the gardens, they felt cold despite the warmth of their equatorial location.[74]

As the war turned against them, and more POWs were relocated back to Changi, the Japanese decided to relocate all prisoners to a small complex centred on the barracks jail. Officers would henceforth be segregated from other ranks. The overcrowding was now acute. 'There are 28 of us in an attab hut' made from palm leaves and bamboo, Tom noted, 'which allows space per man for his bed and 15″ of space alongside it, with a corridor down the middle about 18″ wide'.[75] The upshot was that he would have to set up a desk outdoors, where 'we are exposed to the view and comments of the passing mob'.[76] The gardens that had been tended so assiduously were abandoned in the move, and he was tasked with establishing new ones closer to the jail. Amid it all a plethora of mail turned up, bringing Tom up to date with letters written as recently as eight months ago. More arrived over coming weeks to fill in gaps in the sequence of news from home. Gavin was growing fast, and Margot was staying positive and maintaining as normal a life as possible. 'It is a tremendous comfort to read your letters', Tom remarked. 'I feel you more and more to be the inspiration for my very existence and my ambitions.'[77]

The gardens were now more critical than ever. In mid-1944 the prisoners were told they would need to supply a third of the camp's requirements by August and lift this to half by the year's end. Tom spent several weeks laid up with an ulcer behind his knee, and when it healed, he found himself assigned to reclaim a rubber plantation for farming. One advantage of the shift to the jail was that the sea was closer, making it easier to bring seaweed in as fertiliser. He was a true farmer now, watching the sky anxiously for signs of rain and fretting over caterpillars and pests among the crops.[78] Such concern was understandable. 'One can count the ribs of practically every man and can notice thinness especially around the collar bone and shoulders', he observed at the end of another day's work. 'It is no wonder really because, although in quantity we are getting enough to fill our tummies, the food is really rubbish – the only protein coming from our daily spoonful of whitebait for which incidentally we have now cultivated a very great liking.'[79] Rice rations were soon cut yet again, and there could be little doubt that further reductions were imminent.

For his wedding anniversary Tom hoped for a day off, but it didn't transpire when the Japanese arranged an inspection of the gardens that day. He had the next day off instead and used it to bring his diary up to date. Inevitably, such a prolonged separation from Margot was preoccupying him: 'It's been a long long time Darling but I think that I am still a reasonably normal human being and am more optimistic than ever.'[80] That same day became one of the most memorable of his captivity. A force of forty American planes raided Singapore, triggering a cacophony of air-raid sirens and anti-aircraft fire. It also happened to be Guy Fawkes Day, and the coincidence was not lost on Tom: 'we certainly had an hour's good enjoyment'.[81] Japan was now within range of American bombers, as the Allies worked to recapture the territories lost in the first few months of fighting. Inflation began to soar, dashing any hope for a decent meal at Christmas. Tom looked at prices in the canteen and realised a single peanut had roughly the same value a coconut once had. Christmas day itself was marked by goodwill and festivity, despite these hardships. Another raid occurred in January, and they were common thereafter.[82]

Tom had set a record for yields from his garden during December and broke it again in April 1945. He was still presenting lectures on the Australian timber industry as part of the education program, and his reading progressed from Shakespeare's classics, to biographies of Napoleon and General Haig, Carnegie's *How to Win Friends and Influence People* ('a high-pressure sales textbook but with quite some meat in it'), and a short history of Japan ('very interesting').[83] A swimming carnival was organised during February, in which Tom competed for the 2/4th officers in a relay. They won their heat easily to attract a hefty handicap for the final, only to snatch victory on the last lap by three-quarters of a length. The naked victors were presented with a shield 'amidst a great ovation by the assembled multitude…I felt that at least would have been one of the occasions upon which "clothes maketh the man"'.[84] It was the last sports event held at Changi. A few days later a new ration system was implemented, in which food was allocated on a scale linked to the manual labour each prisoner undertook. For those able to work it meant yet another reduction in the daily intake. For the infirm at the hospital, it meant starvation. Red Cross supplies were now essential to keeping the prisoners alive.[85]

Top and bottom: Card addressed to Tom from Major Bruce Hunt, Army Medical Corps, December 1944. Tom admired Hunt for bravely confronting the Japanese commanders on many occasions to gain medical supplies and improved conditions for sick prisoners (Bunning Family Collection)

Overflights by American aircraft became more common, until they were a daily occurrence. It was obvious the war was drawing to a close. Since leaving Perth, Tom had carried a gold sovereign Helen had given him for his twenty-first birthday. He now exchanged it on the black market and distributed a little over half the proceeds among his fellow officers, keeping the remainder for himself to buy precious food; a month later he was contemplating doing the same with his watch.[86] His weight was down to 9 st. 9 lbs, barely 61 kg. His days continued to be occupied in the garden and with reading, visiting patients in the hospital and chatting with his friends in his spare time. 'Had a yarn to Bruce Hunt this morning as to future plans' he reflected one day. 'Broadly speaking, my idea will be to achieve qualification as a Cost Accountant which will be followed up by a trip to America to gain further knowledge, experience and background'. A course in economics and history was on the agenda and he would not neglect culture and the arts, lest he decide at some point to enter politics.[87] There was little else to do for the time being. 'Afraid things have been very dull and prosaic lately and I have nothing further to report at the moment' read one entry in late July.[88]

The end of the war came a short time later. Reports of the atomic bombs at Hiroshima and Nagasaki and Russia's entry into the war on Japan set off a wave of speculation and excitement. This reached a crescendo on the evening 15 August 1945, when news of peace talks broke at Changi: 'after three and a half years of this life one could not really grasp the significance of the happenings except in small handfuls and I really think that yesterday was my happiest day since the boil up started', he jotted down after a sleepless night.[89] Suddenly there was movement everywhere as working parties returned, Red Cross stores came in and other supplies were dropped from the air. They ate stew made from bully beef and had coffee with cigarettes. 'People cheering and shouting all over the place', Tom remarked, as a few Japanese and Koreans stood around disconsolately.[90] He briefly hoped that he might telephone home in time for Gavin's birthday, but it was not possible in the tumult surrounding the ceasefire. Orders came through to assume command of the 2/4th in Singapore. 'It is good to be back with the troops again and am gradually picking up the strings of administration.'[91]

A wireless set was brought to Changi and connected to loudspeakers in time to broadcast the signing of Japan's surrender in Tokyo Bay. There had been a thanksgiving service at the hospital – 'I really think that it was the finest service that I have ever attended' – followed by a victory parade. The change of diet had caused a lot of sickness and Tom himself had symptoms of beri-beri, which he attributed to the sudden glut of rice.[92] The most pressing concerns, however, were the responsibilities of his command. To an Australian public long starved of information on POWs, reports of high death rates, emaciated men and the horror of the labour camps were producing widespread anger and despair. The surviving men were desperate to contact their families at home, but for some reason the army insisted that all correspondence be censored in the same way it had been on active service, creating a deluge of mail for Tom to work through each day. His other priority was to revise and update the battalion's casualty list as accurately as possible, even though the fate of many still in Thailand and Borneo remained unknown. As the men released from Changi enjoyed the freedom to wander about Singapore, his focus was on attending to these tasks.[93]

There was at least the chance to reach Margot via airmail. 'Darling, I personally have had a very fortunate spin as a POW and am perfectly fit…I have no sickness whatever', he wrote, although his hair had thinned noticeably since 1941 and this was as good a time as any to tell her.[94] A second airmail advised that his diary had been entrusted to a senior officer being evacuated by air, who would ensure it reached Margot. He had maintained it assiduously the entire time, notwithstanding the scarcity of paper and ink, writing with great honesty and insight on his experiences. The idea was that she could read it in advance of his return; 'After that there should never be any occasion to refer to it again'.[95] His final entry had been made on 12 September 1945: 'Cheerio my Darling, see you soon'. It remained only to pen a letter to Gavin on his future plans. 'You have been born under really fortunate circumstances, from stock that have done a tremendous lot for Western Australia and can justly be looked upon as really fine citizens. I am talking now of your grandparents and Mummy and I will be determined to build solidly on the foundations that they so truly laid'. If there was a positive to come from the war, it was that it had broadened his mind.[96] A day later he boarded HMS *Arawa*, bound for Australia.

The route home was nearly as circuitous as their original voyage to Singapore, calling first at Darwin, then Brisbane, followed by Sydney, then Perth. It didn't matter a lot. There was a physical-fitness session each morning, an abundance of cards and other games to occupy the afternoons, and a whisky ration with their meals. 'The troops are behaving themselves in an exemplary way and everybody is thoroughly enjoying himself' he observed. Tom tried to arrange flights home

Tom's Certificate of Service as an Officer, 1941–45 (Bunning Family Collection)

for the Western Australian soldiers in Darwin, but the military would not oblige.[97] There was at least an opportunity to call home on the telephone. He entertained the hope that Margot could fly to Sydney and meet him there, but their course might yet be altered, and she was in the midst of moving back to Cotswold anyway.[98] In mid-October the ship reached Fremantle. Tom finally relented against the orders coming down from above by having Margot and Gavin brought directly on board. It was a reunion four years and one month in the making.

6

Back to work

Tom resumed his post as executive director of Bunning Bros on 2 January 1946. The role he returned to was responsible for financial administration and sales and distribution across Western Australia.[1] He had wanted to go back sooner, but the army had a checklist for rehabilitation and only discharged him on Christmas Eve, then Bob Holmes insisted he take a short holiday to Bunbury before returning to work.[2] On his return, he found that the company was in good shape, 'rolling along on an output of 24,000 loads' and, to his pleasant surprise, with 'money in the bank'.[3] The old faces were there to greet him at head office. Charlie remained as joint executive director, alongside the venerable Petherick as managing director with his long-serving deputy Bruce Johnston. On the desk next to Tom, Joe Bunning still ran Perth Jarrah Mills. Despite these familiar aspects, much about the company had changed. The accounts had been made more complex when new Commonwealth taxes had been introduced and old state taxes revised. Export restrictions and price controls implemented during the war remained in place. Against this backdrop, the company was gearing up for unprecedented demand fuelled by a long postwar 'baby boom' and large-scale immigration. Western Australia's population was barely 500,000 in 1946, yet 70,000 new houses would be needed in the decade ahead.[4]

Tom and Charlie were in a position their father could only have dreamt of, and not simply because there was cash at hand. The opportunity for growth that lay ahead was not dissimilar to what Robert had perceived when he turned to sawmilling and retailing timber, but the company now had size and experience in its favour. Bunning Bros had developed the vertical integration that linked logging and milling to wholesale and retail distribution. Though the building trade had been sluggish since the Depression and in hiatus during the war, it had long been accustomed to sourcing structural timber, cabinets, flooring and other timber products from the company's yards. At Nyamup, the company had the newest and one of the largest sawmills in the state. The company's senior men were close-knit and experienced at operating sawmills, marketing timber and managing contracts.[5] If the second generation had a handicap, it was in the legacy of the family-owned structure they inherited. But the time to address this had not yet arrived.

Tom, of course, had devoted a great deal of thought to Bunning Bros's future during his four years away. His most pressing task was to review the balance sheets for this period, by way of catching up on the company's performance

Advertisement for Perth Jarrah Mills, c. late 1940s. Sales continued until the 1960s (Bunning Family Collection)

during the war. Insofar as the position of the accounts surprised him, it was because he feared Charlie might have been a little cavalier towards money.[6] At Changi, he had devised plans to revise costing systems, implement staff training, improve marketing, reform head-office administration and construct new offices, all of which he intended 'to tear into like a lifesaver into the surf'.[7] By necessity, however, these quickly developed into longer-term objectives that would be implemented when the time was right. The scale and pace of postwar reconstruction was partly a factor in this. Tom had sensed the enormity of it on the eve of his departure from Singapore. He had written in his letter to Gavin: 'conditions generally may settle down to be much different from what they were six years ago. We must study these conditions and make the best of them. Not only that but it looks perhaps as if the time is arriving when Father may be expected to resume some public obligations'.[8] The need to balance work with family obligations was to be another factor shaping Tom's ambitions as he settled back into work.

Tom's Right to Reinstatement at Bunning Bros from the Commonwealth Employment Service, December 1945 (Bunning Family Collection)

On 23 January 1946, Helen passed away. She had been frail for several years, and a series of falls during the war years had robbed her of much of her mobility.[9] The uncertainty of Tom's fate after the fall of Singapore weighed heavily upon her: 'I really have been broken hearted since you left', she had written in mid-1942.[10] 'If we could only hear from you things would not be so bad.'[11] She had a close bond with her youngest child, and when news that he was alive finally reached Australia, it had a visible effect on her appearance.[12] The news of her failing health had been conveyed in the letters he received at Changi and must have played on his mind as his captivity dragged on to an interminable extent. 'I have to thank you and no one else for most of the things about me that are good', he had written to her in 1944:

> Your sense of dignity, pride, duty and your interpretation of right and wrong are so direct and straight forward that the code has been a simple one to follow. Your wonderful sympathy and affection also go along to make you just the best Mother that a man could ever be blessed with.[13]

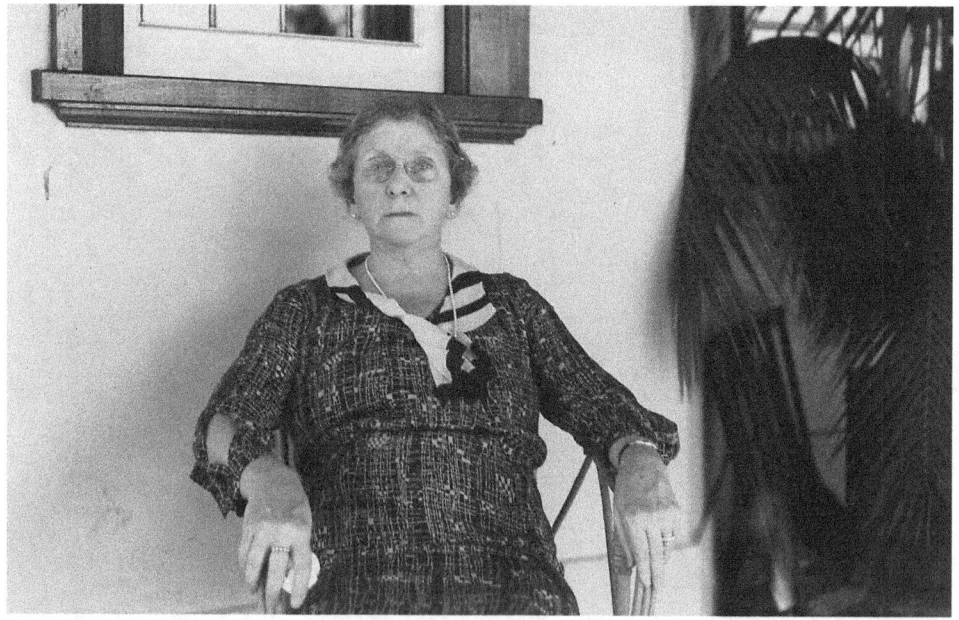

Helen Bunning, Innerhadden, 1935 (Courtesy State Library of Western Australia)

She had been in Fremantle with her other children to welcome him home, and she died only fourteen weeks later. The funeral was held at Karrakatta the next day.[14] Innerhadden was later acquired by St Hilda's Anglican School for Girls, which had moved onto adjacent land in the 1930s, and renamed Whitby House. Gena and Joe were by now well and truly middle-aged. The younger siblings each had established families of their own. In Tom and Margot's case, there were hopes of a larger one to come.

Charlie and Betty's children had all arrived by 1939; they had two daughters, Jenny and Fiona, and a son, Robert (Bob). During the war Charlie had risen to the rank of colonel in the VDC, although it was his role on the Timber Control Board that occupied most of his time, requiring frequent travel to the east coast and several expeditions through remote parts of the Northern Territory and Queensland to survey timber resources there.[15] At home, he worked with Norman Temperley on a partnership between Bunning Bros and Millars to develop a boatyard to supply wooden vessels to the military. 'Millars Bunning Shipbuilders' operated by the causeway at Perth for two years, constructing vessels as large as 85 feet and 100 tons, several of which were repurposed as fishing boats as the partnership wound up in late 1945.[16] This was a rich experience for Charlie and ensured he ended the war with enhanced stature within the industry.

It was on his initiative that Bunning Bros moved in early 1946 to expand their sawmilling operations and source other decorative species that were now difficult to obtain from overseas. In January, the company purchased four mills around Cairns in North Queensland from JM Johnston Pty Ltd, where Queensland maple, silky oak and other rainforest varieties produced the best grades of cabinet timbers available in Australia.[17] There were established markets in the state capitals, and an arrangement with Colonial Sugar Refinery (CSR) Ltd to ship sawn timber to Perth aboard its own vessels made the acquisition particularly enticing. Only months later, a small mill at Muchea that handled timber cut on private land was also picked up.[18] Yet Charlie was only at the start of a push to expand output. The concessions accumulated by Bunning Bros exceeded the permits held by competitors, including the State Sawmills, Whittakers, and each of the Kauri, Adelaide and Worsley Timber Companies. Only Millars controlled more of the Southwest forests; the two companies between them owned half the state's timber. Yet in 1940 Millars had deferred plans for a new sawmill, contributing to a looming undersupply of timber in the context of the building boom now underway. Rival firms such as Whittakers were already planning new mills of their own.[19] Bunning Bros would now do the same.

It was soon apparent that finance was going to be a problem, much as it had been in the past. The cash reserves Tom had found when he returned in January were quickly depleted and, inevitably, the company's board found itself wrestling with the need to restrict outlays to available funds. The board comprised Tom, Charlie and Joe, together with Petherick and Johnston, the solicitor Henry Downing and accountant Harry Merry. It had long been rather loosely organised because, although all of them conferred regularly, formal meetings were rare. One of Tom's early actions was to remedy this through a schedule of monthly meetings.[20] At the September meeting 'a long discussion took place on the question of anticipated capital expenditure within the next two years'.[21] The scale of operations now envisaged added weight to these deliberations. Charlie had proposed a new sawmill on the Donnelly River to work a concession of over 81,000 acres of prime jarrah and karri forest. This represented a strategic shift towards the southern forest belt and signalled that Manjimup would become a regional base for the company's operations. To facilitate the shift, a small engineering workshop was established in the town during 1946.[22] Unlike softwood milling, there was little standard equipment made anywhere for processing the likes of jarrah, with its gum component and uneven grain within a hard timber. The new unit would therefore be gradually expanded with expertise to manufacture, as well as maintain, mill equipment. The board was fulsome in its support of Charlie's plans, but it was conscious of its duty 'that commitments will not be made in excess of available funds'. There was no option but to notify the bank of an impending need to draw upon the company's overdraft.[23]

At Charles Street, there was much to keep Tom busy. The joinery and cabinet shops were being reorganised to better cope with the demand for housing supplies, and the yard needed to be drained and bituminised to cater to the company's expanding fleet of surplus military delivery trucks and to allow more timber to be stored.[24] About 150 men had worked throughout the war due to the essential nature of the industry, with their numbers now swelled by those returning to jobs that were on hold for the duration of their military service. At least twenty-eight men, not including Tom, were in this position, and they all needed to be fitted back into the organisation.[25] Another effect of the war was the

Margot, c. 1945 (Bunning Family Collection)

employment of more women within head-office administration. Tom wanted to meet them all and learn about their backgrounds and family. This was the still the era of the 44-hour week, with a half-day on Saturdays, and often this was the most convenient time for chatting informally to the workforce.[26] A contract to supply timber for houses, jetties and other infrastructure to Broken Hill Pty Ltd (BHP) for their planned iron-ore mine at Cockatoo Island had been signed in late 1945, and it became necessary to push the men and machinery hard in order to meet it. The last new equipment had been purchased in the late 1930s, and much of it now required constant maintenance to remain in working order.[27]

At home, the family settled back into Cotswold. Tom's Buick had sat out the war years in the garage, a victim of petrol rationing and Margot's use of her father's car. He soon had it running again, repainted a shade of turquoise that struck others as not entirely in keeping with the character of the vehicle or the

Top and bottom: Cotswold, 6 Osborne Parade, Cottelsoe (Bunning Family Collection)

man. It soon made way for a Rover imported from the United Kingdom, one of few new cars on Perth roads at a time when the first Australian-made Holden was over a year away.[28] There was less progress on his idea for a farm. Parting company with his batman Brookie was a factor, as the plan had taken hold across countless evenings together inside Changi. Brookie had returned to his job in the coal mines at Collie, so it was inevitable that their friendship waned.[29] Tom did, however, see Bruce Hunt regularly as his physician, and he maintained contact with the battalion through the association he helped establish at the end of the war. In time, more than one man from the 2/4th would find work at Bunning Bros. Tom was an active supporter of Legacy, but he considered this a private matter and rarely spoke about it.[30]

In his spare time, Tom rapidly regained form on the golf course. He no longer belonged to the young generation of players that had made Cottesloe a powerhouse of pennant golf in the 1930s, and now he had to contend with a new wave of golfers determined to make their mark in amateur competitions. Nonetheless, his performances were so strong in his first year back that he was rewarded with the honour of captaining Western Australia's team at Royal Sydney for the first national championship since 1939.[31] He had recovered well from the rigours of three and half years as a POW, and he kept up a routine of physical training that included, in the summer months, a regular morning run and swim at Cottesloe Beach.[32]

In September 1947, Robert Law passed away the day after his eightieth birthday. During the war he had worked tirelessly to maximise the supply of cement, an essential product for the construction of air-raid shelters across Perth and all manner of installations required by the military, delaying his retirement in the process. His health had been poor for the last couple of years, and the strain took a toll on Margot, who twice suffered a miscarriage in these years.[33] For so prominent a businessman, there was surprisingly little comment on his death in the daily press, although the significance of his career has not been lost to posterity; in the words of one historian, Law 'was a captain of industry in the traditional sense, a creator of wealth who knew intimately the industries in which he was engaged, as well as the intricacies of high finance'.[34] He had been a strong role model for Tom, with a subtle-yet-profound influence on his attitude towards the successful running of businesses, the importance of community service and the accumulation of private wealth.

Gavin and Sue, 1952 (Courtesy State Library of Western Australia)

Just over a year later, in October 1948, Tom and Margot welcomed their second child, Sue. It almost ended tragically when a seven-year-old Gavin unwittingly brought measles into the hospital on a visit to his mother and newborn sister, passing the infection onto them both.[35] They soon recovered, however, and went home to Cotswold.

A second child did not have a noticeable effect on Tom's routine. He was content to leave much of the parenting to Margot, and during the week he would spend time with the children only at dinnertime. There was, however, some change to his weekends, as he began to play golf a little less frequently in order to have more time with his family. He had made the state team again in 1947 and captained Cottesloe in 1947/48, but some quieter seasons followed. When he did play competitively, his performances remained strong and he remained among the small handful of amateurs locally to regularly post scores below seventy. He won Cottesloe's Catlidge Cup in 1947 and still placed highly in matchplay events, tying for the win in the annual Christmas Cup at Lake Karrinyup in 1951.[36]

A growing family also meant that his plans for travel would be put on hold. Whereas he had once contemplated spending an extended period overseas, the opportunity for doing so was closed for the time being.

As Tom stayed put, Charlie kept up a busy itinerary of travel. He went frequently to the Southwest, and with the purchase of assets in North Queensland it became necessary to make regular journeys there as well, even if it was at the opposite corner of Australia. In 1947 he attended the Commonwealth Forestry Conference in London and followed it with an extended tour of logging operations in Canada and the United States. What he witnessed was a window into the industry's future. Sawmilling was being transformed by the advent of powered saws and more advanced methods for hauling logs, sorting green timber and seasoning the sawn product. Plywoods and other specialised laminated products were gaining prominence in the North American market. It all shaped his vision for the future of Bunning Bros. The new mill at Donnelly River was to be a benchmark for efficiency, utilising the latest handling equipment, saws and kilns. In addition, rail lines for carting sawn timber would be built to connect the mill to the company's yard adjoining the railhead at Manjimup. Further to the findings of a recent royal commission on housing for mill workers, Donnelly River was also to be a carefully planned community, with a higher standard of housing, and modern facilities that included electricity, a reticulated water supply, a community hall and a general store.[37] To support the new mill, the engineering works at Manjimup would need to be enlarged. By mid-1948, when construction began, the venture's cost was approaching £100,000.[38]

This activity in the Southwest highlighted the need to reform the company's structure. During 1948, Tom worked with the board to orchestrate the reorganisation of Bunning Bros as a propriety company controlling its subsidiaries of Nyamup Sawmills, JM Johnston in Queensland, the new Donnelly Sawmills, the 'Bunning Bros' network of timber yards centred on Charles Street, and Dunbrick, the small cement brickworks at Maddington.[39] This was all very orthodox and reflected the company's growth. To Tom's mind, there were other sensible steps to be taken, even if they were more novel at the time. The outlay on amenities at Donnelly River was soon replicated with new facilities at Charles Street and the smaller mills, with a part-time amenities officer being hired to manage social activities for workers and their families.[40] Tom also pushed for the company to self-insure for workers' compensation. Logging, sawmilling and joinery production were all inherently dangerous by virtue of the machinery used, especially for inexperienced workers. The potential for serious accidents was a constant danger, and in the first few years after the war, several had occurred.[41] Under these circumstances self-insurance was financially sound, with the added benefit of lending every incentive to internal safety protocols. The company also became one of the first in the industry to employ a full-time safety officer. Bunning Bros would soon enjoy the best safety record in the timber industry. As with the focus on amenities, it made sense to look after the workforce's health and wellbeing, all the more so in a context where the postwar labour shortage was beginning to bite.

By early 1949, Donnelly River was coming into production and plans for a second new mill at Tone River were well advanced.[42] The concession here was 143,000 acres, considerably larger than Donnelly River and Nyamup. The mill would cost £24,000, implying a total outlay for the year of £70,000. The problem was that money was needed for equipment and facilities at Charles Street too, so that less than £50,000 was available for projects in the Southwest.[43] Profit was

Donnelly River Mill (Bunning Family Collection)

not an issue; rather it was the company's ability to reinvest it that had become a problem. As a private company, Bunning Bros was subject to undistributed profits tax, which mandated that forty per cent of profit be distributed to shareholders and thus diminished working capital. It was something Tom recognised was holding the company back.[44] To make matters worse, the attitude of the Commonwealth Government was becoming a concern. Chifley's Labor government was approaching the upcoming election with a radical program of bank nationalisation and the maintenance of wartime economic controls. Under these circumstances, the availability of money to support ongoing expansion was as restrictive as it had ever been.

The option of going to the public for funding, long avoided by Bunning Bros, was looking increasingly attractive. On Tom's recommendation, the board agreed in September 1949 to do exactly this. The company's capital would be increased from the existing £100,000, comprising 100,000 ordinary shares nominally valued at £1 each, to £350,000, divided into 249,000 ordinary shares and 1,000 employee shares of £1 each. An agreement was also reached with the Australian Mutual Provident (AMP) Society to sell 75,000 five-per-cent cumulative redeemable preference shares of £1 each.[45] These preference shares represented the first significant external financial backing in the company's history. The timing was good. Chifley lost the election in December, ushering in the stability and prolonged economic growth of the Menzies era. Hardwood exports were to be permitted once more, promising a revival of the sleeper trade that had once been so lucrative to the industry. In Western Australia, tentative steps towards industrialisation made during the war were gathering momentum after the election of a Liberal–Country Party coalition. A charcoal-iron furnace had been established at Wundowie, a tractor factory (Chamberlains) was being constructed at a former munitions works in Welshpool, and a new iron-ore mine was planned at Koolyanobbing. Agriculture, fruit growing, fisheries and other primary industries were all being encouraged to develop. Most importantly of all, population growth was being boosted through the arrival of European migrants or 'New Australians'.[46] The need for timber in housing, railways and other infrastructure showed no sign of slackening. There was therefore every prospect that Bunning Bros would continue to grow.

Indeed, during the first half of 1950 alone the company embarked on several major projects. The first of these was an agreement to supply prefabricated residences to the State Housing Commission. It was a significant undertaking. A new precut factory would be established at Manjimup to process timber coming in from the mills, with the roofing iron, wall cladding, and other hardware sourced in bulk from Perth and forwarded mainly by rail as required. The operation would come under Tom's area of responsibility.[47] A second important initiative was a contract to supply 1,500 louvred railway wagons to the Western Australian Government Railways (WAGR), which involved Bunning Bros working in partnership with Millars, Whittakers, the State Sawmills and the Kauri Timber Company in a new venture, the Wagon Timber Company.[48] At the same time, Bunning Bros won a contract with the Public Works Department (PWD) to construct high cooling towers for the state's new power station at Muja, near Collie.[49] Sales of flooring, mouldings and other finished timber remained strong. The company had opened a new metropolitan sales yard at Victoria Park, and it purchased land at Bunbury that might facilitate future developments.[50]

To oversee these new projects, the company's managerial team would have to expand. Ever since Robert had been in charge, Bunning Bros had benefited from the longstanding service of capable, experienced and loyal managers outside of head office. Ron Drysdale, a hands-on, self-taught engineer, was among them. He had worked with Charlie in the Commonwealth Timber Control Board, firstly to arrange the timber required for the new munitions works at Welshpool, followed by the role of manager of the joint Bunning Bros–Millars ship-building operation.[51] He would be invaluable now in managing the company's new projects, and he was renowned for his ability to find practical solutions to stubborn problems. Tom and Charlie knew he could be trusted with considerable autonomy within clear guidelines for the company's expansion.

Tom's own property holdings had expanded when, in 1950, he purchased the adjacent lot in Osborne Parade from his elderly neighbours. Enlarging Cotswold had been among the preoccupations of his POW diary: 'Are we to going to make another room in the house and are we to continue to have the maid's room upstairs, and if not, where? Then we must make the drawing room more comfortable'.[52] The end result now included an extension to the drawing/sitting room and, on the new block, the addition of a double garage and a housekeeper's flat, with a large attic above as a playroom for the children, plus a tennis court and chicken coop. By midyear he had commissioned a boat to be constructed as a weekend project in the Charles Street yard using plans obtained from England. To be built by Ron Drysdale, *Suzy Wren* was a 23-foot motor sailor, fitted with bunks, an enclosed head and galley, and finished inside with varnished Queensland maple.[53] It became a centrepiece of Tom's time with his family, especially in the summer. Gavin had commenced his schooling that same year at Scotch College. Tom had joined Scotch's council some years earlier, where he would continue to serve for many more to come.[54]

As the new decade began, then, there was every reason for feeling satisfied. In terms of its business activities, Bunning Bros had come a long way in the comparatively short space of time that had elapsed since Tom's return. The company had lifted its supply of sawn timber to the domestic market by nearly forty per cent on prewar levels, at the same time as modernising much of its operations. A new and modern sawmill was already approaching full capacity and another was under construction. The workforce numbered several hundred and continued to grow. A new and valued segment of this labour pool had been established through the recruitment of European migrants. They were frequently hired upon arrival at Fremantle; those skilled in woodwork or machining were always needed at Charles Street, and labourers were in constant demand in the Southwest.[55] Annual turnover was in excess of £1,000,000. Over the preceding five years, Bunning Bros had consolidated its standing among the four larger sawmillers that dominated Western Australia's timber industry.[56] The contracts with the State Housing Commission, WAGR and the PWD suggested the company was in good standing with the government. Yet any feeling of complacency was about to be quashed. As the pace of economic development shifted gear, the relationship between state government and free enterprise began to change. As it did, it signalled a more difficult path ahead for Bunning Bros.

The beginning of this rockier road was the planned opening of a new logging concession at Milyeannup, south of Nannup, covering 82,000 acres of virgin jarrah forest. Charlie had long had an eye on it. The company's logging activities on privately owned land would soon exhaust the available timber, and Lyall's Mill was similarly approaching the end of its useful life. The equipment and men tied up with these operations could instead be redeployed to this new concession to bring it rapidly into production.[57] Both Charlie and Tom had good reason for believing this is what the state wanted. During 1950 the Minister for Forests, Gerry Wild, had criticised sawmillers for not meeting the needs of residential construction, telling a congress of the building trade 'he

Above and right: *Suzy Wren* being launched, c. 1951 (Bunning Family Collection)

Suzy Wren on the Swan River (Bunning Family Collection)

did not think the timber industry has played the game by the people of the state'. It was a statement the timbermen objected to, issuing a defence of their performance via their industry association.[58] To be fair to them, Wild had been no less trenchant in lamenting the 'sorry picture' presented by local brick and cement manufacturers.[59] What made his speech galling was the fact that Wild also held the housing portfolio, creating a potential (if not a real) conflict between responsibility for the stewardship of timber resources and overseeing the government's housing program. Be that as it may, it was only a prelude to a more substantial conflict of interest. Within weeks it became apparent that Wild was intending to sidestep the requirement for a formal tendering process and award the Milyeannup concession to the Kauri Timber Company.[60]

The deal on behalf of the Kauri Timber Company had been worked out behind closed doors by the thirty-nine-year-old accountant, Charles Court, the future Premier of Western Australia. Not yet in politics, Court was a partner in the Perth-based auditor of Kauri's local operations. The Melbourne-based timber and trading company operated a new sawmill at Northcliffe and a smaller operation at Nannup. They were now proposing to invest £200,000 in a second sawmill at Nannup, new kilns, and the development of timber yards in Perth. All of the jarrah produced at the new mill would be reserved for the local market. Court had met Kauri's directors in Melbourne and fixed on a royalty of 11 shillings per load from the concession.[61] In the meantime, unaware of these dealings, Bunning Bros had decided to offer 14 shillings and 8 pence per load, which was the second highest among eight bids submitted when tenders were called for in August. But Wild had already made up his mind. In a clear signal of his intentions, he doubled down on criticism of the industry, saying in a speech at Busselton 'he had no apology to offer for his recent charge that those responsible were not producing sufficient timber'.[62] It only remained to confirm he had the power under the *Forests Act* to accept a tender that was not the highest offered.[63]

To the Bunning Bros board, this warranted something sterner than simply another statement on behalf of the Timbers Industries' association. Charlie was furious and Downing, who also sat on the board of Swan Portland Cement, had been no less irritated by Wild's remarks.[64] It was left to Tom to put forward the company's response in a statement to the *West Australian*. 'It is quite easy for any individual to make a charge that sufficient of this or that commodity is not being produced, but we would expect from a gentleman of Mr. Wild's standing that one may receive some tangible suggestions rather than loose criticism', he argued. The facts indicated Bunning Bros had boosted its output considerably over recent years, and that contrary to the Minister's assertions the company's three larger mills were all producing at close to capacity. Output by the industry as a whole had been affected recently by labour shortages and the loss of sawmills in bushfires, but even so it had nearly doubled since 1938. 'We have always had the helpful co-operation of the Government, the Forests Department and the State Housing Commission in our efforts to build up our production of sawn timber', Tom observed. 'For this reason we have up to the present refrained from making any comment upon the statements made by the Minister in regard to the production of timber in Western Australia, feeling that as he arrived at a better understanding of the present difficulties that the industry is undergoing, and of the all-out efforts that it is making he would have a sounder appreciation of the situation.'[65]

Tom's point about co-operation was well made. In a highly regulated industry for which the government was itself a principal customer, it made sense to maintain good relationships. This was especially the case in Western Australia, where isolation and a relatively small population tended to foster harmony between the state, capital and labour, and all the more so when the memory of the Great Depression and its aftermath remained fresh in the minds of so many. It was for this reason, as much as the questionable figures quoted, that Tom described Wild's speech as 'unfair and irresponsible'.[66] Beyond this, the focus was on lobbying in private. During October a follow-up letter was sent to the premier, Ross McLarty, to protest the 'grave injustice' being done to Bunning Bros by shutting them out of the Milyeannup concession: 'In effect, your Government will be giving a very considerable preference to a company which has done less than any other sawmilling company of its capacity towards the Government's housing programmes', it was suggested, 'rather than considering the tender of Bunning Bros a company which has done everything the Government has asked of it'.[67] To put this in context, Kauri's two existing sawmills at Northcliffe and Nannup were not using even half of their current allowed intake, despite the shortage of timber locally.

What was also becoming apparent, however, was that the government was moving towards a fundamentally new relationship with private enterprise.

The support for BHP to open its mine on Cockatoo Island had been an early example of its intent to attract large-scale capital to invest in Western Australia, and assistance to CSR to establish an asbestos mine at Wittenoom was another.[68] Wild made no secret of his wish to do the same for the timber industry when, at the end of October 1950, a bill to ratify the arrangement with the Kauri Timber Company was put before parliament. This was necessary because the Solicitor-General had looked into Bunning Bros's claims and found the deal worked out by Court likely breached the *Forests Act*.[69] Legislation would have to be passed instead. As Wild told the Conservator of Forests, by way of justifying why a lower tender price for Milyeannup should be accepted, 'there is a company prepared to enter the retail business in Western Australia and I am prepared, if possible, to strike a bargain with it'.[70] The company's size was the critical factor. Kauri was the largest sawmiller in Australia, with significant assets in Victoria, Tasmania, New Zealand and the South Pacific.[71] It had come originally to Western Australia to mill timber for export, but the prospect now was of a major new player in the local building supplies trade.

The attractiveness of Wild's plan was plainly evident to a growing population seeking opportunities for home ownership and a state government intent on promoting it. But as Tom had argued, the process was flawed, and the industry's problems would not be solved by a new mill and sales outlet. Much of this and more besides came out in the parliament. It was resolved to refer Wild's bill to a select committee. This spent the latter part of 1950 examining evidence.[72] What it found was that the issues around production and supply of timber ran deeper than the solution the minister was proposing, recommending instead that a royal commission (the fourth to look at the timber industry) be convened. This would be a wide-ranging inquiry that was to cover every aspect of forestry and the timber trade in Western Australia. In the meantime, the deal with Kauri Timber Company was on hold.[73]

If a reminder that Bunning Bros was in good standing within the industry was needed, it came through the formal opening of the Donnelly River Mill in April 1951. The company arranged for a special train to carry representatives from the government, trade unions, the Employers' Federation and the press to the occasion. The sawmill was opened by the acting premier, Arthur Watts, as McLarty was overseas, and the worker's club was opened by Justice Lawrence Jackson (later Sir Lawrence and Chief Justice) of the Supreme Court.

Top and bottom: Nyamup Mill, paintings by Elizabeth Blair Barber (Courtesy of Bob Bunning)

There was a picnic lunch and demonstrations of felling, log-hauling and sawmilling using the modern equipment obtained for the mill; Watts declared the spectacle 'a complete answer to those who wanted more urgency in building'.[74] Wild attended but did not speak. It was probably just as well, and in any case, his ideas on the way forward for the timber industry were hardly a secret anymore. To meet the state's future needs, much less expand into other markets, investment on a scale beyond Bunning Bros's present capacity would be required. The company already was pushing the limit of its overdraft to complete the Tone River mill. As Tom well knew, there could be no major capital expenditure beyond that point until the bank was repaid.[75]

The time to consider a float had arrived. During 1951 a new company secretary, Ralph Bower, was appointed.[76] This was central to the internal reorganisation Tom had long envisaged, although now there was a more pressing agenda, as the pair worked closely for the rest of the year to investigate a full public listing. The case was becoming irresistible. Undistributed profits tax

Donnelly River Mill, painting by Elizabeth Blair Barber (Courtesy of Bob Bunning)

remained a burden on the reinvestment of profit in ongoing expansion. It was also in the interests of Tom's sisters, Gena, Jane and Angie, to one day have a convenient way of selling all or part of their own holdings in Bunning Bros. And in any case, the company's growth suggested it was the logical step to take. 'As sales increase so you need more money to finance the increase in stocks which you need to cater for greater custom', Tom later explained.[77] Articles of Association were drafted by Henry Downing's firm, with much of the burden falling upon his son Frank, a friend of Tom's since before the war.[78] In March 1952 a prospectus was issued.

The listed company would be named Bunning Timber Holdings Ltd, though it would be known more commonly as simply 'Bunnings'. It would take over the existing shareholdings in Bunning Bros Pty Ltd and acquire all its interests, including the sawmills, the North Queensland operations, and Henry Martin and Co, which operated the prefabricated housing plant in Manjimup. The issued capital in the form of Bunning Bros shares would be acquired for £420,000, paid for by the issue of 640,000 fully paid shares and £100,000 in preference shares. An additional 200,000 ordinary shares would be released to the public at 10 shillings each, and another 480,000 ordinary shares would be held in reserve. This meant a nominal capital of £1,000,000, made up of 1,800,000 ordinary shares and 100,000 5% cumulative preference shares. In the prospectus, the company's net assets were valued at £614,599. The Bunning family would retain control by virtue of the shareholdings of Tom, Charlie and their siblings. The offering of 200,000 shares was heavily oversubscribed and, as the *West Australian* reported, the subscription list 'opened and closed almost immediately'.[79] Working capital had been secured, and within days, Bunnings was moving to expand the engineering workshop at Manjimup that had become critical to its wider operations.[80]

The royal commission, when it reported in early 1952, was a vindication of the stand that Bunning Bros had taken against Wild and his deal with the Kauri Timber Company. 'The forest policy of the state is considered to be sound in principle and soundly administered', it found.[81] The commissioner, GJ Rodger, was satisfied that local sawmillers 'have in most, if not all, cases made every reasonable endeavour to meet the Government's express desire for increased intake'.[82] Furthermore, the 'system of disposal of forest products had been fairly administered and generally satisfactory and no adequate reason can be seen for changing it to a system of purely arbitrary allocation of permits'.[83] The Milyeannup concession would be retained by the Forests Department to be used in the future to boost existing permit areas.[84] Charles Court's deal was dead. To him, as to Tom, this was old news by now. The pair had a thing or two in common, being close in age (Tom was elder by a year) and having both qualified as accountants through the correspondence course offered by Hemingway and Robinson.[85] But whereas Tom was contemplating the future of a publicly listed company, Court was eyeing a career in politics. In 1953 he became the Member for Nedlands, joining what became the Liberal opposition following McLarty's defeat in that year's elections. The affair over Milyeannup would not be the last time their paths would cross.

This was all in the future, however, and for Tom there was a more immediate priority. The successful listing of Bunning Timber Holdings Ltd meant the start of a holiday, or rather, of the overseas travel he had long wished to undertake. The idea of an extended tour abroad had frequently occupied his thoughts inside Changi, and in July 1945, when it was clear the war would soon be over and Bruce Hunt asked him what he planned to do next, 'a trip to America to gain further knowledge, experience and background' was at the top of the list.[86] But it had been a long time coming, pushed to one side as the demands of work, the needs of his family and his commitment to competitive golf all combined to deny him the opportunity. Barely a fortnight after the float, with the ink on Rodger's report still drying, he boarded an aircraft for Sydney. He would fly first to America and then on to England, where Margot was to join him for an extended holiday. Gavin would be initiated into the rough-and-tumble world of the Scotch College dormitory. Sue, not yet four years of age, would be left in the care of a nanny.[87]

Tom's first destination was Hawaii, where he visited timber yards, played golf, and was struck by 'the extraordinary coloured shorts worn by young and old'.[88] He spent a fortnight on America's west coast, travelling south from Vancouver through the heartland of the timber industry, before stopping in Los Angeles, where the design of the city to suit private car ownership offered a glimpse of Australia's suburban future. Another three weeks were devoted to travelling through the South and up the east coast to New York, where every weekday was spent visiting sawmills and manufacturers of flooring and other materials derived from timber. It was all on an entirely different scale to home, and he made careful records in his journal on factory organisation, the equipment used, prices and margins, and labour productivity, along with the names of everyone he met. From New York he travelled by the *Queen Elizabeth* to London and a reunion with Margot.[89]

The English summer would be something more akin to a holiday. Tom played regularly at London's Highgate Golf Club. He went with Margot to the races at Ascot and to St Anne's in Lancashire to watch the Open Championship, where Bobby Locke won by one stroke over Australia's Peter Thomson. They also went to Wimbledon, although their day there was cut short by rain. They caught up with Tom's cousin, Will Bunning, who was by now the Secretary to the Australian High Commissioner, and took a drive through Kent, visiting Chartwell Towers, the residence of Sir Winston Churchill, then in his second term as prime minister. Tom bought a new set of golf clubs and a new pipe and lighter, and he was fitted for a number of suits. On almost every other day there was a lunch or dinner engagement to attend. He continued to visit local timber firms, called into the offices of Millars to speak with his counterparts there, and went down to the West Indian docks to inspect shipments of South American hardwoods. In mid-July they went up to Newcastle and travelled across to Norway and Sweden, before returning to England and going from there to France, Switzerland, West Germany and Belgium. Back in London, he played in the Timber Trades golf day and attended a woodworking and machinery exhibition. It was a 'marvellous day', and a fine end to their trip.[90]

7

Ploughing back the profits

BUNNING TIMBER HOLDINGS had a good first year. The mill at Tone River reached full capacity, pushing the company's output of timber to a new peak. The housing boom ensured that demand for structural timber, cabinets and flooring remained strong. At Manjimup, the precutting plant was now producing a house per day for the State Housing Commission.[1] The mills and processing operations were being converted to run on electrical instead of steam power and the fleet of motor trucks was expanding. Profit after tax reached £94,918 in the second year, and the company group continued to expand its operations. Tom outlined the strategy in a speech to senior Bunning staff in late 1953. 'A point to be noted is that only half of these profits arose from our normal operations as sawmillers and timber merchants and the other half came from our activities which included Sleeper Mills, Precut Houses, Contracts, and Joinery Manufacture'. A modest dividend had been paid and the remaining funds reinvested in modernisation and diversification. 'After providing for taxation, most of the profits are being ploughed back into the business in the purchase of plant, improved amenities, increased stocks, and for the financing of increased turnovers'.[2]

What made these early results so pleasing was that the company achieved them in the face of difficulties that were not of its own making. A protracted strike at the Midland Railway Workshops had obstructed rail freight so badly that it became necessary to quickly arrange for the road transport of timber to meet requirements at Charles Street and the needs of the branches. 'The Directors appreciate the value of the work done by road transport in overcoming such a complete breakdown in rail facilities', the inaugural annual report remarked. 'It is hoped that all governments will realise this value and not compel the public to rely solely on the railways by implementing existing legislation which is aimed at the protection of one form of transport'.[3] Such comment on public policy as it affected the company was to be a common feature of communication with shareholders. And Tom would not find himself speaking out solely on their behalf. Insofar as the fracas over the Milyeannup concession had thrust him into the role of a spokesman on behalf of the timber industry at large, it was a foretaste of what lay ahead.

Dudley and Bertha Law, c. 1960 (Bunning Family Collection)

It certainly looked as though the business climate was shifting within Western Australia. On the one hand, the push for industrial development was materialising in the form of a new refinery under construction for the Anglo–Iranian Oil Company (soon to be renamed British Petroleum, or BP) in the new precinct of Kwinana, a steel-rolling mill for BHP in the same industrial complex, and a new cement works in nearby Munster.[4] Each of these projects had been agreed to in 1952. On the other hand, the election of a new Labor government under the leadership of Albert Hawke at the beginning of 1953 signalled a change in direction away from private enterprise. Hawke was a charismatic figure, less doctrinal and more reformist than many parliamentary colleagues, but with an ingrained distrust towards business and a commitment to the state socialism reminiscent of an earlier political era.[5] Before the election, there had been calls within the union movement for a 'socialisation of building' to meet Western Australia's housing needs. After polling day, Hawke made it clear that state-run enterprises would be given preference ahead of local businesses and would be built up over time in opposition to enticing overseas capital investment.[6]

This new direction was something Tom also took up in his address to senior staff:

> An interesting observation [can be] made on the trading of the State Sawmills as compared with this company…The conclusion is quite irrefutable that disregarding shareholders entirely, our company was worth more than twice as much in revenue to the Government and the community generally than was the Government owned State Sawmills.[7]

This was a pragmatic stance, but it was also one that reflected the evolving nature of his role within both the company and the wider business community. During the year he had been appointed to the local board of the Anglo-Iranian Oil Company, as construction proceeded on the new refinery at Kwinana.[8] This was a £40 million investment, the largest ever made in Western Australia and unprecedented in the scale of works involved, making it his most important board position yet.[9] He was also now a director of the Metropolitan Brick Company (Metro Brick), alongside brothers-in-law Gordon and Dudley Law, and a board member of Peter Ice Cream Ltd.[10] Since 1951 he had been a director of the Nor'-West Whaling Company, a local outfit attempting to revive the humpback whaling industry that had prospered along the Gascoyne coast before the Second World War.[11] As the company grew and as his own portfolio of interests expanded, the health of the state's economy and the way it was being managed were increasingly matters that concerned him.

Any clouds looming on the horizon were at least tempered by the ongoing strong performance of Bunnings. During 1954, the company's subsidiary delivered its one-thousandth house to the State Building Commission. When the original contract for prefabricated housing was filled, a new one was negotiated to keep the Manjimup plant in operation. A sideline in the sale of kit houses to the public had been established. The partnership with Millars, Whittakers, the Kauri Timber Company and the State Sawmills to construct wagons for the Western Australian Government Railways (WAGR) had proven to be a profitable undertaking. Sleepers were being delivered in greater numbers after orders came in from the Commonwealth railways and South Australia.[12] This helped to alleviate concerns that overseas sales would struggle to recover when export restrictions were finally relaxed, due to the advent of cheap hardwoods from Southeast Asia and South America and the rising cost of shipping during the intervening period. Labour shortages continued to be addressed with the aid of postwar migration schemes, as the mills in particular needed men, and though they often lacked skill, the new migrants were capable of working hard and learning on the job. At Donnelly and Tone River, single men were accommodated in individual huts with a communal dining hall and ablution blocks, and migrant families were housed in larger cottages.[13] In mid-1955 the company reported an annual profit of £146,762, and it could contemplate a future where the imperative of overcoming chronic shortages in timber products for residential construction was no longer the most pressing concern of the day.[14]

These circumstances naturally affected decisions being made around growth and diversification. Safety remained a priority, especially with so many inexperienced men now employed. The company's safety officer, its innovative practices and the commitment to safe practices from the top led by Charlie and Tom underlay the lowest accident frequency in the industry. An emphasis on the rehabilitation of injured workers, together with the company's

Charles Bunning with mill workers (Bunning Family Collection)

self-funded workers' compensation scheme, also saved the company money in the long run.[15] Access to standing timber remained a concern from a longer-term standpoint. Charlie had long advocated for the development of pine plantations to reduce reliance upon imported softwoods at the same time as supporting the established sawmills and the communities linked to them. Since the mid-1930s, the company had held timber rights over 24,000 hectares near Boddington, where jarrah and wandoo were sourced and cut for sleepers and to augment the supply of hardwoods at Charles Street. The land was suitable for *Pinus radiata*, and when it was learnt the concession might be sold to a local outfit producing tannin, the company set out to acquire the land itself. The owner, an elderly Englishwoman, had inherited it from her father (an old friend of Robert) and was not necessarily predisposed to part with it. It took some careful negotiation by Tom before she agreed to a sale.[16] At Charles Street, an adjacent property was acquired around the same time. The joinery section was relocated to the new site, freeing up space to warehouse timber and builders' hardware for retailing direct to the public.[17]

The strategy of increasing sales through the main yard and branches by adding hardware products appealed to Tom, but achieving that diversification was not a straightforward proposition. The housing boom increased demand not only from building contractors, but also from an expanding home-handyman market as well. However, the difficulty of expanding any further into hardware lay in gaining purchase arrangements with suppliers. These arrangements were tightly controlled by distributors, who maintained close and, in some cases, exclusive relationships with established manufacturers, most of whom were British. Indeed, it was almost guild-like in its organisation, little changed from the Edwardian period of Tom's birth.[18] Local firms like Boans, Bairds, Sandovers and Drabbles maintained a tight hold on the retail hardware trade, benefiting from exclusive agreements and price controls that would be illegal in the twenty-first century. These were the sort of strategic and administrative challenges that Tom embraced and worked on during this period. It would take careful planning and persuasion to realise the potential generated by residential construction and the rising rates of home ownership in Western Australia during the 1950s.

Petherick had remained at the helm since the company went public. Tom greatly respected his business acumen and personal qualities, though by the mid-1950s he began to concede privately that his tenure was beginning to drag on.[19] When Petherick retired at the beginning of 1956, it ushered in a transition that was timely, if not overdue. Tom and Charlie assumed the roles of joint managing directors of Bunning Timber Holdings. Charlie remained focused upon the challenges and opportunities within the company's forest and timber processing operations. Bold in his ideas and aspirations for this side of the business, he had a practical, 'can-do' approach to innovation and improving efficiency, and he worked closely with the mill managers and the other subordinates working for him. On occasion, Tom would caution Charlie that his aspirations may not be viable or were stretching the company's finances, but the two were rarely seen by others to disagree, and their respect for each other was such that any differences were quickly resolved. Petherick remained on the board until he passed away in 1958. H. P. Downing retired as chairman a short time later, allowing Charlie to ascend to that role and Tom to become vice-chairman. This arrangement related to Charlie being five years older, and Tom was happy to defer to him as his senior. As managers, they would henceforth run Bunnings jointly and retain their separate day-to-day responsibilities, with Charlie taking care of production and forestry matters and Tom handling sales outlets and administration. It remained the closest of partnerships, all the stronger for having matured across three decades of hands-on experience in business together.[20]

Outside of the office, Tom's various commitments inevitably constrained his free time. His board appointments not only involved formal gatherings, but also came with social obligations, especially when BP executives and other interstate or overseas businessmen were in town. Visitors were invariably invited home to Cotswold. He and Margot enjoyed entertaining, so it was rarely a burden, even if it did sometimes come at the expense of time with their friends and families. His regular schedule and frequent travel meant that much of the parenting continued to be left to Margot. On an ordinary day he would stop past the Weld Club after work for a quick beer out of his favourite tankard and arrive home at 6.30 pm. After a whisky with Margot the family would have dinner, when he would quiz the children about their day, before retiring to his study in the evening. Like most fathers, but also because of the seven-year age difference between his two children, he was inclined to spend more time with his son, taking Gavin for a swim at Cottesloe before breakfast in the summer months, or bringing him along when he called in at the West Perth yard on Saturday mornings. Saturday remained part of the normal 44-hour week, and Tom enjoyed the opportunity to chat with the machinists and yard hands. In the school holidays, both Gavin and Sue were taken on visits to the mills, just as Robert had done with his children. Sue was escorted by Margot, and Gavin 'worked' under the wing of the mill manager. When summer holidays came, the family spent them aboard *Suzy Wren* at Rottnest, or occasionally at a holiday house at Palm Beach owned by Margot's mother.[21]

By the start of 1956, Tom could look back on a decade of virtually uninterrupted progress and prosperity since the war. He and his brother were running one of the largest and most-modern timber firms in Australia.[22] His career outside of the company was thriving, with directorships that spanned brickmaking, food manufacture, whaling and, later that year, heavy engineering in the form of an appointment to the local board of Vickers Hoskins Ltd. But any satisfaction with these achievements was soon to be tempered by a marked shift in the business climate. Early in the year it became apparent the building industry was cooling off, as lags in the construction of new homes were finally dealt with and the sector began adjusting to a new pace.

Gavin in *Suzy Wren*'s tender (Bunning Family Collection)

The tender alongside the dinghy which Gavin built himself (Bunning Family Collection)

Another use for the tender (Bunning Family Collection)

The easing of supply problems domestically prompted the Commonwealth to remove restrictions on timber exports, though increases in shipping costs and competition from Southeast Asia and South America meant that overseas markets would not be as lucrative as they once had been.[23] For producers supplying the Australian market, it suggested a new and more-competitive era lay ahead.

What made the downturn worrying, however, was not the situation overseas so much as at home. Within Western Australia, the conditions long prevailing were such that timber supply barely matched demand, leaving Bunnings or the industry at large with little incentive to promote timber against alternative building materials. That situation had begun to change. At the end of the war, the state faced an undersupply of bricks that had now steadily improved as new brickworks opened and production expanded. For example, Metro Brick had doubled its output by joining a syndicate making bricks at the site of Robert Law's old brickyard in Armadale, which was up and running by 1953.[24] Midland Brick Co. Pty Ltd had also been established by the energetic Rick New, and it was soon shaking up the sector with innovative production methods, the creation of a bricklaying training school, and a hard-hitting advertising slogan promoting double-brick construction over timber framing and brick veneers.[25] It had a lasting effect on the building industry as, unlike the rest of Australia, almost all Perth houses have been double brick ever since. The response from Bunnings reflected this more-competitive marketplace. A sum of £2,500 was committed to advertising in 1956, much more than had been spent in the past.

There were other reasons for promoting the company and its products. The Hawke government's preference for state-run enterprises was beginning to bite. By the mid-1950s, the old tendering system had been practically abandoned in favour of government building and construction being undertaken solely by an expanded Public Works Department. This utilised a day-labour system and drew its supplies from the State Building Supplies into which the State Sawmills and State Brickworks had been merged. When the company's contract with the Housing Commission was filled, there was no option but to close down its prefabricated housing plant.[26] Bunnings was now effectively debarred from supplying materials in connection with new public projects for the foreseeable future.[27] This was in keeping with Hawke's mandate, and there was more to come. After Labor was re-elected in April 1956, a new 'Profiteering and Unfair

Trading' bill was introduced to parliament. It was unfinished business for Hawke, as the legislation proposed to re-establish wartime price controls that had lapsed in 1953 and that he had tried but failed to have extended during his first term; his aim was to keep inflation and the cost of living in check.[28] To the opposition and the business community at large, it represented an unjustified impost on free enterprise and placed large-scale capital investment at risk. Controversial from the outset, the *Unfair Trading and Profit Control Act* (1956) strained an already fraught relationship between state government and industry.[29] Credit restrictions introduced by the Commonwealth to help curb inflation added further to the building sector's misfortunes.[30] For Bunnings, it pointed to a new cycle of diminishing profits, casting a shadow over the company's dividend for the first time since its public listing.[31]

Amid this challenging climate, Tom had been pushing ahead with administrative reform, an ambition long contemplated and made easier by Petherick's retirement. The nucleus of a new team was soon in place to pursue sales growth to the building industry. Ralph Bower, recruited originally as company secretary, was promoted to the new position of sales manager. The position of hardware manager was also established and opened to application. The company was fortunate to attract Wally Anderson, managing director of a local firm, Raphael & Co, which had recently been caught up in a takeover. Anderson had nearly three decades of experience in the trade and maintained the relationships that would be vital to allowing Bunnings to improve its range and competitiveness in the hardware market. In essence, it was a question of positioning the company as 'A grade' merchants rather than 'B grade' purchasers in the eyes of the industry association, unlocking the distributors' lists that this body controlled (and of which Anderson was a past president). His experience would also prove essential in light of the specialised nature of most product lines, and the fact that the knowledge of the company's existing sales representatives was limited mainly to timber.[32] Both Bower and Anderson were experienced men, and Tom trusted their judgement, delegating considerable authority to each. There would be no overnight transition, but the direction was clear.

Another strategy was to seek opportunities outside of Western Australia. Charlie led the way in the new year by embarking on a tour to India, Pakistan, Ceylon and Singapore to investigate the market for sleepers and heavy section timbers that had once been a mainstay for the state's sawmillers. Some new sales resulted, helping to offset the loss of orders at home as demand from WAGR dried up and other states pushed ahead with closing old and unviable railways. Freight costs remained a problem. The expense of shipping timber between Bunbury to Adelaide was roughly the same as shipping it from Malaya – no minor issue in light of the reliability of the South Australian market to Bunnings in the past.[33] The Northern Territory was a more enticing prospect. Darwin was on the route of Western Australia's State Shipping Service, which meant shipping was both economical and reliable so long as labour on the wharves was quiescent. More importantly still, the Northern Territory was ending years of stagnation, as the Commonwealth moved to encourage mining and pastoralism and to rebuild old defence bases neglected since the war. Tom went there in 1957 to appraise the situation and consider opportunities for establishing a presence for the company.

The result was one of the more colourful associations of his career. Remote and under-developed, Darwin was a rough-and-ready town with a population made up of civil servants on temporary postings, Indigenous residents, recent migrants and an odd assortment of characters that had found their home in the tropics. It was a far cry from the boardrooms and private clubs he frequented on his visits to other Australian cities, although day-to-day dealings with the shopfloor staff and his time in the army all helped when it came to rubbing shoulders with such mixed company. On his visit he met a prominent local, Dorothy De Fraine, and the two quickly established a good rapport. De Fraine was a former Australian executive for Warner Bros Films, who had married (and divorced) four times before moving to Darwin and becoming one of the town's more colourful local identities. Known as 'Mumma', she had been among the few women to remain in residence during the war, where she had run a hostel for single men, developing a reputation for keeping them check through an ability to swear as badly as the worst of them. Post-war, she had built an impressive list of contacts among the Territory's administrators and business community. In an era when the Northern Territory was run by federal civil servants posted out of Canberra, she had made a point of keeping in contact with the senior government personnel stationed in Darwin. Tom recognised the value in a partnership and took steps to engage her as a local representative of Bunnings. It yielded immediate results by providing the company with a major new outlet for karri, and it marked the beginning of what quickly became a successful business partnership.[34]

Later that year, Tom took time away from his assorted responsibilities to complete a business administration course in Hawaii. The Advanced Management Course had been established in the mid-1950s by the University of Hawaii in conjunction with the Harvard Business School and offered an intensive, full-time course for senior executives lasting six weeks, targeting Australia and the Pacific region.[35] Such programs were still a novelty for Australian businessmen, but for Tom it marked the fulfilment of a long-held ambition, one of the last of his wartime plans to come to fruition. It wasn't just the curriculum that was of interest either. There were valuable contacts to be made among his cohort, some of which became lasting friendships. With Honolulu developing rapidly as a tourist destination, there was much of interest to see in terms of the products and techniques being applied in the construction of expansive new hotels.[36] There was even time for some golf, something that was becoming harder to retain as a regular part of his schedule at home.

Fathers and Sons competition at Cottesloe Golf Club, c.1960 (Bunning Family Collection)

If travelling kept Tom abreast of new technologies and trends in business organisation, it also helped to clarify the problems he was returning to. Both he and Charlie had become involved in the Western Australian Trade Bureau, a centrepiece of the private sector's response to what it perceived as an ideologically-driven crusade against free enterprise.[37] Comprising representatives of commercial, construction, manufacturing and professional interests, the bureau was dedicated to opposing the state's antiprofiteering legislation through publicity campaigns and assistance to members facing investigation by the new Unfair Trading Control Commissioner.[38] Tom had been appointed to the bureau's executive in 1957, around the same time he was elected President of the Associated Sawmillers & Timber Merchants of Western Australia (ASTMWA), an amalgam of the Sawmillers' Association and Timber Merchants' Association (of which Robert had been president throughout Tom's childhood).[39] In the meantime, the Hawke government's determination to curb excessive profits was continuing. Two actions during 1958 indicated Tom would be in for a busy time of it. The first occurred when prosecutions were initiated against Cockburn Cement for offences under the *Unfair Trading Act*, a worrying precedent for industry as a whole.[40] The second was the formation of an Honorary Royal Commission into the 'administration, management and control' of the state's railways.[41] The administration of WAGR was a perennial issue, but it also thinly masked the real intent of this inquiry. In practice, it would investigate the Associated Sawmillers & Timber Merchants' control of the sleeper trade in light of the same legislation now being wielded against cement manufacturers.

The timber industry was hardly a stranger to commissions of inquiry. What made this one unusual, however, is that it was based entirely on departmental records and made no attempt to obtain evidence from interested parties.[42] An interim report in late 1958 laid out the complaint against the association. The background was that sleeper production had been entrusted to the association during the Second World War (in fact, on the eve of the Battle for Singapore) and then retained in its management during the era of postwar price controls. Thereafter, WAGR had continued to draw its annual requirement from the association, which in turn divided the contract among its members; in practice, it was uneconomical for large or 'trade' mills to produce sleepers, so the bulk of supply came from subcontractors operating throughout permit areas and on private land, as had occurred prewar.[43] This arrangement held until the State Sawmills (now renamed the State Building Supplies) and the Kauri Timber Company defected in 1957, leaving Millars, Bunnings and the Adelaide and Worsley Timber Companies as the association's members. When the government opened the next sleeper contract to competitive tender, the association's members submitted uniform bids that were slightly higher than some former subcontractors, but which together accounted for the quantity required. 'Obviously, this tender price must have been agreed on between the firms concerned', the report determined, 'and this is the very practice against which the findings and recommendations of the Honorary Royal Commission were directed'.[44] Prosecution by the Unfair Trading Control Commissioner was recommended accordingly.[45]

At face value, there was a basis for a complaint against the sawmillers. Yet Hawke chose to rail against the association even before the interim report was released, with rhetoric that was disquieting to more than just the timbermen. Sawmillers and timber merchants had been 'battering, plundering, and robbing' the railways for too long, he told parliament, all at the behest of 'some of the high priests of private enterprise in Western Australia'.[46] Relationships had already been strained by the announcement that a large new sawmill would be built for the State Building Supplies at Dwellingup through the Public Works Department's day-labour system.[47] There could be little doubt the government's attitude was as uncongenial as it was towards other industries. Dialogue between the government and cement manufacturers had certainly taken a turn for the worse after the prosecution of Cockburn Cement was announced. The managing director of its English parent company, the influential entrepreneur Sir Halford Reddish, had been quoted in the *Financial Times* warning against further investment in the state. The charges against his company, he wrote, were 'wild and irresponsible', and the *Unfair Trading Act* 'repugnant to a sense of British justice'. 'No, Mr Hawke, it just won't do', Reddish concluded. 'Repeal your Act and then let us join together in a real effort to put Western Australia on the industrial map.'[48]

Against this backdrop, Tom responded to the Honorary Royal Commission's report. 'The somewhat dramatic reference to this association being a sleeper combine', he explained in the *West Australian*, was 'quite untrue'. The report had made basic errors on points such as the association's membership and the details of the recent tender, although it was the means of gathering evidence and the allegation of profiteering that he focused on in his reply.

> The Star Chamber tactics are quite unfair and if the Government chooses to waste further money on matters such as this my members would welcome an enquiry in open court based on sworn evidence. I am confident that such an enquiry would reveal that over the years, including times of keenest demand for all forms of timber, the major suppliers have fulfilled all commitments to the entire satisfaction of the WAGR and in cases to their own disadvantage.[49]

'With reference to unfair profits', he continued, the Royal Commission 'knows very well that the price structure adopted for the supply of sleepers has followed a formula laid down by the Prices Control Commissioner in the days of price control and has not been departed from'.[50]

Tom beside the karri log at King's Park donated by Bunning Bros, 1958 (Bunning Family Collection)

The unspoken reality was that the economy was in a slump and business conditions were less favourable than any time since the war. Bunnings was effectively debarred from the government contracts that had once been a reliable source of income. A large sleeper order had been finalised for India after Charlie's visit there, but the local sleeper trade had been lost, and with several British railways in the process of switching to concrete sleepers and crossings, the outlook for this traditional activity was looking bleak as well. After more than a decade of sustained growth, revenue had begun to fall. The company would go on to record a profit for the financial year of only £70,719, less than half the amount recorded four years earlier.[51] Still, whatever enmity towards the government that did exist was limited to the forums Tom had been active in. During a 1958 'festival of trees', Bunning Bros had donated the trunk of a giant karri for a permanent display in Perth's King's Park. It was nearly 48 metres long, measured 7.6 metres in circumference at its base, and was thought to be 363 years old when it was felled; it would be sufficient for the building of nine timber-framed houses and required three company trucks to transport it from Donnelly River. Charlie was away, so Tom was called upon to present it to the King's Park Board at a ceremony opened warmly by the Minister for Forests, Herb Graham.[52] At times like these, such exercises in good public relations more than made up for the lost value of marketable timber.

Another lesson to take from the difficulties that had been encountered was the importance of embracing innovation. Even when government policy was put to one side, it was clear that markets were continually evolving. Aluminium frames for windows and doors, steel framing for houses and concrete flooring were among the products seeping into Australia, alongside the growing use of particle boards and timber laminates. Timber merchants, it seemed, 'had to run faster in order to stand still'.[53] The Bunnings group had by no means been reluctant to test emerging manufacturing processes and timber products, though it would need to keep doing so to remain competitive in the future. Engineered timbers offered the most promising option, so two new production units were soon established at Charles Street: for the manufacture of 'Glulam', or glued laminated beams and trusses, and 'Tim-Aic', a style of laminated timber flooring. In North Queensland, the group was expanding its production of timber veneers through the purchase and installation of a timber slicing plant utilising timber from its operations there. Overhead costs and the need to market these new products domestically meant that each unit was modest in size and something of a gamble, yet it marked another important step in the company's development.[54] Anderson continued to work on expanding hardware sales through the company's yards. At Boddington, some 55 acres of *Pinus radiata* had been planted and was doing well, with a program in place to expand this annually with the support of the Forests Department.[55]

Parliament closed at the beginning of December, and with an election scheduled for the new year, further action against sawmillers and timber merchants was in abeyance. As the new year approached, Tom could reflect on a different milestone altogether. Gavin had graduated from Scotch College and was spending the summer working at Bunnings. At work, Tom handled his son in much the same way that Robert once treated him – that is, at arm's length, under somebody else's authority and in roles where he could learn from the men who had worked in the industry for decades and risen through the ranks by virtue of hard-work and ability rather than formal qualifications.[56] His hands were full anyway. The Trade Bureau had been reorganised in 1958 to embrace a wider ambit than antiprofiteering legislation. Its long-serving president had resigned when the forthcoming state election was announced, to avoid a conflict of interest with his dual role as State President of the Liberal Party and, a few days before Christmas, Tom was elected to replace him. It was a mark of the esteem in which he was held within the business community and no small responsibility either, in light of the economic situation and the rancour with Hawke. The bureau's revised mandate was to educate voters on the risks associated with a re-elected Labor government.[57]

What followed was a campaign stridently in support of free enterprise and ruthless in its critique of 'state socialism' and its handmaiden, 'state trading'.[58] The main tactic focused on statewide newspaper advertising across the summer period, with the election due in the third week of March. Hawke was unsettled and fought back with propaganda of his own, arguing the Trade Bureau had an agenda to sell off or close down state-run enterprises including the vital State Shipping Service, with mass unemployment the inevitable result.[59] But Labor had the problem of rivalry from the Democratic Labor Party in addition to the usual opposition from the Liberal–Country Party coalition and a cutting and efficient campaign from the nominally unaligned Trade Bureau. When the polls closed and the votes were counted, it was clear at once that Labor had lost. According to one considered postmortem, 'the Bureau's campaign was well-organised and hard-hitting. Its biting commentaries on State business undertakings were a considerable embarrassment to the Hawke Administration'.[60] The era of Labor dominance in Western Australia dating back to mid-1930s was over, and though it may not have been fully apparent at the time, a new era of coalition ascendency was about to begin. For Tom, it would be the closest he came to a foray into politics.

The irony of the election was that he didn't witness its outcome first-hand. A long-planned business trip stood in the way, and so, at the end of February, he boarded a flight that would take him back to the Pacific Coast of North America. Following a stopover in Hawaii and a fortnight of commitments in Los Angeles and Portland, he went on Vancouver and a rendezvous with Margot. It was left to 10-year-old Sue to report on the election via an aerogram to her parents: 'I haven't much news today...Mr Hawke is no longer Premier. It's different and awful without you both'.[61] Gavin was now at the University of Western Australia, his summer at Bunnings behind him. Tom and Margot's vacation in British Columbia was a welcome break after such a taxing time in his professional life. Among the attractions of the Pacific Northwest was that golf was as popular as at home, meaning he could play at almost every stopover in the United States and Canada.[62] It was good for his form. In 1959, at the age of 49, he would win his third Club Championship at Cottesloe.[63]

The return trip gave Tom the chance to inspect Asian markets. He called at Hong Kong and Singapore for meetings with Australian trade officials. He also spent a week in Tokyo. This was his first visit to Japan and the experience was enlightening, as the nation's postwar 'economic miracle' was underway. The rudimentary Japanese he had acquired at Changi came in handy for the first time since the war. Tom's attitude towards his captors had never hardened in the way it had for many ex-POWs; indeed, he found Japanese culture fascinating, and although he understood the brutality of strident Japanese nationalism only too well, it was the conduct of Nazi Germany (most of which came to light only after its surrender) that he regarded as the more unconscionable aspect of the war.[64] It was probably just as well, as there would be more dealings with the Japanese ahead. He went back there a year later as part of a delegation representing the Australian whaling industry. Nor'West Whaling had just recorded its best season after taking over the whaling station at Carnarvon from the Commonwealth, but the catch by Japan's fleet around Antarctica was threatening the humpback population that migrated between the South Pole and the Australian coast. The delegation hoped that some sort of quota would be agreed to, though as Tom quickly appreciated, the grace of their hosts masked a determination to not concede an inch in negotiations.[65]

The mood at home was one of a corner being turned. The new government under Premier David Brand had lost little time in repealing unfair trading legislation and abolishing the system of day labour on infrastructure projects.[66] Bunnings could once again bid for government contracts. But there was more to aspire to than simply this. The government was determined to revive industrial expansion through the development of mineral and petroleum resources. Brand's deputy, Charles Court, was now the Minister for Industrial Development. He moved quickly to establish an Industries Advisory Committee, which would be headed by Sir Russell Dumas, the now-retired civil servant who had helped drive the establishment of Kwinana and been central to negotiating deals with BP, BHP and Cockburn Cement.[67] Efforts were directed at once towards lobbying the Commonwealth to remove its restriction of exporting iron ore, which had been imposed shortly before the Second World War in the erroneous belief the nation's resources were only limited.[68] Lifting this barrier had the potential to unleash development on a vast scale and to the benefit of companies like Bunnings, which had long been a key supplier of construction materials to mining operations.

Even before these announcements, there was rising confidence internally. During 1960 the company had been contracted to supply its Tim-Aic flooring to the main Commonwealth Bank building in Perth. A commission to install Glulam trusses for a new dining hall at one of Perth's elite private schools also came in, helping to lift the profile of these new product lines. In the space of twelve months, Bunnings boosted its profit by nearly eighty per cent. Once again, it was ploughed back into growth and diversification. Rail haulage between the depot at Manjimup and the mills at Nyamup and Tone River was taken over by the ever-increasing fleet of trucks. There was a growing feeling that too much of the company's funds were invested in the production of jarrah and karri for local needs, relative to the returns being realised, lending impetus to the push for diversification.[69] A small timber and building-supplies outfit in Adelaide was purchased to help grow sales in that state. A second subsidiary to produce parquetry flooring for the South Australian market was soon established as well.[70] Tom continued to stay alert to opportunities in Darwin, which had quickly become one of the company's largest markets for karri. He went there again in 1960, flying with sales manager Bower (who had a pilot's licence) in a small Cessna, travelling up through the North West and across to the Northern Territory to liaise with De Fraine and meet some of the customers she had lined up.[71] Papua New Guinea offered similar potential due to the increasing scale of Commonwealth investment, leading the company to seek out opportunities there as well.[72]

Internally, the company was also becoming more sophisticated. Such matters of administration remained Tom's forte. He oversaw the creation of a share scheme for employees and drove the formation of a new subsidiary to provide insurance against accidents and injury. Self-insurance made financial sense because of the high premiums that applied in the timber industry, and all the more so in light of the company's strong emphasis on safety and track record of good employee relations.[73] Another of his initiatives was establishing a business-training program for senior staff. The first of these was undertaken in 1960.[74] It coincided with the launch of a new Property Improvement department, the next significant step in expanding the company's range of services. The focus was on product advice and the provision of credit facilities to the small-scale and self-employed builders and renovators that Bunnings had been servicing for several years. With an eye on Perth's growing northern suburban corridor, a new yard for imported timber was opened on Scarborough Beach Road in Osborne Park. A property was also purchased in Norma Road, Melville, in Perth's southern corridor, in preparation for opening an outlet there. This site also housed the joiner's shop, transferred from West Perth, and a specialist section where complete houselots of materials were assembled for dispatch to the northwest (and which Gavin was to manage for a few months as part of his 'cadetship').[75] A new figure had also been rolled out in the company's advertising, the 'Bunnings Man'. Created initially for the Property Improvement advertising, in the 1960s 'Call the Bunnings Man' became a popular jingle on Perth's airwaves.[76]

By the end of the year, it looked as though the economy had come full circle. In December the Commonwealth announced it was finally lifting its embargo on iron-ore exports. This was followed in the new year by a commitment to rebuild the railway line between Kalgoorlie and Fremantle in standard gauge

The Bunning Man, 1962 (Bunning Family Collection)

and support a new branch line to the rich iron-ore deposits at Koolyanobbing, which the state had leased to BHP in return for an commitment to build a smelter at Kwinana.[77] Other major projects had been approved by the state government, including Alcoa's new bauxite mine and processing facility, also on the Kwinana strip. In the northwest, the first leases were being pegged by local entrepreneurs. Western Mining Corporation, Rio Tinto and assorted American and Japanese interests were soon exploring partnerships to develop mines on an unprecedented scale.[78] The timber industry stood ready to reap the benefits in the form of large-scale sleeper contracts, and the sale of prefabricated houses, structural timber and a full range of building materials needed for the new mining towns. Rather abruptly, Bunnings was faced with a situation not dissimilar to the immediate postwar period. The years ahead promised great opportunity, but this would have to be balanced against the challenge of retaining an adequate pool of labour, given the wages on offer to skilled men willing to relocate to the northwest and the imperative of maintaining a sufficient supply of standing timber.

A bad bushfire season that summer burnt through 1.5 million hectares of state forest. Bunnings was lucky to escape relatively unscathed, and although its main concessions at Nyamup, Donnelly and Tone River could in theory sustain these mills in perpetuity, new permits were essential to keep production costs low and increase output in the long-term.[79] Naturally, the board had been watching carefully for any movement in regards to the State Building Supplies. The coalition's preparedness to sell off state-owned enterprises had been revealed when it let go of six state-owned hotels during its first year in office.[80] Early in 1961, the sale of the State Building Supplies was announced. On offer were large mills at Dwellingup and nearby Banksiadale, with their trained workforces and permits over the northern jarrah forests, in addition to concessions over karri forest near Pemberton, branch timber yards, and the state brickworks facility at Armadale.[81] Finance was never a straightforward proposition, but Tom worked carefully on a bid for the sawmills and timber assets, based on a fair assessment of value. The tender was submitted in March 1961.

This acquisition would have positioned Bunnings strongly in the context of the resources boom about to begin. The company was acutely aware of this, and it was rumoured their bid for the entirety of what was formerly the State Sawmills operation was the highest the state received.[82] Tom, however, was never entirely confident.[83] On the one hand, the quarrel with Court over the Milyeannup concession was a distant memory, and Court himself had been at the forefront of defending the Associated Sawmillers and Timber Merchants from Hawke's attacks in parliament.[84] On the other hand, as Minister for Industrial Development he was as determined to attract overseas capital as he had been when he worked out the arrangement that would have handed such a large area of prime forest to the Kauri Timber Company. A related rumour doing the rounds was that negotiations were taking place with Hawker Siddeley, the British heavy engineering and armaments manufacturers. Building supplies would be a new branch of activity for them, and although Western Australia was a sound proposition on the basis of its housing market alone, the speculation was that an initial investment on the ground might be a prelude to the construction of an aircraft factory to supply and service the Australian market.[85] If this were true, a sale to homegrown interests was an unlikely prospect.

The tender would be Tom's last substantial undertaking for some time. With it in the government's hands, he departed overseas on what would be his most extended journey abroad in nearly a decade. Business commitments would take him to Rangoon, Delhi, Calcutta and Cairo during May. He reunited with Margot in Rome for a tour through Vienna and Stuttgart, before they settled into a London flat that would be their home for the rest of the European summer. There were the odd business commitments to keep, including a meeting of the International Whaling Commission, where the question of Antarctic whaling and its impacts on migratory populations was on the agenda. There was also a major hardware and building-supplies exhibition to attend in Hamburg, at which all the latest products were on display. At a number of places around the United Kingdom, opportunities beckoned to establish new stockists and to inspect new machinery and manufacturing techniques.[86] But there would be time for relaxation as well. They had close friends throughout the country, so many that it made sense to acquire a car to get about in. Moreover, although Sue had been left behind at an equestrian school at Busselton, Gavin had relocated to the University of Cambridge twelve months earlier to complete his Bachelor of Economics at Jesus College, so there would be an opportunity to spend time with him as well.[87] Tom was able to take in the British Open at Royal Birkdale. With Gavin, they caught the British Grand Prix at the Aintree Circuit as guests of Tom's friend, Sir Eric St Johnston, the Chief Constable of Lancashire, which entitled them to a visit to the pits and a lap of the circuit in the chief constable's car.[88] A week in Scotland followed, before they returned to London, taking in Wimbledon, the Bolshoi Ballet and the Ashes Test at Lord's, which Australia won by five wickets.[89]

At this stage, Tom put their itinerary momentarily on hold and made a call to Sir Russell Dumas in Perth to follow up on the tender he had left with the government. It turned out the rumours circulating at home were true – a deal with Hawker Siddeley had been worked out.[90] The whole of the State Building Supplies was being sold to the British-based conglomerate for £2 million, in return for a commitment to spend £500,000 on upgrading these assets.[91] The revelation was hardly a surprise to Tom, but neither did it sit comfortably with him. He would have plenty of time to reflect upon it, as the holiday continued into the autumn. In his new Jaguar Mark IX, they drove to Madrid, Valencia, Avignon and Florence, before farewelling Gavin and boarding the brand-new SS *Canberra* at Naples for the voyage home, via Aden and Colombo.[92] It was three years since the royal commission had indulged Hawke's rhetoric by lumping Bunnings in with its competitors into a 'timber combine', an unjustified allegation in light of the circumstances that had led to the creation of Millars Timber and Trading Co as the industry's original 'combine'. For his whole career, Tom had engaged in a long struggle to win market share back from the behemoth created before he was born. Yet whereas the company he jointly managed with his brother had been too large and successful for Labor to stomach, to Brand and Court it was simply a local firm and not in the league of big business at all. But if the recent past had taught him anything, it was that, in terms of innovation and diversification, the company was ahead of the bunch. What was needed now was to stay the course through the boom that lay ahead.

8

Hard-headed innovation

THE *SS Canberra* was 36 hours late arriving in Fremantle, irking Tom, who had a lot waiting for him upon his return. The AGM had been held a fortnight earlier, and he had yet to pour over the accounts of Bunning Timber Holdings for the preceding financial year. Trading conditions had improved, contributing to a net profit of £157,842, a new record for the company. But the rebuffed bid for the State Sawmills continued to rankle. Charlie had addressed it in his annual address for 1961. 'An event of far-reaching importance which occurred this year, has been the sale by the W.A. Government of the State Building Supplies', he had said in his chairman's address. 'Your Company submitted an offer for the purchase', Charlie continued, and 'it is understood that our offer was better than that of the Hawker Siddeley Group. However, our offer was not accepted by the West Australian Government, and this is disappointing and difficult to understand'.[1] To Tom, it was an unambiguous signal of the government's priorities in developing the state's resources. Clearly, they would not hesitate 'to roll out the red carpet to outside investment', as he would later explain it.[2]

At the same time, his reflections on the long voyage home had focused on the importance of innovation. Homegrown companies could prosper in the economy being remade by the resources boom by tempering the drive for expansion with sound business judgement, or what he liked to refer to as a 'hard-headed' strategy. This was the maxim he had returned with.[3] Bunnings had a surplus of capital that was now uncommitted and had lost ground in the industry to make up for. With his brother's energy and entrepreneurial spirit never in doubt, it would again be necessary to balance opportunities for growing the core business in sawmilling and timber trading with ongoing opportunities to diversify operations. Before the end 1961, a series of decisions were taken that reflected this imperative.

The most pressing need remained additional standing timber, and this was met in a modest way by acquiring a controlling stake in a sawmill at Walpole established by the Swarbrick family. It was licensed to cut 4,000 loads of karri annually, plus a small quantity of tingle (*Eucalyptus jacksonii*).[4] A calculated decision was then taken about the North Queensland mills that supplied furniture timber. The arrangement with CSR that subsidised shipping costs had ended, just as import restrictions on foreign timbers were being relaxed. JM Johnston Pty Ltd, which had never made much money but had served its purpose until now, was duly disposed of. Bunning's head of imports, Brian Hoar, went to Borneo and Sarawak to investigate replacement supplies of Southeast Asian timbers.[5] More reorganisation soon followed. The company's Adelaide-based operation was beset with problems in local management. In Queensland, the veneer plant jointly owned by Bunnings was also failing to meet expectations. Both were soon dispensed with. Tom was relieved not only because each netted a good price; these businesses had become a distraction and were burdensome when it came to travel.[6] There were other needs for this capital anyway. When it became apparent that rezoning could lead to the resumption of the company's Bunbury yard, the nearby buildings, stock and plant of a rival timber business were purchased outright. Additional plant for producing glued and laminated beams and roof trusses was installed at Charles Street, in time for the arrival of a qualified engineer Tom had recruited on his recent trip abroad. A partnership to pressure-treat poles for the Postmaster General's department was set up. This venture utilised pine, underlining the anticipated value of the plantation at Boddington, which was continuing to expand.[7]

The Property Improvement department continued to develop. During 1961 Bower was sent on a tour of the United States, following up on Tom's visits in previous years. He returned with insights that would be useful in expanding sales of hardware and building supplies to complement the merchandising of sawn timber and other timber products. The strategy would be to redevelop

Bunning Bros yards as 'One Stop Centres' for the building trades. Several were redesignated accordingly over the next eighteen months, with other new facilities planned. The tenth centre, in Bunbury, was opened by Premier Brand in October 1963. It showcased the strategy in full, stocking paint, tiles, doors and cabinets, baths, basins and other plumbing supplies, and all manner of hardware, alongside timber of all sizes and grades.[8] There was an eight-page feature in the local newspaper inviting builders to call in and see 'the Bunnings Man', who had the attributes of being 'knowledgeable, courteous and attentive', and was the ubiquitous representation of the company's sales staff.[9]

The disappointment surrounding the sale of the State Building Supplies was quickly put to one side. Charlie had moved to bury the hatchet at the launch of the first One Stop Centre in 1962, built on another new property recently purchased at Albany. Court was invited, and some generous remarks had been prepared. It was 'an honour to have with them as the representative of a Government which had done so much for the development of the State, the Minister for Industrial Development, Mr Court', Charlie exclaimed, 'who had personally played such a very big part in building up Western Australia's industrial resources'.[10] Court was no less magnanimous in reply. Bunnings had been in existence since 1886, he observed, making it 'thus very truly a Western Australian' entity. The company was a mainstay of Southwest communities and had driven technological change in timber production. Now outlets such as the one he was opening were assisting further with economic decentralisation. But the focus of his praise was the second generation of Bunning brothers, whom together 'had taken a leading, and indeed an aggressive part in developing the timber industry'.[11]

Behind this magnanimity, however, lay an awareness of the expediency of staying on good terms. Brand's government had been re-elected only months earlier and was focused firmly on developing mineral and petroleum resources. Bunnings was benefiting already from a buoyant local market and was primed to benefit further from any new boom in residential construction or industrial development. Yet industrialisation remained largely concentrated in the Kwinana precinct. 'Decentralisation', one of the government's maxims, was a byword for spreading growth across the state's vast and thinly populated regions. This meant exploring every opportunity for economic growth, and the timber industry stood to benefit from the determination to unlock the full potential of the state's natural assets. Barely a month after opening the Albany One Stop Centre, Court departed on a tour of forestry districts in Victoria's Gippsland region to inspect the emerging paper-pulp industry. The government, he announced, hoped to establish a similar industry locally within the next decade. What made pulping so attractive was that it could potentially draw on the mill waste that no longer had a ready use now that mills ran on electricity rather than steam power, adding value to established operations.[12] This would benefit all sawmillers, even if the funding necessary to establish a new pulpwood mill would, presumably, be sought from outside the state.

In Tom's eyes, the decision to target a wider consumer base was simply a natural progression for the company group. The state's population was continuing to grow, rates of home ownership were rising, and the standard of living was increasing. This meant a wider consumer base, beyond the building trades, for building supplies, hardware, and allied products. On the other hand, new materials such as fibrous cement, aluminium and plastics threatened to replace timber products in residential construction. Brisbane and Wunderlich, for example, had introduced steel framing for doors and windows, followed by aluminium framing and cladding.[13] It was simply good sense to respond to this changing marketplace.[14] Millars was also making efforts to increase retail trade through its yards, while in other states, the establishment of the Mitre 10 buying and marketing cooperative pointed to a trend of timber merchants diversifying their product range. Other local firms were innovating in other ways. The family-run Cullity Timbers had been manufacturing plywoods and veneers from locally grown pine since the 1950s.[15] Bunnings still saw itself as primarily a forest products business, and there was no prospect of this outlook changing for the foreseeable future. Yet through Tom's initiatives in merchandise and marketing, it was continuing to evolve in its own way.

The company's changing character was also reflected in its ranks of middle management. Tom's influence was paramount here as well. The practice had long been to promote from within, and that meant a pathway for men with sawmilling experience to progress from mill and branch management to executive positions. The appointment of Wally Anderson and Ralph Bower had, however, opened the door to further targeted recruitments from outside, especially as the product range expanded. Olly Rees had been poached from Brisbane & Wunderlich to act as cost accountant, and Mal Pickles was similarly poached to run the credit department. Each was highly regarded in his field. A young accountant, Ian

Kuba, had also joined the team at head office. There was a new safety officer, and new management roles in sales and marketing and branch administration. The most senior men under Tom and Charlie, such as Ben Bryant and John Scott, had backgrounds in sawmilling and engineering respectively, but a more diverse team was slowly being put together.[16] There were changes at a lower level too. Gavin had returned from his year at Cambridge and completed his economics degree at the same time as Bob, Charlie's son, graduated in engineering. Both had joined the company full-time by 1964. Tom had placed no expectations around his son's choice of career and was not about to show him any favours now. Rather, he would work his way up, just as Tom had once done himself. In practice, this meant gaining hands-on experience in the bulk hardware section at Charles Street, before a posting as manager of the Kalgoorlie branch.[17]

During 1963, Bunnings purchased the 14-acre site of a building company at Melville, in Perth's south. The property included a planing mill, kilns, joinery works and storage sheds, and all joinery production was quickly transferred from West Perth. Building a presence around the expanding suburban fringe addressed the objective of growing the timber trade and emerging retail business, so planning was soon underway for a new One Stop Centre on the site.[18] There were other strategic priorities that needed to be acted upon too. Back in 1955, the state government had received the Stephenson–Hepburn Metropolitan Region Development Plan, which proposed a network of roads and development corridors to provide for the cities' long-term growth. This effectively cast a shadow over the company's headquarters, as large areas of West Perth had been earmarked for resumption for a planned freeway interchange. It seemed inevitable that the company would eventually have to relocate some or all of the operations carried out at head office.[19] To cover such a contingency, Bunnings purchased vacant land at Welshpool and Spearwood, two emerging light industrial estates.[20]

These were not the only real estate investments that Tom made during the mid-1960s. When Joe retired from his role at Perth Jarrah Mills, it created an opportunity to leave its dwindling firewood business behind and reorientate the company, which had remained family owned, as predominantly an investment company. His old pennants teammate at Cottesloe, Justin Seward, was now one of the state's leading real estate agents and remained a close friend. Acting on Seward's advice, Tom arranged for Bunnings and Perth Jarrah Mills to form a

A young Justin Seward in the 1950s (Bunning Family Collection)

syndicate to acquire parcels of land at Bentley, southeast of the city, and on the outskirts of Bunbury.[21] The objective was to hold onto this land and begin to subdivide each for residential development when the time was right.

Not all acquisitions, however, were planned so far in advance. It also helped to be in the right place at the right time. Ever since the Milyeannup dispute, neither Tom nor Charlie had seen eye to eye with the Kauri Timber Company's directors. When Kauri opted to quit its Western Australian holdings in 1963, an arrangement was made to sell its assets to the Swan Timber Company, a subsidiary of the Borneo Timber Company. It was known around the industry that Swan was mainly interested in jarrah, so when Tom bumped into their local manager at a cocktail party hosted by Margot's sister a short time later, the question he put casually was whether or not there would be any interest in on-selling Kauri's old sawmills and accompanying permits in the karri belt at Northcliffe. Bunnings had been left wanting more karri when the bid for the State Building Supplies fell over and, on this occasion, luck was on their side. Within days, a sale was agreed for a sum of £100,000. The company acquired two sawmills, one of them a large and modern operation capable of producing up to 24,000 super feet of karri per day. Just as significantly, it had acquired substantial new permit areas and picked up a trained, loyal workforce of men happy to be joining a locally owned firm. Being nimble in decision-making had proven beneficial, though as Tom also knew, the purchase demonstrated the importance of being in good standing with the bank.[22]

By 1964, the company had therefore made up a large part of what had been foregone to Hawker Siddeley only a few years earlier. Bunning Timber Holdings controlled assets totalling more than £2.2 million. In terms of shareholder funds, it was similar in size to Cockburn Cement and Peters Ice Cream, but it was still dwarfed by local giants like Swan Brewery, the BP Refinery or Western Australian Newspapers.[23] The company employed nearly 1,100 workers and produced 26 million super feet of timber a year, almost one-fifth of Western Australia's total production.[24] Output was returning to its mid-1950s peaks, but less than a third was now being exported, a key factor in Kauri's decision to sell out.[25] The overseas markets that had long sustained the industry were becoming ever more precarious in the face of competition from North and South America and Southeast Asia, and the use of concrete and steel in place of timber. Kauri's exit had led to some consolidation within the industry, which ranked behind only mining, wool and wheat in order of economic importance to the state.[26] Bunnings now sat alongside Millars and Hawker Siddeley as one of the industry's three dominant players. Though the company still lacked the capital reserves of its two London-based rivals, it controlled permit areas comparable to them, and it had established an edge on either when it came to general retail trade.

Across the years, the one constant at Bunnings, other than Tom and Charlie, had been its headquarters. While Charlie looked after operations in the Southwest, Tom had overseen head office's expansion from a basic operation to one encompassing sections for purchasing, sales, stock, transport, pay, safety and branch administration, among others.[27] As it marked a half-century at the premises, however, it was clear the Charles Street property was on borrowed

Tom and Charlie welcoming the Governor-General of Australia, Lord Richard Casey, to Charles Street, 1967 (Bunning Family Collection)

Tom and Charlie with Lord Casey, at Charles Street (Bunning Family Collection)

time. Planning for what was known as the 'ring road' to run through the site had culminated in the creation of the Metropolitan Region Planning Authority (MRPA) to overhaul and administer Perth's modern town-planning scheme. The company would have to make way for an expanded freeway system, though the timeline remained unclear, and the terms upon which it would be resumed were up for negotiation.[28] Charlie would take care of designing a new and upgraded replacement complex, and Tom would handle the claim for compensation from the state.[29] On top of this, he was also overseeing preparations for the impending switch to decimal currency. The task was so large it became necessary to appoint somebody full-time to coordinate the changeover across the company's branches and other divisions.[30]

Amid these developments, Tom and Margot had been preparing a move of their own. Cotswold had been their home for almost a quarter century, but the time to upgrade to a new residence was about to arrive. A few streets away in Peppermint Grove, a property known as 'The Cliffe' was coming onto the market. It had been owned originally by the railway entrepreneur Neil McNeil, before winding up in the hands of Sir David Brisbane in the 1930s. Located at the junction of McNeil Street and The Esplanade, adjacent to an S-bend known locally as 'Devil's elbow', the property occupied two and a half acres (one hectare) and had commanding views over Freshwater Bay and towards the Darling scarp.[31] Tom had mentioned to Brisbane that he would be interested if he ever desired to dispose of it. Although Sir David had died in 1960, he had evidently told Lady Brisbane of Tom's interest, because Tom had received a phone call from Justin Seward when he was overseas to advise that the property was for sale, and that he had three days to accept it at the nominated price. Tom had done so, before proceeding to subdivide the property, retaining the prime corner block for himself (not one to boast about his achievements, he later told Gavin with some pride that after selling off the rest, he effectively walked away with his block for free).[32] The renowned Perth architect Mervyn Parry was then commissioned to design a residence that Tom and Margot intended would serve them for the rest of their lives.[33] The house featured an expansive living space, formal and family dining rooms, a large kitchen and generous master bedroom, with additional bedrooms upstairs and separate wings for a home office and games room that enclosed a swimming pool and courtyard.[34] Margot's fiftieth birthday was the last to be celebrated at Cotswold. With construction completed by late 1964, she and Tom moved the short distance to McNeil Street.

Middle age was doing little to slow either of them down. Only a year earlier, Margot had won the Ladies Championship at Lake Karrinyup, despite playing on a handicap of fifteen and being involved in a car accident on the way to the course that day, injuring her knee in the incident.[35] Tom's form had hardly wavered at all. He and his old rival Justin Seward were now a formidable pairing in foursomes competition, playing in consecutive finals of the state championships and only narrowly losing both.[36] He and Margot still played tennis regularly on friends' courts, and Tom occasionally played at the Weld Club. *Suzy Wren* was, however, not used as frequently as in the past, as Tom now had access to BP's larger motor launch. When BP's chairman commissioned the leading Western Australian naval architect Len Randall to design a new VIP vessel in the mid-1960s, he realised it was probably time to relinquish his own boat. The new vessel, which inherited the name *Manitoba*, was built in Fremantle and launched in 1965.[37]

McNeil Street (Bunning Family Collection)

Suzy Wren after modifications by a later owner (Bunning Family Collection)

Tom's directorships and additional commitments weighed on his decision to part with *Suzy Wren* in other ways, too. Spare time was not a commodity enjoyed in abundance. He had been an executive member of the Empire (later Commonwealth) Games Committee, hosted in Perth in 1962, and he served as chairman of Scotch College's School Council throughout the early 1960s. He had also been the local chairman of a nationwide drive to raise funds for the construction of the Anzac Memorial Chapel at Canberra's Royal Military College, Duntroon, and on top of all this, he was president of the Weld Club during 1963–64. Just as this was ending, he was invited onto the full board of BP Australia and only months later to a directorship at Vickers Australia, necessitating regular travel for meetings in Melbourne and Sydney. His board positions at the local subsidiaries of each company continued, alongside his directorship at Peters Ice Cream and a new board appointment at the state branch of AMP.[38] He remained active alongside Gordon and Dudley Law at the Metropolitan Brick Company, joining its board following its public listing in 1962.[39] In fact, the only interest discontinued in this period was in the Nor'West Whaling Company. This was a troubled industry, caught between collapsing whale populations and the emergence of synthetic oils as a substitute to its main product, and beset by failure to obtain an international agreement to regulate harvests in Antarctic waters. The company was wound up after the International Whaling Commission extended complete protection to humpback whales in 1963.[40]

Towards the end of 1965, the board of Bunning Timber Holdings settled on a statement of its objectives for the future. The company should always provide a good return to its shareholders, it declared, by growing sales commensurate with Western Australia's economic growth and exploiting new market opportunities outside of the state.[41] An important step in this direction had been taken only months earlier, when the agency at Port Hedland was upgraded to a full Bunnings branch. Sales in the North West were booming, making it the right time for this move.[42] The company had acquired a significant shareholding in the Metropolitan Brick Company, a step Tom was convinced would generate strong returns in due course. When a bonus share issue was announced at the release of the most-recent yearly results, the financial position appeared sound, to say the least.[43] Such results were attracting the attention of the national financial press, and with it came interest from investors in other states. In February 1966, when the changeover to decimal currency occurred, the price of a Bunnings share was around $2.10; the equivalent in 1952 had been $1.00.[44]

Other objectives included the development of the company's pine plantation, maintaining its excellent record in industrial safety, providing the best possible working conditions for its staff, and offering opportunities for promotion from within. Alongside his office-based executive duties, Tom frequently walked among the departments at head office and continued to visit the branches regularly. He had always encouraged younger men to pursue self-education opportunities, just as he had done himself. Bunnings also kept up its annual family Christmas party for its workforce at West Perth, held in an adjacent park, with games and presents for the children, alongside short speeches from Tom and Charlie. The statement also mentioned catering for the homebuilder in timber and hardware and fostering goodwill among the customer base. In the early 1960s, Bunnings revived its prefabricated housing arm through a large contract for cyclone-hit Mauritius, and some of this capacity had recently been redirected to the construction of holiday homes. A farmer's home service department had also been created to assist with improvements to rural properties. Credit facilities were available for all products, and services were aimed at the general public. To ensure the building trades were well catered for, the company had opened an enlarged product showroom at Charles Street, despite knowing it would have to vacate the site by the end of the decade. The effort would be justified if it increased sales in the short term, at the same time as helping Bunnings to meet its broader objectives.[45]

All the same, not every promotion came from within. Expertise was brought into the business when new skills were needed, as it had with the recruitment of Anderson and Bower. Another example was the appointment of a professional forester to manage the Boddington plantation. Much of the executive and nearly all the branch managers, however, were experienced men who had risen their way up through the ranks. The question of how to address labour shortages had to be continually addressed, with high wages on offer to workers willing to relocate to the Northwest, and migration unable to keep pace with the demand for labour in the mills, the joinery shop, the branches and other parts of the company. One solution was to open jobs previously filled exclusively by men to female workers, something that began to occur during the mid-1960s.[46] Succession in senior ranks was something that remained in the back of Tom's mind. When Bruce Johnston retired at the start of 1966, the last of the men to have worked for his father had finally moved on from head office.[47] The company remained tight knit at the top, but who filled the senior roles was not something to become complacent about.

Inevitably, not every appointment worked out for the best. Ralph Bower was sacked by Tom after the pair had a falling out over a proposal to replace an agency arrangement in Esperance with a full branch. The district was being opened to broadacre farming, with most of the land sold on a conditional purchase basis to a customer base that collectively had a high credit risk. While the district was growing rapidly, Tom decided that the best approach was to minimise the company's exposure by continuing to sell through an agent. Bower saw it differently, believing that the expansion of farming in the area created a significant opportunity that should be exploited, much as the company had done by opening a branch in Port Hedland on the back of the resources boom in the Northwest. However, what he had not disclosed was that following Tom's discouraging response, he had set about making his own plans for an Esperance branch as well as floating the concept to various Bunnings agents of joining the Mitre 10 marketing group, which had yet to expand its reach into Western Australia. Tom got wind of Bower's machinations through the grapevine and called him in for a meeting. It was a short conversation, ending with Bower's immediate departure from the company.[48]

There had been another misstep, of sorts, in Darwin. The company continued to do well as a major supplier of karri for the construction of high-level framed houses built by the Commonwealth government under a deliberate policy of populating the Northern Territory. Contracts of up to forty house lots at a time were being let to builders who often had little or no experience as contractors (many were tradesman who had only recently migrated to Australia). For the past eleven years, Dorothy De Fraine had given invaluable assistance as the local Bunnings agent. She had been a linchpin for the Territory's administrators tasked with sourcing the materials needed for the government's housing program, and she retained the trust of building contractors to manage their progress payments and to pay their suppliers. Tom had worked closely with her throughout this period and not once had the company suffered a bad debt. But problems had emerged in the partnership. De Fraine had become an alcoholic, and Darwin's rapid growth had overtaken her capacity to adequately service the company's increasing sales. Tom determined it was time to establish the company's own facility and management. He went to break the news, and softened the blow as best he could by offering her a directorship of the Northern Territory subsidiary. As he expected, she didn't take it well. In what was another of his rare misjudgements in company appointments, Tom appointed Ted Smith, a devout Christian and teetotaller, as the first manager of the new branch. It was quickly followed by Gavin's dispatch to Darwin with a dual role, one part being to keep the peace between Smith and De Fraine, and the other to oversee the construction, fit out and stocking of what would be, when completed, the largest Bunnings store.[49]

Not every problem was so easily fixed. Bunnings had suffered a major blow in 1966, when a fire took hold at the larger of its Northcliffe mills, burning it to the ground. This sawmill had been substantially modified after its purchase to be the company's largest producer, and its destruction put a significant dent in production until it could be rebuilt.[50] That year, the housing market experienced a downturn, eating away at turnover.[51] Then, mid-year, a new road tax came into effect that had an immediate impact on the cost of transporting logs to the mills and sawn timber from the mills to the various workshops and branches. There were more headaches to come. The Forests Department had announced its intention to hike royalty payments, and the industry, via its association, was working on a unified response. Security of tenure had become a concern against the backdrop of proposals to develop open-cut bauxite mining in the northern jarrah forests and the ever-present prospect of losing forest to agricultural expansion.[52] There was also an emerging threat to the sustainability of the entire industry. Forest dieback had been spreading from pockets of the northern forest to areas throughout the Southwest. A pathogen that attacked the roots of jarrah had been recently identified as the cause, although little was known about it and no remedy was immediately apparent.[53] Bunnings was fortunate insofar that none of its permit areas appeared to be affected. But it was an issue of growing concern, and one that the industry would have to deal with collectively.[54]

As Tom well appreciated, this made for a delicate situation. Relations with the Forests Department had improved since his own term as president of the ASTMWA, and the current conservator, Allan Harris, was a respected figure. At the same time, however, there was no longer the same rapport that had been a hallmark of Kessel's career in the 1930s.[55] The industry was replete with forceful personalities, Charlie foremost among them, yet Harris was hardly one for bending under pressure. There had been one or two instances already when Tom's quiet diplomacy had been needed to keep the company and the Forests Department on good terms. The royalty increase was looking inevitable, but the question of tenure remained a sticking point. A united voice was needed now as much as ever. With this in mind, the association had framed a proposal to establish of a consultative committee that would provide a formal channel for advising on policy changes.[56] At the start of May 1966, a deputation of the industry's leaders called upon Harris to put the case to him.

But Tom was sitting this one out. Only days earlier, he and Margot embarked on a tour of South Africa before continuing on to a vacation in the United Kingdom. Stepping away was never easy, yet there was always something to be gained by venturing abroad, to say nothing of the chance for a holiday. He met with counterparts and other business contacts in Johannesburg, Pretoria and Cape Town, taking in Victoria Falls, the diamond mine at Kimberley and the game reserve at Malamala along the way. They reached England in time for Tom to compete in the Lucifer competition at Walton Heath. He tied for the highest Stableford score in the first round and, although his results on the two subsequent days were mixed, the weather was splendid and the entire event 'thoroughly enjoyable'. The dinner was chaired that year by the former Australian Prime Minister, Stanley Melbourne Bruce, with the former British Prime Minister Clement Attlee as the guest of honour; 'as they were both 86 the speeches were not up to the usual standard', Tom wrote to Charlie, 'but none the less it was a very fine occasion'.[57] In London they attended Ascot, Wimbledon and the Lord's test match to see the touring West Indies side. They also went along to a garden party at Windsor Castle and were in St James for the Trooping of the Colour: 'a magnificent spectacle', Tom commented, except the crowds and bustle of the city were beginning to grate. For the rest of the holiday, they went down to Kent, where many of their English friends had their homes. Here, he could play daily at either Royal St George near Sandwich or the Royal Cinque Ports Golf Club outside Deal. Their journey home went via the United States, through Boston, New York and Chicago, before a quick stay in Honolulu to break up the flights (by now, they preferred to travel by aeroplane).[58]

Tom and Margot on the way to Ascot Racecourse (Bunning Family Collection)

On this occasion, Tom arrived back in time for the AGM and its announcement of a result he had long known would fall short of expectations. Bunnings had exceeded its overdraft in his absence, and he needed to visit the bank at once to sort it out.[59] But beyond these setbacks, the outlook was brightening. While Tom was in the United Kingdom, the company had sealed a contract on the Hejaz railway linking Damascus with Medina, its largest sleeper contract for some time.[60] As he continued on to America, moreover, the first consignment of iron ore had been shipped from Port Hedland.[61] This heralded the opening of the Pilbara's new industry, and with several large mines at an advanced stage of planning, the company was in the running to supply sleepers to what were expected to be among the largest railways projects in the world. There was sufficient optimism at this time to proceed with replacing Lyall's Mill, which Bunnings had operated since its inception. The new mill would be built in Collie itself, taking its timber from the same northern jarrah forests that had sustained Lyall's Mill for more than sixty years.[62]

Another matter needing his attention upon his return was the resumption of Charles Street. The kiln-yards section had already been handed over and the Glulam shed and old stables area had followed, forcing some activities to be shifted temporarily to Melville as site works and initial construction was carried out at Welshpool. The difficulty at this time was about compensation. It was a complex issue, legally and financially, requiring careful assessment of land and asset values, relocation costs and disruption to trade.[63] The company's case was far from complete, even as expenses were being incurred. Prior to his trip, Tom had worked out a proposed schedule of interim payments by the MRPA, even before the final sum was fixed. The priority now was to secure the first of these.[64] The company had purchased an adjacent block at Welshpool, bringing its holdings to more than fourteen hectares. It had pushed ahead with building new kilns and storage sheds on the site, and with an initial compensation payment secured, it could move on to the construction of a joinery works and caretakers' facility. This was still only the beginning of works, with new sawmill and timber-engineering plants to follow. The complex, when complete, would be among the largest and most-advanced timber-processing and distribution facilities in Australia.

With the Welshpool complex taking shape, Charles Court was invited in the new year for an inspection of the site developments and to open the railway siding that would service the operation.⁶⁵ It was another amiable occasion, though a rude shock lay ahead. At this very moment, the government was working on a secret deal with Hawker Siddeley. Court's vision of a local paper-pulp industry had never died, and neither had his belief that the London-based conglomerate would follow up on its initial acquisition with capital investment on a large scale. Negotiations to achieve precisely this had been underway during the early part of 1967, involving Court, Harris, the Minister for Forests, Sir William Bovell, and Hawker Siddeley's state manager, Roger Bryce. Court's initial interest had gone nowhere due to the limited domestic market for paper products and the need to blend hardwood chips with large quantities of softwoods, which Western Australia did not possess.⁶⁶ What had changed was that hardwood chips were now in demand overseas. Japan's paper industry had grown spectacularly during the 1960s as part of the same economic miracle driving demand for iron ore and other minerals. Although their needs were being met at present, long-term supply had to be shored up to facilitate ongoing expansion, as suppliers in the United States began to redirect their produce towards the growing paper industry there. Enquiries had been made accordingly with the Forests Department about the prospect for establishing new woodchip sources.⁶⁷ The response, as it was now unfolding, had every hallmark of the government's signature approach to industrial development and decentralisation.⁶⁸

The proposal being considered was nothing less than transformative for the timber industry. It centred on exploiting marri (*Corymbia calophylla*), a species distributed widely in the Southwest forests and especially common in the karri belt of the southern forests. Marri had traditionally been shunned by the industry as unmarketable on account of the gum pockets that weakened its strength and limited its utility as a structural timber. It was also a relatively fast-growing species that could out-compete the slower-growing karri in areas that had been cut over, given karri would drop seeds at up to seven-year intervals. This meant that careful management was required to prevent areas of valuable karri forest becoming marri forest that held no value as a commercial resource. However, Japanese technicians were increasingly confident of developing processes to deal with marri gum and process it with jarrah and karri chips for blending with softwoods to produce pulp for their paper mills.⁶⁹ The door had been opened to a new pulping industry in Western Australia. Each stage would require new facilities and upgraded infrastructure, hence the need for adequate capital. In the meantime, export contracts had to be sealed to provide a basis for initial investment. This helps explain the secrecy surrounding negotiations. 'We are keeping the whole matter very quiet', Bryce advised Court in mid-1967, prior to visiting Tokyo. 'I feel we should try and reach some agreement with the Japanese before making an announcement.'[70]

What neither of them realised was that their secret would soon be out. Only days later, Tom was surprised by an approach from one of Japan's leading trading houses, Toyo Menka Kaisha Ltd, in relation to a prospective woodchip supply. Two representatives were on a tour of Australia and asked to meet him to discuss the matter. He not only obliged but arranged for Bryant to take them on a flying visit to Manjimup and for Don Stewart, one of his most trusted colleagues, to escort them on a visit to the Forests Department in Perth. It was at this stage, and during a call to Harris, that he became aware the government had previously been contacted by a rival Japanese trading house before proceeding to discussions with elements of the timber industry.[71] Harris would not divulge anything more, but it hardly took any imagination to deduce that Hawker Siddeley was involved. It was a situation Tom could not abide. Three critical steps were taken. The first was to contact Charlie, away in Europe, to suggest he meet with Toyo Menka officials on the return trip.[72] A second was to have samples of marri dispatched to Japan for analysis. The third was to register a new entity, Toyomenka–Bunning Bros. Pty Ltd, to provide a vehicle for exploring a potential export arrangement.

When Bryce returned, he was confident of finalising a deal between Hawker Siddeley and their overseas partner, Sumitomo Shoji Kaisha Ltd. He advised Harris to this effect and encouraged him to also visit Japan at the earliest opportunity to affirm the government's support.[73] He certainly seemed to have matters running his way. The parent company made chipping and other mill machinery in the United States and was prepared to sink $3 million to establish an export trade locally. An integrated pulping operation could be expected to follow. Sumitomo were working on plans to build ships to carry chips to Japan.[74] What Bryce still lacked, however, was a licence from the government to harvest marri. Questions such as the location of new mills, transport options and harbour facilities had also yet to be worked through. These were the questions that Tom was now focused on. He wrote to Harris to say that his company understood sufficient marri existed to supply the needs of both Sumitomo and

Toyo Menka. Their preliminary discussions with Toyo Menka had also been promising. He continued:

> The stage has now been reached when we would appreciate an assurance from you that your department would be sympathetic to the establishment by Toyomenka–Bunnings, of an operation for the production of hardwood chips from Marri logs and mill waste and that you would be prepared to make available standing timber for this purpose.[75]

This resolve to be part of the new industry had only hardened following Charlie's return. Bunnings had to contend with the prospect of having its existing permit areas opened to cutting marri by other firms, and its established sawmills obliged to on-sell byproduct for chipping at prices fixed to guarantee profits to the exporter.[76] The company was therefore undertaking its own detailed feasibility study and expected no rushed decisions by the government. As Tom advised Harris: 'we would trust that no arrangements would be finalised with another organisation during the time that our study is being made which would preclude the Government from negotiating an agreement with Toyomenka–Bunnings.'[77]

There was an element here of what Tom would later call 'stirring the pot'.[78] The government had committed to working with Hawker Siddeley and was not about to put discussions on hold. But there were also principles of proper business conduct at stake. Harris made several points in response, arguing that forest resources would support only one company exporting at the volumes required, affirming the government's plans to move from woodchip exports to an integrated pulp industry, and suggesting that recent experience with iron-ore projects showed that Japanese customers sought to play Australian companies against each other to obtain the best prices possible.[79] Tom was buying none of it:

> it is surely of vital importance to examine the proposals of more than one interested party before the total reserves of the state are committed. In general terms, is there not an availability without allowing for further growth, of over 30 million tons of Marri?[80]

Harris could hardly have been any more discouraging but, in effect, the government's hand had been forced. He had discussed Tom's letter with Court and Bovell and received their advice; 'I am to inform to you', he replied, 'that there is no objection to your conducting a feasibility survey of the operation and submitting concrete proposals to the Government when you are ready to do so'.[81]

Tom had obtained the result he wanted. The matter was now open, even if the Bunnings group was a rank outsider. The government was in tricky position, caught between its encouragement of Hawker Siddeley and the need to evaluate rival proposals fairly. Political considerations could not be ignored. No state government had ever won a fourth term, yet Brand would be seeking one in the new year. The State Building Supplies sale had not gone down well after Hawker Siddeley laid off mill workers at Pemberton, whereas Bunnings was a homegrown firm that had over eighty per cent of its ownership in Western Australian hands. A statement was duly issued to the effect that discussions with Hawker Siddeley were at an advanced and promising stage and that interest by other timber firms was also being encouraged.[82] Bryce, interviewed at this stage in the press, seemed to regard it as a fait accompli.[83] The reality, however, was that hard negotiations lay ahead. Millars and other local firms had been contacted by Japanese interests and were exploring options for developing a woodchip trade.[84] A second delegation from Toyo Menka visited in October, bringing samples of paper made from marri with them. Tom escorted them to meetings with Brand, Court and Harris, before Charlie took them to Manjimup.[85] The Bunnings-led consortium was now considering plans to acquire purpose-built ships and, in light of this, an assurance was sought for the rights to cut marri for a period of twenty years.[86] The government finally buckled. 'As a matter of government policy', Court explained to Bovell, 'the opportunity must be given to more than one firm to participate if they consider they can put forward economically and otherwise viable propositions'.[87] Days later, the Forests Department advertised formally for applications for a woodchip concession.

The proposal needed to address all aspects of the new industry. The Bunnings consortium would construct a mill at Manjimup capable of producing 500,000 tons of marri chips annually, and a second at Collie to produce 225,000 tons. Each would also take in as much of the industry's current timber waste as could be procured. Specialised shipping facilities would be constructed to handle exports on this scale. Flinders Bay was identified as the most economic option due to its depth and the fact it was entirely undeveloped, though the government's preference for redeveloping Bunbury harbour to accommodate larger vessels was noted and addressed. A plan for transitioning to pulp production was also specified by addressing needs for a water supply and the treatment and disposal of the chemical effluent that would be created, though the proposal noted that a pulpwood mill was not a viable prospect in terms of costs relative to prevailing market prices. The consortium would form a partnership involving Bunning Timber Holdings, Toyo Menka, who would build two 25,000-ton vessels, and the Kokusaku Pulp Industry Company, which would construct a new pulp and paper mill specially designed to handle marri, jarrah and karri. Ownership would be sixty per cent Australian and forty per cent Japanese. Bunnings would contribute up to thirty per cent of the Australian component and open the remainder for subscription, giving preference to its rival Western Australian timber companies ahead of the general public. Altogether, the project would involve an investment in excess of $10 million.[88]

Tom, as always, had made the project's finances his special responsibility. To ensure its commitments could be made, he arranged a deed of trust that would allow Bunnings to repay $1 million off a loan to ES&A Bank, catering for any new loan in the event their proposal succeeded. To give it the best chance possible, he also had been working on involving one of the industry's heavyweights in the consortium. Australian Paper Manufacturers (APM) Ltd had led chip and pulp developments at Gippsland and elsewhere on the Australian east coast, and the Bunnings group had gone to the company for technical advice as they worked on putting their proposal together. With a market capitalisation of $95 million, it was comfortably within the top one hundred Australian corporations and in the same league as Kokusaku, itself the third largest paper company in Japan. Tom knew that bringing APM on board would take away much of Hawker Siddeley's comparative advantage. Early in 1968, APM's commitment was secured. Court was advised immediately. The consortium's proposal had impressed him already, and he now wanted additional detail from each of Hawker Siddeley and the Bunnings group before a decision was made.[89] The contest, it seemed, had become an even one.

These had been tense and busy times for Tom, although the performance of the Bunnings group helped alleviate any anxiety surrounding the woodchip

Tom speaking as President of the Western Australian Chamber of Manufacturers, late 1960s (Bunning Family Collection)

deal. The company recorded its best result ever in 1967, only to improve it again a year later, despite a sharp increase in company tax.[90] The mill at Northcliffe had been rebuilt and was back in operation. Bunnings had contributed to a large sleeper order for the Mt Newman iron-ore project and been named as contractor for a second railway from Mt Tom Price to Dampier.[91] The company was also poised to benefit from a new boom in nickel mining. Western Mining Corporation was developing its project at Kambalda and had put in a modest order for prefabricated housing. With West Perth operations being wound down and the Welshpool property undergoing site works, the decision was made to develop a new transportable-housing division on vacant land at Cannington. Rather than the kit homes built previously, the new facility constructed ready-made residences that could be transported by road in two

Tom speaking in his capacity as President of the Western Australian Chamber of Manufacturers, late 1960s (Bunning Family Collection)

Tom officiating in the presence of Prime Minister John Gorton (left) and State Premier David Brand (right) (Bunning Family Collection)

halves.[92] It was a good move by the company. The initial order was quickly followed by a far more substantial one and, in the meantime, a range of designs had been developed to meet the needs of other mining companies and appeal to the general public. Barely a year after being established, the new division, Bunnings Manufactured Homes, was among the largest builders of timber-framed housing in Western Australia.[93]

All this time, Tom had been working on the case for compensation from the MRPA. By late 1968 it was apparent the parties were wide apart in their valuations: whereas Bunnings was seeking $2.25 million, the MRPA was offering considerably less. Arbitration was looking inevitable.[94] In the meantime, site works at Welshpool had been continuing. A new planing mill, kilns and storage facilities were already completed. Bunnings had expanded its urban footprint with a new One Stop Centre at Armadale, in Perth's south-eastern suburbs. Port Hedland continued to trade well by supplying construction projects throughout the Pilbara, as did the Darwin branch, where fresh contracts with the Northern Territory administration had been sealed. The land developments at Bentley and Bunbury had been progressing and were nearing the point where the first stages could be released to the public. Tom had been elected President of the Western Australian Chamber of Manufacturers, another prestigious post reserved for the most respected of local business figures. It was a little quieter at McNeil St because Sue was spending the term at a finishing school outside Paris, though he and Margot continued to entertain regularly. They each still played golf regularly and played a little tennis from time to time. He had regular access to *Manitoba*, and they enjoyed heading over to Rottnest when the conditions suited.[95]

During August, rumours began circulating around Perth that a decision had been made on the woodchip project. The share price for Bunning Timber Holdings had been rising, going from $2.25 to $3.35 on reports the company was the winning contender.[96] The official announcement was made two months later. At the start of October 1968, Brand formally notified Charlie of what was, by now, a poorly kept secret: the Bunnings consortium would be awarded the concession to produce and export woodchips in Western Australia.[97] It was a deal of proportions that could scarcely have been comprehended in Robert's day. A new entity, the Western Australian Chip and Pulp Company Ltd (WACAP), would be established by the new partners, with Bunnings having a 35% stake.

Tom and Margot at McNeil Street, late 1960s (Bunning Family Collection)

Tom, Margot, Sue and Gavin attend one of the last Law family Christmas lunches to be held at Bertha Law's home in Waratah Avenue, Nedlands, c. 1969 (Bunning Family Collection)

The company would build and operate a new chipping mill, purchase rolling stock for the railway, and make a major contribution to upgrading Bunbury to a deep-water port. More than a hundred new jobs would be created in the Manjimup district.[98] The agreement was finalised in Brand's office, with Court attending as the minister responsible. Television cameras filmed the occasion for the nightly news as Charlie signed the document, with Tom looking on from the side. Everybody was smiling and shook hands to complete the formalities.[99] It had been a hard-won victory. Brand later admitted privately that it had been the government's intention from the beginning to see Hawker Siddeley lead the development of a woodchipping and pulping industry in Western Australia.[100]

Such an admission underlines how successful Bunnings had been. Brand and Court were in no way unsupportive of local companies, but their commitment to attracting overseas capital was grounded in the conviction that such investment would flow on to medium and smaller businesses and thereby benefit the entire community. As they saw it, the key was to make this happen by enticing big business.[101] By prospering from a strong housing market and through contracts supplying resource developments, Bunnings had been doing precisely this. But it was never envisaged they would trounce one of the largest corporations on

Signing the Woodchip Agreement (Bunning Family Collection)

the London Stock Exchange. Ultimately, their proposal was too compelling to overlook. It was the clearest example yet of the capacity of each brother to complement the other and work closely with their colleagues and advisers to achieve the outcomes they desired. It equally reflected Tom's own financial acumen and his quiet resolve to manage the company in the interests of all – his extended family who remained its major owner, the other shareholders, and the employees and the families they supported.

Some recognition would be inescapable. The story of a timber firm founded by two brothers in the early days and built up by brothers in recent times was an image the company liked to project, and it was catching on.[102] According to one feature piece, the Bunnings brand 'is almost a household word in the State'. It singled out Tom as an example of the local boy made good. He was among 'the State's captains of industry', a term once applied to his father and father-in-law, but unlike them he was entirely a homegrown product, 'who has resided most of his life in WA and yet has made his mark on the international and national business scene'. For a parochial Western Australian audience, this was high

Tom (centre) farewelling Charles Street with Don Stewart (left) and John Scott (right), 1969 (Bunning Family Collection)

praise indeed. And it was not entirely out of order, against the backdrop of the woodchip agreement and the move to Welshpool steadily taking place. 'In the 40 years since Tom Bunning started in the company as a boy in the West Perth timber yard', the profile continued, 'the company's assets have increased from $250,000 to $7.7 million last financial year'. He had qualified at night school, served in the Second World War and survived his captivity, going on thereafter to prestigious board appointments and important posts in the community. What would have struck the readers was that a man who had been a prisoner of war had now formed a successful partnership with Japanese interests. 'To be involved in all this has meant that "life has been full of interest" for Mr. Tom Bunning', it continued.[103]

It was rare for Tom to engage publicly in such self-reflection, but the journalist was persistent, and the occasion seemed to warrant it. 'Asked if he had any regrets or unfulfilled ambitions, Mr. Bunning said this week that he would like to have more time to devote to his golf'. At the age of 58 he was still playing off scratch; however, 'because of the lack of opportunity and practice, he has become a Saturday afternoon golfer at Cottesloe Golf Club'.[104] There was some truth to this, as Tom no longer played inter-competitions and was content instead with the friendly rivalry of the best young players coming through the club's ranks.[105] However, there was also more on his mind than he was prepared to disclose to the journalist. Sue was back now and enrolled at university. With her twenty-first birthday approaching, the next stage in family life could be contemplated too. Joe had died two years earlier, and although his own health was good, it was never something to take for granted. At work, he could contemplate Gavin's experience over the past few years as a branch manager in Kalgoorlie, consolidating the Bunnings presence in Darwin, planning and implementing a large hardware warehouse at Welshpool and in his current senior role in the company's marketing division. Gavin had lately proposed to spend a year undertaking advanced study at Stanford University, something Tom had encouraged. Renewal of the company's executive and promotion of men who could be trusted in senior roles was something that Tom counted among his accomplishments, and he recognised that leadership involved knowing when it was the right time to step away. Though he was not quite ready to announce it, he had determined that this would be his last year as the company's joint managing director.[106]

9

Buying back the farm

ONE OF THE factors weighing on Tom's decision to step aside as managing director was the demands on his time away from the company. The woodchip project had only added to this burden. Lengthy negotiations would be required before the Commonwealth granted an export licence and the Japanese settled on a price for export contracts. The ink on the agreement had barely dried when he boarded a flight for the east coast to speak with federal agencies, before continuing on to Tokyo for meetings at Toyo Menka and the Kokusaku Pulp Company and discussions with Australia's ambassador and trade commissioner.[1] He was still President of the Chamber of Manufacturers, and in the new year he would take on the chairmanship of the Heart Foundation Appeal. On top of his various directorships, he had been recruited to the executive of the Australian Industry Development Corporation (AIDC), a new body established by government to support Australian participation in projects requiring finance on a large scale.[2] The relocation to Welshpool was underway, and this contributed to a sense of transition within the company. He would soon be sixty and remained in good health, but it had never been his intention to stay in his managerial role indefinitely, as those who reached the top in business were sometimes prone to do. It was in the company's interests, as much as his own, that he wanted to step down.

As ever, he had weighed up the matter carefully. And yet, having made his announcement, he just as soon shelved his plans. It all changed one morning at Charles Street in March 1970, when Tom received a surprise visit from Desmond MacQuaide, a director of the parent company of Hawker Siddeley Building Supplies. MacQuaide was in Perth to review the business in light of its failed bid for the woodchip concession, and he had become concerned at its longer-term prospects in light of the economic forecast for the years ahead. He had a simple proposition – that Hawker Siddeley and Bunnings merge their timber operations.[3] If a deal could be struck, it would create one of the largest integrated timber and building-supplies companies in Australia.

Tom immediately understood it meant something else as well. Even before the original 'combine' had created the Millars company in 1902, overseas interests had dominated Western Australia's timber industry. From its humble beginnings, Bunnings had persisted on what was often an uneven playing field, as the furore over the Milyeannup concession and the company's failed bid to purchase the State Sawmills had demonstrated. The latter sale had transferred yet another segment of the industry into offshore ownership. Now, they could buck the trend and begin to 'buy back the farm', as he would describe it.[4] Work towards a deal commenced at once. Given the implications at both the operational and strategic levels, he would need to carry on at head office for the time being. Quietly, Tom put his plans for retirement on hold.

To progress the deal, it would be necessary to meet Hawker Siddeley's executives in London. Fortuitously, he had a trip with Margot already planned. They departed in April, travelling via Bangkok and Tehran. Their first stop was Sandwich to visit their friends, the cricket commentator Jim Swanton and his wife, who were due in Perth later that year for the inaugural test match at the WACA (a highlight of Charlie's long tenure as WACA President).[5] Tom also went to St Andrews, where he had become a member of the prestigious club. Then, in London, he settled down to negotiations on the merger. Charlie soon arrived and, within a fortnight, an agreement acceptable to both parties had been hammered out. Each company would transfer its respective timber assets to a joint operating company, with Hawker Siddeley receiving a one-quarter shareholding and an additional cash payment.[6] 'Saw MacQuaide again', Tom noted in late May, as he and Margot waited to board a hovercraft for Calais, 'and all is generally clear'.[7] They spent the rest of their vacation in the Low Countries,

Charlie Bunning (Bunning Family Collection)

Switzerland and Italy. He was home again at the start of June, with the merger at the top of his agenda.

Until this stage, the matter had remained confidential. With MacQuaide set on returning to Perth to work through the fine print, the time for an announcement had arrived. The board and senior staff at Bunnings were the first to be told, followed by the state government. This was a relationship in the best of health. Tom had been generous in his comments recently: 'That the state is so dramatically "on the move" is largely due to the drive and imagination of our Premier and his team', he declared to the Chamber of Manufacturers in late 1969.[8] Consolidating ownership within the timber industry was looked upon favourably in return. 'I think the proposal is an excellent one', Court remarked, 'particularly as it looks as though the Western Australian company [Bunnings] will be the major interest in the new project'.⁹ The timing helped, as Court had been criticised recently from an unlikely quarter, after both the Prime Minister, John Gorton, and the leader of the Country Party, John McEwen, had accused him of 'selling the farm' through his dogged pursuit of overseas investment.[10] There would be full cooperation from the state government in relation to red tape surrounding the merger.[11] Employees of both companies were notified via a joint statement from Charlie and Roger Bryce, his counterpart at Hawker Siddeley Building Supplies; they guaranteed no jobs would be lost and that all pay would be maintained.[12] A press release was then issued to shareholders advising that a merger was in the offing.[13]

That same day, Tom wrote to MacQuaide with a simpler proposal. Instead of establishing a joint operating company, Hawker Siddeley would transfer its sawmills, logging concessions and retail outlets in return for 600,000 shares valued at $2.50 each, equal to a 25 per cent stake in the company, and $1.45 million in cash, to be paid across five years, with the AIDC to assist with arranging finance for the purchase. Bunnings would acquire modern sawmills at Deanmill, Dwellingup, Manjimup and Pemberton, kilns at Manjimup, and five yards around Western Australia. All the stock and equipment at these locations would be handed over, along with a fleet of trucks, tractors and bulldozers, and a locomotive and functioning railway. To the 540,777 acres held under permit were added an additional 661,405 acres, a combined area comprising one-quarter of all allocated state forest. In effect, Hawker Siddeley's timber assets would be taken over by the Bunnings group. There would also be no change of name – Bunning Timber Holdings Ltd would remain the holding company and Bunning Bros Pty Ltd the principal operating subsidiary.[14] The deal was finalised in time for that year's AGM. It would take effect almost immediately and see Bunnings double in size.[15]

The practical side of the acquisition would take the rest of that year to work through. More than 700 staff had to be integrated with 1,100 existing employees. Some problems arose when it was found that Hawker Siddeley Building Supplies' mills and yards were both overstaffed and overstocked, a legacy of the State Sawmills era that remained unaddressed. Tom became aware of it on his first visit to the largest yard at Carlisle. It was inefficient and disorganised by Bunnings standards. The company now owned the timber and equipment, paid the workers and were liable for the rent – 'how bloody long for us to quit this place?', he asked after an hour.[16] The fact that activity in the building trade had begun to fall away was not at all helpful.[17] The company was fortunate in that its relocation from Charles Street was ongoing, with ample space available at the 40-acre Welshpool complex to rationalise these operations. In the Southwest, sawmilling was on a scale sufficient to absorb the new workforce, and the injection of experienced men proved most welcome in light of the labour shortages that had persisted for quite some time.[18] The output of timber from the company's mills was soon approaching 140,000 cubic metres per year.[19] Bunnings maintained its cabinet works at Melville and its manufactured homes division at Cannington, along with its engineering works at Manjimup. All other manufacturing and distribution activities were now based out of Welshpool.

On the administrative side, two systems of office organisation needed integrating as quickly as possible. This was also facilitated by the departure from Charles Street. The plan had always been to set up new head offices in the city and use this opportunity modernise administrative processes. Suitable premises were found at a new, multistorey building on Adelaide Terrace, and in November 1970, the company moved in. What was left at Charles Street was demolished soon afterwards to make way for the expanding freeway system, with the compensation finally set at $1.6 million.[20] It had been fifty-seven years since Robert had established his headquarters there, in the aftermath of the fire that destroyed his premises on Wellington Street. Tom had never worked anywhere else. Now, he was moving from the office he had long shared with Charlie to a modern set-up at the heart of the central business district.

It remained to consider the merger's strategic implications. Tom had consistently advocated for diversification and seen headway made across more than a decade in engineered-timber products, merchandising, and the manufactured-homes and property-improvement divisions. In terms of the asset base, however, this had all been set back through the acquisition of so much capital tied up with the production and sale of hardwoods. It meant the group's performance would remain closely tethered to conditions in the building and construction trades. This became obvious during 1971 when recession set in, exacerbating the problem with excess stock inherited from Hawker Siddeley Building Supplies. Barely a year after taking over its mills and yards, Bunnings was faced with the prospect of curtailing production.[21] Neither was the threat posed by substitutes going away. 'Timber producers face the continual problem of maintaining the range of timber in competition with other structural and finishing materials', Tom would explain to the staff. 'Once it was the traditional material. Now it is just a material. We must be constantly alert to ways and means of keeping timber effective and competitive'.[22] The nature of the marketplace was about to change in other ways as well. Later that year, the impending sale of Millars Timber and Trading Company was announced.[23] It was bought by the British conglomerate Inchcape Group, which had previously purchased what was formerly the Western Australian interests of the Kauri Timber Company, among which included the timber merchants Douglas Jones Pty Ltd. All these holdings were now set to amalgamate and compete against the Bunnings group in almost every activity the company was involved in.[24]

Another issue to grapple with was the long-term outlook for the timber industry. At the peak of the postwar boom, more than half a million cubic metres of hardwood were produced annually in Western Australia. But output had now slipped below 400,000 cubic metres, and it was becoming apparent that the decline would only gather pace. In theory, the industry could be sustained in perpetuity. But there were indications that sawmillers would be forced to adapt to reduced access to jarrah and karri resources. Jarrah dieback was spreading to affect both cut-over sections and areas where logging had yet to occur. Areas of jarrah forest were also being lost to open-cut bauxite mining. The government's policy for the state forest was moving in the direction of 'multiple use', balancing forestry with the competing demands of water catchment, recreation, and the conservation of flora and fauna.[25] Western Australia had also recently set up an Environmental Protection Authority (EPA), and the agency had moved quickly to establish a committee, the Conservation Through Reserves Committee, to devise a strategy for the systematic protection of the natural environment. Even at this early stage, it was clear that native forests would be included in any expanded conservation estate.[26] Inevitably, there was going to be less hardwood resource available for logging in the future.

All of this shaped the agenda Tom took on before revisiting his plans to step aside. On his initiative, Bunnings was restructured into semi-autonomous timber and trading divisions. These would be placed in the hands of the next generation, with Bob Bunning to run the timber division and Gavin to look after trade and retail merchandising. Bob had overseen the relocation and rationalisation of timber operations at Welshpool and would now run the company's sawmilling

Tom with Sir William Kyle, Governor of Western Australia 1975–80 (Bunning Family Collection)

and manufacturing operations, a research and development department, and the plantation at Boddington.²⁷ Gavin would take charge of the Welshpool hardware warehouse and the branch outlets, of which there were six in Perth, five elsewhere in Western Australia, and one in Darwin. It was a good time to revisit their roles and purpose within the company. Lately, the One Stop Centres had been falling short of expectations, with a lack of accountability and specific reporting as individual profit centres. Bunnings had an advantage in its well-located metropolitan and regional sites and its existing, well-trained staff, but the underlying challenge was to protect and grow the traditional market to builders at the same time as aggressively pursuing the emerging home-handyman customer. Potentially, the two strategies were in conflict. Whereas the trade customer was best served by a traditional model of stock and service from behind a front counter, the retail customer generally required product advice and was better served by well-displayed products and prices marked in small quantities.[28] There would be a lot happening in the merchandise division in the years ahead.

The other matter for Tom to address was leadership at board level. Bruce Johnston was almost seventy and would soon stand aside. Gavin and Bob had been made associate members, but both had limited experience, and all of it had come from within the company. Ben Bryant, who would take over as managing director when Tom retired, remained on the board, as did Frank Downing, Tom's trusted adviser on all legal matters. Two Hawker Siddeley representatives would be joining the company's board. What Tom wanted, however, was an extra injection of corporate expertise. He found it in Dolph Zink, an American businessman attracted to Perth because he thought it a good place to live and bring up a family, before landing a job as the inaugural dean of the Western Australian Institute of Technology's business school. Zink had met Tom shortly after his arrival, and the pair had become friends.

Margot and Tom at McNeil Street (Bunning Family Collection)

Top and bottom: After Bertha Law died in 1974, the Law family's Christmas gathering moved to McNeil Street, where it continued until 1983. One further Law family gathering occurred in 2015 at a rebuilt McNeil Street. The guest of honour was Mary Davies, aged 92, the last remaining member of Robert and Bertha's children (Bunning Family Collection)

Impressed by Zink's management background and wide experience, Tom recruited him to the company's board in 1972.²⁹ The path was finally clear to pursue his own change of direction. 'I think that I have indicated to you during the past two or three years that I had it in mind to retire as an Executive Director of the Company when this could sensibly be arranged', he wrote to Charlie. 'I would now like to inform you that I wish to retire'. The feeling that his father had stayed on for too long, stepping away only when his health deteriorated, was something he had reflected upon in the past.³⁰ All the same, it was only a retirement from his executive role. 'I would like to remain a Director of Bunning Timber Holdings', he continued, 'and be retained to advise on such things as investments, land development, corporate planning, and any other special purpose that might arise'. His resignation would take effect in the middle of 1973.³¹

These had been among the busiest times of his career. After joining the AIDC it had been necessary to keep up with a steady stream of information and updates on the national economy and travel each month to the board meeting in Canberra.³² At home, the social diary was always full. 'Mum and I attended a dance given by the Prisoner of War Association', Tom wrote to Gavin, who was nearing the end of his course at Stanford. They had stopped in for dinner at one of Perth's newest hotels on the way and lost track of time:

> We got to the dance rather late and I had wrongly told Mum to put on a long frock and appeared myself in a dinner jacket. When we got there we found that we were the only people dressed like that and when the President said "of course you have just come on from the Lodge" I agreed with him. This is the first time in my life I have sailed under the false colours of a Freemason.³³

For years they had been regulars at vice-regal functions and were on good terms with the Governor, Sir Douglas Kendrew, and his wife. When the Duke of Edinburgh came to Perth that summer, he was told he could stop past McNeil Street if he felt like a swim. At short notice, the duke turned up. Margot found herself having to serve afternoon tea to the prince consort. 'In England, we put our milk in after the tea has been poured', he told her. 'Really?', she responded. 'In Australia we pour the milk in first'.³⁴

Top and bottom: Gavin's marriage to Helen Clarkson, 1970 (Bunning Family Collection)

The occasions that mattered far more were those they had celebrated together as family. Gavin had become engaged to Helen Clarkson, with most of their courtship carried out by letter and phone calls between Perth and Darwin. They married at St Lawrence's Church in Dalkeith in 1970, and Gavin's stint at Stanford had become part of an extended honeymoon. Tom and Margot's first grandchild, Robert, was born early the following year, followed by a second, Daniel, a short time after Tom's retirement from Bunnings took effect. Sue was now engaged herself to a capable young solicitor, Clive Hovell. The couple had been nervous about their prospects right up until the evening that Clive asked Tom for his permission, though it ended up being only the shortest of conversations. Their engagement party was one of the largest functions held at McNeil Street in many years, followed by the wedding in November 1973.[35] It had been almost two years since Tom's sister Gena, his eldest sibling from Robert's first marriage, had passed away. These milestones helped to sharpen Tom's focus on his own affairs, and he began to use some of his newfound time to plan these more methodically. As a major shareholder in Bunnings and a savvy investor of his own funds, he had accumulated considerable wealth. The question he was working through was the sort of future he would put it towards. With both his children married, it was the right time to be putting appropriate arrangements in place.

There were other reasons for attending to these private matters. Perth Jarrah Mills, the family enterprise he had been associated with his entire life, was demanding some of his consideration. It had ceased operating as a firewood venture after Joe's death, and now it functioned solely as the holding company for his extended family's shareholdings and property investments. These included the real-estate projects at Cannington and Bunbury that were reaching a final stage. Dissolving the company after Gena's estate was settled was briefly considered, though with his three remaining sisters not yet ready to sell out of their stake in Robert's old private company, it would continue on and invest its cash in equities, including more Bunnings shares.[36] There were also decisions to be made at Metro Brick, in which he and Margot held a substantial interest. It had prospered in the seller's market of the long postwar building boom, but all the signs suggested that the market would be far more competitive in the future. The conundrum facing the company was whom would take it forward into a new era. His brothers-in-law and fellow directors, Gordon and Dudley Law, had run it between themselves for decades and were now poised to retire without an obvious successor. It therefore came as no surprise when a takeover was attempted by the rival brickmaker Calsil Ltd, followed by a counteroffer from Brisbane and Wunderlich, another prominent Western Australian firm.[37] After decades in one family's hands, the company's future was up in the air.

To Tom's way of thinking, a takeover was not only inevitable but would also resolve the problem of succession. In September 1973, Metro Brick was acquired by Brisbane and Wunderlich.[38] They had held out long enough to get the price they wanted and, in his view, this the best outcome possible.[39] It also

Sue's marriage to Clive Hovell, 1973 (Bunning Family Collection)

The Law family. From left: Mary, Margot, Gordon, Dudley & Muriel, c. 1968 (Bunning Family Collection)

underlined precisely what he hoped to avoid occurring with his own company. When the negotiations with Hawker Siddeley were taking place, there was every reason to provide a third generation of the family with the opportunity to maintain a controlling interest. Accordingly, he had sought, and obtained, a letter from MacQuaide stating that should Hawker Siddeley choose to dispose of its stake in Bunnings, it would be offered for sale in the first instance to the Bunning family.[40] Uncertain if and when this commitment would expire, Tom set out to confirm the arrangement a few years later. A second letter from Hawker Siddeley dated 18 April 1975 committed both parties to consult each other before buying or selling their major shareholdings, and gave each party an informal right of first refusal over the other party's stake; Hawker Siddeley's commitment was that 'it is not our intention to sell or dispose of our shares without first consulting with you to arrange for an orderly sale or placing of the shares in the open market to our mutual advantage'.[41] The agreement could be terminated with three months' notice, and it was not entirely clear if it would actually be enforceable in the event of a dispute. Rather, it was a gentleman's agreement, albeit one that Tom trusted as a safeguard against the type of fate confronting Metro Brick.

Planning for the future certainly made sense when the present was looking so uncertain. During 1973 it had become obvious the economy was in trouble. Inflation was out of control, increasing by as much as two per cent each month. It only got worse when, shortly after control over Metro Brick was relinquished, the Arab oil embargo began. The Prices Justification Tribunal, newly established by the Commonwealth in an attempt to reign in the cost of living, made it difficult for Bunnings to recoup their spiralling expenses through higher prices for the products they produced and marketed, eating further into the profitability of the timber and manufacturing division.[42] The outlook for the woodchip industry was also far less sanguine than it had been when Tom had first dealt with Toyo Menka. A recession in Japan had overshadowed final negotiations on an export contract, and it was only in June, as he relinquished his role at Bunnings, that an arrangement was finalised.[43] The final shareholdings in WACAP had been settled as Millars, Hawker Siddeley's parent company, Whittakers and the Worsley Timber Company all signed on, with the necessary export licences soon following. But the new mill, railway stock, harbour facilities and other infrastructure would have to be purchased or constructed against the backdrop of rising expenses in materials and wages. In the new year, it became necessary to renegotiate a base export price.[44] The implications were clear. Japan's economic miracle was evaporating and with it, the long postwar boom was drawing to a close.

The playing field for the new industry was changing in other ways as well. In New South Wales and Victoria, the industry had become a target for conservationists alarmed at its impact on the environment. Images of clear-felled forests were striking and a harbinger of what was in store for the Southwest, at a time when environmentalism was emerging as a social and political movement. Calls had been made for an investigation into the likely impacts of the new industry on native fauna and the quality of water supplies. In response, the EPA had undertaken to monitor the new industry and its contribution, if any, to the problem of salinity.[45] In the meantime, its Conservation Through Reserves Committee had thrown down a challenge to the licence granted to WACAP. The company had been permitted to remove some 680,000 tonnes of woodchips per year from an area covering 400,000 hectares. About fifteen per cent of this area would be clear-felled across a fifteen-year period, and the rest cut selectively as an extension of established logging operations. The committee, however, had called for the preservation of an area of 50,000 hectares covering the Shannon River catchment in the area south of the Bunnings Tone River sawmill.[46] The industry, when it began, was going to be scrutinised carefully by scientists and the subject of opposition from some sections of society, even if it had its supporters in politics and among businesses and communities with ties to the timber industry.

As these issues were emerging, Tom embarked on what quickly became the costliest misstep in his career. In 1973, Bunning Timber Holdings made a substantial investment in a somewhat unlikely venture known as Fish Protein Concentrate Pty Ltd. Zink had been its chief proponent, after a chance encounter in an airport lounge with a fellow American businessman seeking backers for his plans to establish a fish-meal production plant in Tasmania. Tom had been persuaded, and with the board's support, a substantial sum had been invested in a new factory and two large, purpose-built fishing boats.[47] It was in trouble from the outset, after technical problems were encountered with the production plant, and poor weather and other factors led to catches falling far short of expectations. Less than a year into the project it was clear that considerable losses would be incurred.

The debacle in Tasmania could not have come at a worse time. Profits were down and the outlook in the building sector remained gloomy, due in no small way to the fact that interest rates had reached record highs. In these circumstances, rehabilitating Hawker Siddeley's underperforming assets would be more challenging than anticipated. Timber production remained an area of concern. The sawmills, Donnelly River and Tone River were each nearing the end of their working lives. It had been decided to replace them with a rebuilt sawmill at Deanmill, on the site of the old State Sawmills number-one mill, though in the current climate it seemed inevitable that costs would blow out.[48] Knowing there was no sense in throwing away good money after bad, Tom had lost patience with the fish-meal venture. He was on good terms with Perth businessman Michael Kailis, and after calling him in to review the operation, it was offloaded to the Kailis group. A rather unfortunate experiment had ended, and as Tom later acknowledged, 'in our history we have never lost so much money so quickly'.[49] The one positive outcome was a lifelong friendship with Michael and a partnership in the ownership of *Manitoba*, which carried on with the next generation of both families.

Michael Kailis (Bunning Family Collection)

Manitoba in the Kimberleys (Bunning Family Collection)

On the merchandising side, a transformation was underway. At Stanford, Gavin had observed the beginnings of 'big box' hardware retailing in California and, with Tom's support, he developed his own recommendations on the future of Bunnings as a broad-based materials supplier shortly after returning to Perth. The major first step away from the traditional trade-focused retailing had occurred in 1972, when Bunnings emptied out its 1,200-square-metre timber storage shed along Scarborough Beach Road, before cutting an entrance door on one side of its corrugated-iron wall, placing a couple of cash registers inside and filling the shed with a range of products individually packaged and priced by Bunnings staff. To support the new store, advertisements aimed at the home handyman began appearing in the *West Australian* each Saturday. The concept took off, exceeding the expectations that had been held for it. Behind the scenes, the reorganisation of the merchandise division continued, with a clearly delegated structure developing for head office, marketing, and administrative support of individual location managers in their accountable roles as profit-centre managers. To gain further knowledge of the hardware industry and learn about the latest ideas in marketing and management techniques, Gavin travelled interstate and to the United States regularly during this period, often accompanied by one or more senior members of his team. The executives of building-supply companies also came to Perth to examine the new retailing phenomenon, although it would take many years before they agreed to supply pre-packaged products with accompanying promotional materials.[50]

A lot had been learnt in a short space of time, and the merchandise division had soon developed plans to roll out the new approach to timber and hardware retailing in the form of Bunnings 'Super Centres'. As a member of the board that would carefully scrutinise all plans for expansion but which lacked retail experience, Tom's support was critical in supporting Gavin's proposals. He never shied away from asking tough questions, but he always moved from criticism to support in his comments.[51] Charlie was supportive too, but he maintained the view that Bunnings was first and foremost a timber company – on one occasion, Gavin had been called into his office to explain why the weekend's newspaper failed to include timber among the products advertised. Tom also took a keen interest in developments on the ground, as he continued to visit the company's stores and speak with their managers, and, as always, he kept a close eye on the financial reports of both the division and individual outlets.

Alongside the advances that were being made in product range and display, another development he encouraged was the commitment to customer service. Training of new staff and mentoring by senior staff who were experienced at servicing trade clients was a key element of the business model for expansion.⁵² Their challenge was to balance the provision of product and project advice to handymen with prompt attention to trade customers wary of the new retail concept taking priority. Just as a spike in interest rates was threatening to cause a downturn in the building sector, the company moved to support the merchandise division's strategy. During 1973, the first of the new Super Centres were opened, at Riverton and South Perth.⁵³

Bunnings Super Centre Advertising, 1978 (courtesy State Library of Western Australia)

It was another good day for the company, and for its Southwest operations in particular, when the first woodchips were loaded aboard a Japanese vessel at Bunbury. As chairman, Charlie presided over the ceremony at WACAP's new berthing facility. It was a momentous occasion, he explained, and without parallel in the timber industry's history. Charles Court, now the Premier, used his speech to take a swipe at those who were opposed to the venture. 'People in the Southwest should be defending the Manjimup woodchips project against the conservationists', he implored. 'The people of the south-west are letting the foresters and the Government defend the project. It is your project and you should speak up more if you want to keep it', Court said.[54] A small but vocal group of conservationists, concerned at the environmental impacts of woodchipping, had recently been rallying against the operation. The proposed National Park at the Shannon River was also continuing to attract scientific and public support.[55] But neither Court nor anyone at Bunnings was aware of the lengths that some conservationists were willing to go to. Only months after its opening, on 18 July 1976, two conservationists had arrived at the new facility, laden with explosives stolen from a Perth mining magazine. After taking the nightwatchman of the woodchip terminal hostage at gunpoint, some 1,000 sticks of gelignite were placed around the loading machinery. Only some detonated, destroying a gantry used for stacking woodchips. The facility itself resumed operation almost immediately and the perpetrators were quickly arrested at their commune in the forest near Manjimup.[56] Nonetheless, it marked a most dramatic escalation in opposition to the new industry.[57]

The pair responsible for the bombing at Bunbury each received seven-year sentences and the ire of many Western Australians. Court had immediately labelled it 'a gross act of terrorism'.[58] The response within Bunnings was more circumspect. Another bombing or violent protest was not anticipated, and the incident at Bunbury, in all likelihood, was a setback for the movement to protect forest areas from woodchipping. Nonetheless, Bunnings had a sizeable investment to protect and the wider interests of their industry to uphold. Tom felt that there was a need to reinforce the company's name and reputation, and to bolster the image of the timber industry and its workforce. An opportunity to do so arose later that same year via commemorations of the company's ninetieth anniversary. A weekend of activities was held in Manjimup, which included a procession of logging equipment through the main street and culminated in a public picnic in the town park. In his speech, Tom emphasised the company's long connection to the Southwest and the contribution that Bunnings and its employees had made to the state's economy.[59] The anniversary theme was then carried into advertising for the Super Centres. Focusing on the company's proud history and its links to the Western Australian community via a series of vignettes about the old days in the building and timber industries, it was a great success from a marketing standpoint, winning one of the national advertising industry's most prestigious awards.[60]

After he stepped away from his day job, Tom and Margot made a point of travelling overseas at least once a year. They had recently been to London again before travelling on to Egypt and the United States. Tom had then detoured to Tokyo on the way back. He had been appointed as a director of Dampier Salt, a company that had grown rapidly from its beginnings earlier in the decade.[61] Back at home, he returned to the good news that Bunnings had seemingly turned the corner and was on track for its best result in years. The company's Darwin outlet had been one of the few buildings left standing after Cyclone Tracy, leaving it well placed to supply materials for the city's rebuild. During 1976, one of Tom's pet projects had come to fruition with the launch of an employee benefits scheme. Offering workers the opportunity to own shares in Bunning Timber Holdings, it was the first scheme of its kind to be established in Western Australia. The most recent result had encouraged the decision to start the scheme, following a record profit of $2.9 million. The merchandise division was continuing to expand. With its warehousing space running out, it was relocated to the old Hawker Siddeley head office and timber yard, just down the street from the Bunnings Welshpool complex. The company was continuing to roll out its Super Centres, with a new outlet at Warwick and refurbished stores at Osborne Park and Albany.[62]

When, later that year, the government called for tenders to develop the state's softwood resources, Bunnings was determined to be a part of it. The Forests Department had been developing pine plantations since the 1950s and was ready to authorise milling by the private sector. This had been anticipated for some time, and it would clearly be an important component of the industry's future. Bunnings had been proactive in building up its own *Pinus radiata* plantation at Boddington, but those trees were still some years away from maturity and, in any case, it was not on the scale of the plantations the state was now set to release.[63] During the early months of 1977, the company's submission was put together. Bunnings would join forces with Millars and Whittakers to establish Softwood Products (WA) Pty Ltd. The consortium would purchase a small sawmill at Grimwade, near Greenbushes, and build a new mill on the site to handle large volumes of pine. All the necessary infrastructure to transport logs and distribute timber would also be constructed.[64] They would be bidding against another consortium, Wharnecliffe Pty Ltd. The driving force here was Westralian Forest Industries, or Wesfi, the listed company controlled by the Cullity family. Wesfi was already sourcing *Pinus pinaster*, a low-grade species, from state-government plantations, and was a leading manufacturer of veneers, plywood and particleboard. They were tough competition. Wesfi had recently won government backing to construct a mill and particle-board factory at Dardanup that drew its supply from plantation thinnings. Their proposal involved a substantial upgrade to this facility and other related investments in the Southwest.[65]

Just as the Softwood Products proposal was being finalised, another matter arose to demand the attention of Tom and his fellow directors. The board of Brisbane and Wunderlich were on the lookout for an investor to take over a twenty-per-cent shareholding, currently held by CSR Ltd. The two companies had a gentleman's agreement of their own, ensuring that CSR's stake would be placed with a friendly shareholder if and when they chose to divest of it, or in other words, that CSR would attempt to prevent its shareholding becoming a springboard for a takeover bid by another investor. There were obvious synergies between Brisbane and Wunderlich and Bunnings, as both were leaders in the building-materials industry. On this occasion, however, the board was hesitant about buying in. Doing so would mean tying the company even closer to the performance of the local residential-construction sector, thus replicating the risks perpetuated through the Hawker Siddeley takeover and running counter to Tom's push for diversification in the group's activities.[66] They decided to pass. CSR's stake was duly taken over by Whittakers instead.[67]

Only days after settling on this decision, Tom took off to Tokyo for another round of meetings for Dampier Salt. He was home again in time for the birth of Duncan, Gavin and Helen's third son. This was his and Margot's fourth grandchild, as Sue and Clive had welcomed a daughter, Devika, two years earlier. A fifth, Rory, Sue and Clive's first son, arrived only three weeks later. Margot had become involved in the push to construct a new art gallery for Perth and the

Tom would always find time for a round of golf during his travels (Bunning Family Collection)

A charter up the Croatian coast with Raymie and Kathy Rigg (Bunning Family Collection)

committee raising funds to purchase artworks for it. Work on the gallery, the most significant new cultural building in Western Australia in decades, was soon underway. Tom had himself been approached to assist the Cottesloe Golf Club in renewing its lease with its landlord, the Education Endowment Trust, and a related and protracted campaign to have the City of Nedlands designate the land at Swanbourne as a recreational reserve to protect the course's future. He now played off a handicap of six, though he maintained his rivalry with Cottesloe's other longstanding members and remained a tough opponent at match play for even the most promising of younger players.[68] After Michael Kailis had straightened out the mess in Tasmania, he and Tom had worked out a plan, together with another local BP board member, Keith Edwards, the managing director of Wesfarmers, to purchase BP's corporate vessel, *Manitoba*, on a shared basis. Tom was fond of the boat after having access to it as a member of BP's board and could look forward to being able to use it much more freely with friends and his growing family.[69]

By now, the search for new timber supplies had been narrowed to Papua New Guinea. Tom would soon head there himself to inspect a local outfit Bunnings was looking to pick up. At Manjimup, a major rebuild of the engineering workshops was underway. The company had also purchased a substantial property at Mundijong, on Perth's southeastern fringe, as a base for its own softwood operations. The first thinning from Boddington would soon become available and their investment in the new facility would prove to be even more timely if they succeeded with the softwood proposal. It was therefore a setback when, at the beginning of 1978, the government announced that Wharncliffe had won out with their tender to develop the first modern and substantial pine sawmilling operation in Western Australia.[70] It was an outcome Tom had feared. Bunnings would have to pursue other avenues to avoid being shut out from the production and manufacture of softwoods, as the volume of hardwoods available for logging continued to decline. In his typical manner, he had been quietly preparing for such a scenario. 'There is no possibility of this Company expanding its sawmilling operations in Western Australia and no prospect of doing so within Australia', he had reminded his fellow directors at the end of 1977:

> Studies are being made in adjoining countries and if these bear fruit we could in due course have other sources of supply available to us. But

the raw materials for our traditional operations – Jarrah and Karri – are a diminishing resource and this in the near future places a very real constraint on our sawmilling operations and availability of supply.

Even before the Softwood Products consortium's bid was rejected, he could see the writing on the wall: 'our vulnerability is more apparent and so our need to study more diversified activities becomes more urgent', he argued.[71] Serious thought had to be given to the company's prospects and direction.

Nobody, least of all himself, doubted for a moment that Bunnings would always be in the timber business. The campaign to protect the Shannon Basin from logging was continuing, but the state government remained fulsome in its backing of the industry. 'The poet Joyce Kilmer made herself famous by remarking that only God could make a tree', explained the Minister for Forests that summer, at the opening of a new administrative building at Welshpool. 'I will be a little more prosaic and add that while that is undoubtedly true, it takes people like Bunnings to know what to do with a tree once God has completed his handiwork'.[72] The issue that Tom had raised, however, was that timber alone could no longer sustain growth. Since the Hawker Siddeley acquisition, the company had grown its assets from $9 million to in excess of $32.5 million. The push for diversification had seen the split between timber and other activities falling from almost two-thirds in the milling, processing and marketing of timber in 1972 to an even fifty-fifty split five years later. Sawn timber no longer accounted for the majority of company turnover.[73] Price control continued to weigh against the performance of the timber division and when, only months later, the Forests Department announced another hike to royalties for jarrah and karri, the outlook for profits only worsened. In the short term, the company needed to maintain its return on shareholders' funds. From a longer-term perspective, it remained vulnerable to downturns in building and construction. The worrying part of this equation was that inflation and high interest rates meant the average wage-earner now required double the savings to enter the housing market compared to only four years earlier. And as the 1970s had amply demonstrated, companies with underperforming assets were vulnerable to takeover, friendly or otherwise.[74]

What also troubled Tom was the prospect of Hawker Siddeley's shareholding becoming a wildcard in the company's future. Collectively, the Bunning family controlled about 33 per cent of the issued shares in Bunning Timber Holdings. The agreement reached during the merger and reaffirmed in 1975 gave the family preference in purchasing the 25-per-cent stake they had parted with in the sale, or the right to thwart any effort to offload it to a party they viewed as hostile. He remained on good terms with Hawker Siddeley's executives, and for as long as this was the case, there was every reason to believe the agreement would be upheld. But in the world of corporate takeovers and high finance, nothing could be taken for granted. There was no way of knowing what would happen if Hawker Siddeley were itself taken over one day, and Tom had some reservation in his own mind as to whether his agreement would be enforceable at law, should it ever reach that stage.

How to navigate these uncertain waters had been exercising his thoughts. Towards the end of 1977, he and Margot had attended the AGM and dinner of the Stoneware Pipe and Pottery Company, the old Western Australian company founded by Robert Law's business partner, William Atkins. However, it was no regular engagement, because prior to the meeting it had been decided to liquidate the company. The firm had always been profitable, until it recently began to lose market share to plastic pipes and concrete roof tiles. Its main asset, the land in East Perth it had occupied for sixty-five years, had been sold for $1.2 million and distributed to the shareholders. 'So you can well imagine that the dinner was a happy occasion', Tom recorded, 'and many congratulations were bandied about to the Managing Director and his colleagues for their excellent work'. But he had been dismayed. There had been no return on investment beyond the appreciation of its real estate, no vision for utilising these funds elsewhere, and no future for the company's forty employees. Neither was it an isolated case. To Tom's mind, the fate of Metro Brick was not dissimilar insofar as this company had done nothing to renew its executive or diversify its operations until it was too late. 'It is absolutely essential to plan ahead for management succession', he continued in his notes, which he intended to distribute privately. 'If the policy of the Company is not constantly guided to prepare for the future and to adapt for change, then the organisation is coasting onto the rocks'.[75]

The issue confronting the company thus had two dimensions. The first was the gap that had opened in the performance of the two divisions he had established as one of his departing actions as a managing director. That these were in the hands of his nephew and his son was not by itself a concern, but he

Tom and Charlie aboard *Manitoba* (Bunning Family Collection)

saw it as vital that each of them was supported as fully as possible when it came to corporate appraisal and strategic planning. Don Stewart, one of his closest friends and most trusted lieutenants, had retired in the middle of 1977, and Ben Bryant, Tom's successor as managing director, would also be stepping down in the near future. It was imperative that the right appointments continued to be made to the company's leadership, and this meant the common path from the management of a mill or branch to the executive might be a little less common in the years ahead. It was vital, his notes concluded, that these decisions be made without fear or favour: 'We must further strengthen management so that executive time absorbed in new activities is not taken at the expense of our present business'.[76]

The other side of the issue he was addressing was a thornier one. Tom and Charlie had spent almost a half-century in business together and enjoyed the strongest and most successful of collaborations. Together, they had grown their company to a size that Robert could scarcely have dreamt of. Those who had worked with them closely across this period had never witnessed so much as a word of discord between the pair.[77] Charlie was unrivalled in his knowledge of the timber industry and deeply respected and admired by almost everyone within it, especially the company's own mill workers and other employees. But lately, one or two matters had been irking Tom. He didn't think Charlie needed to contest a drink-driving charge all the way to the High Court, for example, and there had been moments when his brother's abrasive personality had ruffled the odd feather within the Forests Department, requiring some tact to restore good relations. Charlie also saw no reason to hide his disdain for Hawker Siddeley's representatives at board meetings, whereas Tom was always anxious not to

Charlie had a 25-year reign as President of the Western Australian Cricket Association (Courtesy Bob Bunning).

undermine their accord with their largest shareholder's executive team. He had always been willing to defer to his brother's seniority and back his judgement. But Charlie had been chairman for twenty years and given no indication of any plan to step aside. Increasingly, Tom was feeling that it was time for his brother to hand over the reins.[78] In what was left of his own executive career, he wanted to do what he could to position the company for handing over to the next generation.

10

Raiders and white knights

It was another eighteen months before Charlie relinquished the chairmanship. Approaching seventy years of age, Tom would finally assume the senior role at Bunnings. Whatever misgivings he had been harbouring in private were quickly forgotten. 'Mr Bunning served as Chairman of the Board for over twenty-one years', he said of his brother at his first chairman's address, 'and not only during this period but for many years of his close association with the company, he has been a driving force in the development of the activities of the company and largely responsible for whatever successes we might have enjoyed'. During this time, the company had grown its sales from $2 million to $58.5 million, its assets from $4 million to $49 million, and its shareholder funds from $3 million to $35 million.[1] Two years later, when Charlie stood aside as a director altogether, Tom was essentially alone as the elder statesman of the Bunnings group. It had never been his intention to hang around himself any longer than he thought was necessary, and in the end, his term as chairman was relatively brief.[2] But the mid-1980s were to prove among the most successful, the most tumultuous and the most consequential years in the company's long history. In these circumstances, his advice and interventions as a company director would be needed for some time to come.

In a certain way, Tom's manner changed as he took on the chairman's role. He had long been known for a quiet and diplomatic approach, and for being somebody who was as good at listening as he was as communicating his own views.[3] It was changing now, however, as he became more forthright in setting out his agenda. The company's long-term outlook continued to weigh upon his mind, and in early 1979 he wrote to Charlie, Bob and Gavin to share his thoughts on this subject. Since acquiring Hawker Siddeley, there had been four bonus share issues, with a fifth on the way. Reinvesting for growth had helped to maintain the share price despite modest dividends. To his mind, this would only entice corporate raiders on the lookout for firms rich in assets but offering unattractive returns. He wanted it on their collective agenda as the company's controlling interest. To maintain the status quo, they would need to remain alert for attempts at a takeover and maintain adequate defences in advance.[4]

The matter of Hawker Siddeley's shareholding was obviously critical. But if it was put to one side, the question was clear in Tom's mind. It came down to good management, 'provided the effect of good management is readily recognizable by the shareholders'; they could be confident in retaining control for as long as the market held faith in the established leadership and ownership structures.[5] He had already flagged his concerns with the long-term outlook for the timber division, and the need for intergenerational renewal and a broadening of expertise at the executive level. These would remain priorities for his chairmanship. The economic outlook remained uncertain, with a quiet residential construction industry and tensions in labour relations, fuelled by persistent inflation, rising unemployment and the trade union militancy as bad as he had ever known.[6] On the trading front, their own push for expansion during the 1970s had left the sector overcrowded and set for a shake-out.[7] The company had come a long way under their stewardship, but it would be results, rather than reputations, that would inevitably be the measure of its success in the years ahead.

In other ways, however, Tom's manner and approach hardly changed at all. As chairman, he would make the same effort to stay in touch with the workforce he always had, even though it numbered more than 1,900 people across Western Australia (with another 230 outside the state).[8] That meant calling regularly at the branches, remaining on a first-name basis with the senior staff, and being familiar to everyone as 'Mr Bunning' or 'Mr Tom'. There was always a benefit to these visits. Maintaining good relationships made sense against a backdrop of industrial strife nationally. He observed at this time:

> There seems to be strong pressure at work throughout Australia to develop a feeling of antagonism between the "workers" and the "bosses". As far as this company is concerned we are all workers and have common interests. Also we have the responsibilities of doing the right thing by our shareholders and by the community at large.[9]

It was no vacuous statement. The company was among the state's ten largest private employers, led its industry in occupational safety and by introducing a profit-sharing scheme, and had recently expanded its apprenticeship program in response to rising youth unemployment. A 'Twenty-Five Year' social club for longstanding employees had immediately enrolled 145 members.[10] It came as a shock when the Metropolitan Timber Workers Union organised a strike. Tom's response was to double-down on theme of common interests, which he genuinely believed in. 'We have a splendid spirt in this company', he said during 1981. 'Let us maintain and foster this and so go on to greater things'.[11]

Keeping an eye on the retail shopfloor was important too. He would invariably find something to remark upon: at one suburban outlet, a clutter of old stock among the hand tools, and in particular, a large variety of hammers taking up more shelf space than seemed warranted; at another, a shabby frontage needing urgent attention; and at a third, a query about whether or not good recent turnover could be attributed to the large number of sales assistants. He thought stock control could be improved across the board, and wanted to ensure store managers were being adequately paid wherever extended trading hours applied. It all went in a memo promptly dispatched for Gavin's attention.[12] It was axiomatic, by now, that retailing would be vital to long-term performance. While the branches continued to emphasise and expand the market for the company's own timber production, its percentage of total sales was declining as the range of hardware products grew. To better reflect the group's widening trading and manufacturing activities, the company changed its name in 1980 from Bunning Timber Holdings Ltd to Bunnings Ltd. Following his retirement as chairman, Charlie had been appointed the group's inaugural president, which was an honorary role, though he still nominally retained his place as a director. Ian Kuba had succeeded Bryant as the group's managing director and chief executive. Bob continued as head of the Forest Products division, and Gavin remained in charge of merchandising.[13]

The Balcatta store had 8,000 square metres of retail space under one roof (Bunning Family Collection)

Tom, of course, had supported the development of merchandising from the outset. The expansion continued after he became chairman. During 1980, Bunnings took over seven metropolitan and a further four country stores from Sims Products Pty Ltd. Originally a national scrap-metal business, Sims had earlier acquired a local company, Krasnostein, which ran a successful hardware store alongside its scrap-metal yard. Sims had then decided to develop this side of the business, commissioning an American hardware consultant to oversee the expansion. The strategy of putting a consultant in charge of something the owners knew little about had not paid off, leaving the Sims hardware operation vulnerable to a takeover. Several Sims stores were quickly merged with existing outlets, and a new phase of rationalising retail operations began.[14] A new One Stop hardware centre, covering 2.5 hectares, opened in O'Connor later that year. A second site, spanning 3.5 hectares, was soon developed at Balcatta, in the northern suburbs. It would replace the trade centre at Osborne Park and the retail store at Warwick, catering to the building trades and retail customers under the same roof. The Balcatta development took Bunnings to a new level, attracting an estimated 3,000 customers weekly and employing 75 staff on a rostered basis.[15] The recent success of the large format Home Depot stores in the United States had been observed by Bunnings, and this was their response to that development. With 8,000 square metres under roof, it was more than double the size of any other store in Australia.

The purchase of Sims showed acquiring established businesses could be a good way to advance the company's strategic goals, especially when they complemented existing Bunnings management experience and expertise. A raft of further acquisitions followed: a glue company in New South Wales that produced products widely used in laminating and jointing; Bristile's glass division, which was merged with the company's own glazing department at Welshpool; and a 50 per cent stake in a joint venture making engineered roof trusses, thereby placing full ownership with Bunnings. In Darwin, a truss manufacturer and successful outer suburban hardware store were acquired and consolidated under the existing management team. The two major capital investments in the timber division, the rebuild of the Manjimup engineering works and the foray into sawmilling in Papua New Guinea, were also coming to fruition. The former resulted in a substantial new facility that would service both the company's extensive logging operations and regional agricultural and mining industries.[16] The latter had materialised as the Vanimo Timber Company, which was up and running but experiencing problems with both the production and marketing of a previously unknown hardwood species.[17] To shore up this venture, steps were being taken to take it over as a wholly owned subsidiary. The push to mill pine was looking better. Though it had lost out to Wharncliffe in the tender for the larger share of the state's pine plantations, Softwood Products Pty Ltd had pushed on with its purchase of the Grimwade mill and obtained a smaller share of plantation resources.[18] Bunnings had also taken a controlling stake in South West Forest Holdings Pty Ltd, a new initiative to purchase or establish pine plantations on private land.[19]

The limelight that came with being chairman was something Tom had not sought. He was a good public speaker, strong and outwardly confident in his delivery, although he once confided in Gavin that he invariably felt a few nerves whenever he gave a speech.[20] The back page of his diary continued to be reserved for jokes and anecdotes he found amusing and could recycle, at an address to the staff at Welshpool or an after-dinner speech in the city: the man who boasted to his wife when he was promoted to manager, or the one about the priest and his bicycle.[21] In 1980, he was named on the Honours List as Officer of the Order of Australia (AO) for his services to industry and the community.[22] Charlie had received a Commander of the Order of the British Empire (CBE) for services to the timber industry back in 1969, and although Tom had also been offered a British-based order, the Officer of the Order of the British Empire (OBE), he had declined in preference for waiting until the new Australian awards were introduced, which had happened in 1975.[23] Allowed only two guests for the service at Government House, he took Margot and chose eight-year-old Rob, his eldest grandchild, to be the other one.[24] The rest of the grandchildren were still all very young. A sixth, Kirsty, Sue and Clive's second daughter, arrived in June the following year. None of them were prospective Bunnings recruits at this stage, although there was every reason to believe that a fourth generation might eventually work for the company.

Tom had begun to wind down his external commitments, beginning with his place on the board of the AIDC. This had been his most prestigious appointment, but also the most demanding from the standpoints of travel and time. He stood down next from the board of Peters Ice Cream, where he had lately been chairman, followed by Vickers Australia, the Confederation of Western Australian Industry, AMP Society and finally British Petroleum. A board trip to Western Australia that included a reception at McNeil Street and a cruise aboard *Manitoba* helped to bring his formal commitment to BP to an end.[25] His board position at Dampier Salt followed a year later. The company had been busy over the preceding decade, taking over the Lake McCleod facility established by the Texada Salt Company and building up its capacity to the point where it had become one of the world's largest producers of solar salt.[26] Among these retirements, he accepted only one new position as the Chairman of WA Chip and Pulp (WACAP) in 1982. Its fortunes had been mixed of late. A long-awaited milestone had been achieved with an inaugural order for jarrah woodchips, previously rejected by the pulp industry, but always readily available from sawmill waste. However, the sector was hamstrung by slack global demand and the poor state of the Japanese economy, and exports were well below capacity.[27]

It had been apparent for some time the local economy was also weakening. There had been hopes at the start of the 1980s that the North West Shelf resources project would help to boost residential construction, but there was

Tom at the award of his Officer of the Order of Australia (AO), 1980 (Bunning Family Collection)

Grandchildren Rob and Daniel, waiters at Tom and Margot's 50th Wedding Anniversary dinner, November 1998 (Bunning Family Collection)

no sign of it showing up in the company's sales figures.[28] Nationwide, inflation remained a persistent problem, contributing to high unemployment and ongoing tensions in industrial relations. This contributed to the cautious tone Tom struck in his second annual address. 'I cannot help but be cautious in forecasting the happenings and results for the ensuing year', he said.[29] By early 1982, it was clear a recession was underway. Considerable capital expenditure had been committed to the engineering works, the sawmill in Papua New Guinea, the purchase of manufacturing operations and the upgrade of retail outlets. Yet net profit in the following year was $2.79 million, down from $4.26 million the year before. Moreover, Tom's concerns about the company's uneven performance had materialised. For the first time ever, merchandising had outstripped the timber division in profitability.[30]

Behind this poor result, and the rare note of pessimism anticipating it, lay the larger question of the timber industry's future. As anticipated, the annual log intake had been reduced recently, and it was beginning to seem inevitable that further cuts would be made in the years ahead. Jarrah dieback and the loss of forest areas to bauxite mining remained factors, but the main issue had become the movement for forest conservation. The campaign to protect the karri forest at Shannon River was continuing and, recently, the opposition Labor Party had flagged its intention of designating further wilderness reserves in the forest area if it was to form government.[31] It all pointed to lower hardwood allocations in the future. Tom was intent on preparing for it well in advance. During 1981 he directed the board to investigate sawmilling and allied timber operations, with a view to company's operations into the 1990s and beyond.[32] Research and development of new product lines remained a priority. Collectively, the industry was also maintaining its commitment to public relations and information campaigns. A revised body, the Forest Products Association, had been established to promote the industry's environmental and economic credentials. It had produced a film, *Forests Forever,* and was actively promoting the versatility of the products the industry produced.[33]

The long-term outlook was in no way enhanced when, at the beginning of 1982, Charles Court retired as the state's premier. He had been among the industry's strongest proponents, even if his support had tended to run against Bunnings and in favour of its competitors in the past. Now, he was stepping away without an obvious replacement, rejuvenating Labor with the promise of an end to their long period in opposition. Privately, Tom believed that Court had deliberately failed to cultivate a successor to ensure there would be no obvious rival during his time in the top job. It was a shortcoming he was determined to avoid himself. That year, he interviewed each of the company's directors on what they would recommend in the event he 'bowled over tomorrow'; in effect, a succession plan was in place.[34] In the political sphere, it was looking increasingly like an end to the long phase of Liberal dominance. That end came early in 1983 with the election of the Burke Labor Government. Almost immediately, a section of forest along the Darling Range was added to the conservation estate. The incoming government also quickly announced a major review of land and resource management in the Southwest region. The timber industry and the forests it relied upon would be at the centre of inquiry, and the demands of conservationists could not be ignored.

In his discussions with fellow directors, Tom had flagged his intention of finishing up in about eighteen months' time. But at his third annual address, later that year, there was no indication of any intention to resign. Instead, in the face of stagnant profits and looming cuts to hardwood allocations, he struck an optimistic tone:

> It is a time honoured obligation of the Company Chairman to enunciate what he considers to be the prospects of the Company in the ensuing year. In presenting my opinion I somewhat naturally adopt a conservative attitude, but I am heartened in speaking with our representatives in the marketplace to learn that, although sales have taken a downturn and competition has heightened, conditions are not as bad as the printed word and our economists would have us believe.[35]

Crucially, there was more to this confidence than his words revealed. The difficulties facing the company were not confined to them alone, confronting the industry at large. Only weeks earlier, Tom had learnt that Millars could soon be for sale. Although now eclipsed by its longstanding rival, the once-mighty combine remained a profitable business, with modern sawmills, permits for state forest and pine plantations, and its own chain of branches. The long-term forecast, however, had persuaded its owner, Inchcape Group, that it was time to sell out. To Bunnings, the door was open to a rationalisation that would shore up log supplies and promote new economies of scale in the production and marketing of timber. For Tom, it would be the capstone for his chairmanship.

The process that followed was dubbed 'Operation Wattle'. A select group of senior staff worked solidly for several weeks on a feasibility study, aided by the AIDC, which came on board to assist with financial arrangements.[36] A prospective takeover was announced in the new year and by March 1983, the boards of the respective companies had agreed to terms. For $16 million, Bunnings would acquire the net assets of Millars (WA) Pty Ltd via two equal payments one year apart. In addition, debts of $9.5 million owed by Millars were to be repaid and invested in redeemable preference shares in Bunnings Ltd.[37] Some 800 staff were affected by the deal. Unions feared more than 300 jobs would disappear. Tom saw it differently: 'In the current depressed trading conditions, the steps now being taken are essential if the industry in Western Australia is to progress', he argued at this time. 'Although some reduction may occur in employee numbers, this will be considerably less than would have been the case if the merger had not taken place'.[38] In the end, only 100 jobs were lost, a number easily accounted for through natural attrition. Tom had reassured the Millars workforce they would be merged into the business; 'Always our aim is to offer more security of employment to more people', he explained to one journalist.[39] The enlarged company emerged with more than 2,500 employees.

When the merger was announced, Tom had predicted that profits would not begin to turn around for over a year. There would be considerable integration costs, as five sawmills and twenty-one retail outlets were being taken over. Several stores were quickly closed and others amalgamated with the company's sixteen existing branches. In Perth, stores at Midland and Morley were expanded as joint trade-retail outlets comparable to the company's other suburban centres. A new and much larger facility soon opened in Kalgoorlie to consolidate local merchandising activities, followed by a second new store at Darwin, reckoned to be the largest timber and hardware store in Australia. Further afield, the company was looking to expand further by starting is first eastern states outlet in Townsville, putting $2.5 million towards a greenfield development. It was quite a stroke of good fortune, then, when the new Commonwealth Labor government established a first-homebuyers-grant scheme in its inaugural budget. The effects were quickly being felt, with a sharp rise in approvals for new residential constructions in Western Australia. Sales picked up noticeably before the end of 1983.⁴⁰ The merger was increasingly looking like the right move at just the right time.

By acquiring all the issued capital in Millars, Bunnings also increased its ownership of WACAP and Softwoods Products Ltd. In effect, each had become a subsidiary company. It gave Bunnings control over 80% of the state's available jarrah and karri forests, plus additional access to the state's pine plantations. This was on top of the 2,600 hectares growing on the plantation at Boddington, where a $2.3 million deal to allow bauxite mining and processing had also just been signed. Construction on the company's first softwood mill at Mundijong was underway.⁴¹ Within a year, the buy-out of WACAP was completed via a three for two swap with shares in Bunnings Ltd. From the standpoint of timber resources, it was a striking turnaround from the position only a few years earlier. In this sense as well, the timing was impeccable. During 1984, the state government

Tom with Professor Gordon Reid, Governor of Western Australia 1984–89 (Bunning Family Collection)

announced the creation of a new entity, the Department of Conservation and Land Management (CALM). It involved merging the Forests Department with agencies responsible for national parks and nature reserves, in fulfilment of the policy of managing forest areas in the combined interests of industry, recreation and nature conservation.[42] For the timber industry, it confirmed what had long been known: the peak days of hardwood production were over. What Bunnings held, in terms of licences and infrastructure, was of substantial long-term value, and the competition had been largely eliminated.

Tom was finally ready to stand down. He had consulted Bob and Gavin, hinting that he preferred Jim Rutherford, a company director, as his successor. Rutherford was an old friend, a past managing director of the public company William Adams, and widely respected around Perth. But he had been retired for some time, whereas another Bunnings director, Dolph Zink, was younger and more active in the business community. Tom duly accepted Bob and Gavin's preference for Zink, who would succeed him as chairman, with Tom retaining a position on the board. The company had largely completed the rationalisation of its operations with those of Millars and, now a much larger entity, would soon be restructured into a more decentralised organisation. Four separate companies would henceforth operate as wholly owned subsidiaries of Bunnings Ltd. The Timber and Merchandise divisions became Bunnings Forest Products Pty Ltd and Bunnings Building Supplies Pty Ltd respectively; a new Management Services subsidiary was formed to handle administrative, management and financial services; and WACAP would continue to operate independently.[43] Bob and Gavin remained in charge of their respective divisions, or, more properly, of the newly created companies. It was a good time to step away. 'Apart from his commercial acumen, Tom Bunning has epitomised a spirt of friendship and loyalty throughout the company' concluded the notice in that year's annual report. He had been five years in the role.[44]

His final duty was to oversee the opening of the pine mill at Mundijong. Burke was the guest of honour. As a new Labor premier, he was no follower of John Scadden or Albert Hawke, and instead led a government determined to promote economic development by encouraging private enterprise. Bunnings was a fine example of a local firm made good, and in his comments that day, Burke complimented the company for its longevity, its success and its commitment to good corporate citizenship.[45] Tom's speech dwelt upon some of the consistent

Top and bottom: Boddington Pine Plantation, Australian leg of the World Rally Championship, 1989 (Bunning Family Collection)

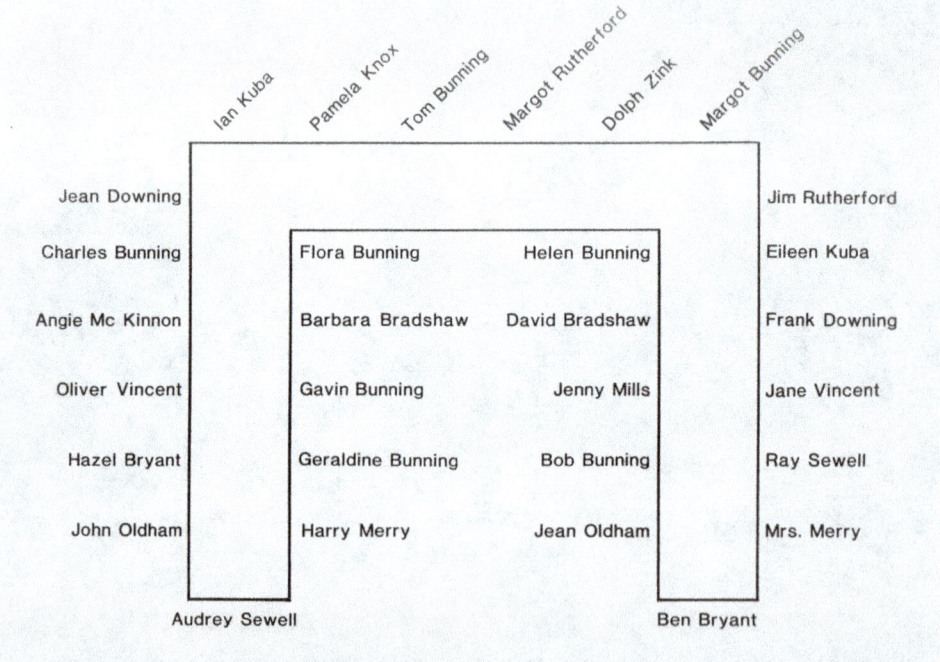

Top and bottom: Tom Bunning's Retirement Dinner, June 1984 (Bunning Family Collection)

messages of his chairmanship. The new sawmill, he suggested, was a visible reminder of the need for long-term planning, 'blending sound conservation practice, economics and common sense'; what the company was doing 'was a small, sensible start to what will one day be a large sawmilling and processing operation'.[46] Then it was all over – he had retired, after five years as chairman. He had been true to his intention not to remain in the role for too long.

Only days later, he and Margot left for a holiday in Adelaide. Tom played in the McIntyre Trophy at Royal Adelaide, a tournament for senior golfers, as a member of the Western Australian side. He had recently been president of the Cottesloe Golf Club, where he was one of only four members of more than

Tom in retirement (Bunning Family Collection)

fifty years' membership still actively playing. The club had finally prevailed in renewing its lease over the Swanbourne course, a cause Tom had been heavily involved in, and his support had recently been called upon to assist with organising the funding of a new clubhouse. That winter, they travelled to London for an extended stay there. Sue and Clive had relocated there some years earlier, and Tom and Margot were keen to spend time with their grandchildren, though Tom also made sure he spent a week at St Andrews. They visited again in 1985, travelling via the United States, where Tom played at courses in California and Vermont. That November, on a golf tour of New Zealand with fellow Cottesloe members, he aced the fifteenth hole at Maungakiekie. Others in Cottesloe's

Tom in retirement. In 1990, he played a round with a stroke score (79) lower than his age. (Bunning Family Collection)

touring party enjoyed making fun of him for having become a pensioner; he was glad to collect a pension, he told them, 'because it keeps me in scotch'.[47] There was a fair amount of it consumed during the tour, which included excursions for trout fishing and sightseeing in the South Island. His friends at the club were almost taken aback at how enthusiastically he joined in it all. They had never known him to be so absorbed in enjoying himself.[48]

There were opportunities now to better attend to his own investments. The share portfolio, in particular, was something he was glad to have more time for. Tom was not averse to taking risks with it, having been an earlier backer of Ralph Sarich's orbital engine company, though the preference for a diversified holding of blue-chip stocks remained the guiding principle.[49] When it came to Perth Jarrah Mills, his philosophy was broadly similar. He was content to see cash build up gradually before expanding its holdings in similar ways. Picking up parcels of Bunnings shares as they became available from time to time remained a core objective, including those owned directly by Flora, Jane, Angie, and Joe's widow and son. As they aged, it might suit them to divest even more their holdings in the main company, and this way, they could do so without diluting the family's ownership. In the mid-1980s, it remained at about 31.5 per cent, when all holdings and associated interests were taken into account. Through Cotswold, his personal family investment company, Tom owned about six per cent of the company.[50] The share price had surged past $6.00 and peaked as high as $7.60, levels unheard of a year or two earlier. Hawker Siddeley retained its 25 per cent stake, with much of the remainder held by investors within Western Australia.[51]

The idea of winding up Perth Jarrah Mills had been dispensed with a long time ago, though questions remained around arrangements for maintaining family control of Bunnings Ltd. Inevitably, the next generation would want a greater say in this matter. During the mid-1980s, Tom was obliged to consider a proposal devised by his nephew, Charles Mackinnon, Angie and Don's youngest son. Mackinnon had been building a career in finance in an era when the sector was being deregulated in Australia, and was at this time the state manager of Wardleys, a merchant bank owned by the Hong Kong and Shanghai Banking Corporation (HSBC).[52] Mackinnon's plan, which he put before Perth Jarrah Mills, was to establish a new subsidiary company, to be named 'Innerhadden' in acknowledgement of its ties to Robert and Helen's children. The Bunnings shares held by Perth Jarrah Mills would be transferred to it, before capital was raised to invest in further shares on the open market. It would remain securely in the family's hands via majority control by Perth Jarrah Mills. In Mackinnon's eyes, this would shore up family ownership at the same time as cutting them all in on a new investment platform.[53]

Tom was sceptical. Whereas he favoured diversification when it came to his own investments, this seemed to involve placing all of the family's eggs in the same basket. Moreover, he viewed the rationale around maintaining control of Bunnings as flawed. The Hawker Siddeley shareholding was still the key to unlocking their own control of the company in his opinion, the same as it had always been. In his eyes, their best defence against hostile takeover remained their collective expertise as managers, administrators and executives. Be that as it may, he also recognised the imperative of maintaining unity across his extended family. It was also possible that he was wrong, and Mackinnon had hit upon a strategy that would work for them all. With this in mind, he lent his support to the plan for Innerhadden.[54]

Tom with Flora Bunning. His financial advice was always valued by his sisters (Bunning Family Collection).

What they could also agree upon was that the company was doing well. Turnover had doubled in the space of two years, as the economy rebounded and the takeover of Millars took effect. The first full year as an enlarged operation resulted in a profit after tax of $7.4 million, a result eclipsed a year later by a net $13.8 million profit. Woodchips exports to a resurgent Japan exceeding $30 million contributed to a third of all earnings.[55] The company was operating thirteen sawmills and producing about 160,000 cubic metres of hardwood annually, making it comfortably the largest hardwood producer in Australia[56]. In Papua New Guinea, the first logs had finally been exported. The performance of the Building Supplies division remained positive. The revamp and addition of suburban and regional stores was continuing. There were now twenty-seven stores and outlets in Western Australia, three in the Northern Territory, and the new store in Queensland. Several new products had been introduced from the Forest Products division to make use of shorter and harder to sell lengths of timber, in the forms of kits for garden furniture, pergolas, backyard fencing and ornaments. These fitted in well with the expanding range being offered in the stores. Altogether, some 16,000 product lines were now stocked.[57] This was a far cry from the days when the company had to convince wholesalers to let it sell basic hardware alongside its timber products. It ensured Bunnings retained a competitive edge against its rivals such as Mitre 10 and the Alco chain, which had recently been working with a sister company, W.A. Salvage, to expand its footprint in Western Australia.

There had been an awareness for some time that the Bunnings name held considerable brand value. One survey in the mid-1980s suggested it was familiar to nineteen out of every twenty Western Australians.[58] Several factors went into this. The image as a homegrown and respected company had developed within the building and timber industries over many decades, tracing all the way back to the company's beginnings. More recently, it had been cultivated deliberately by Bunnings following the rise of the forest conservation movement in the 1970s. Its advertising was one element of this, and its sponsorship of community events and projects was another. In one project, Bunnings had created half of all places available within the state in a national program to provide job pathways for unemployed youth.[59] The company's public image also benefited from its commercial success. By taking over what was formerly the State Sawmills and the old industry giant Millars, the nostalgia associated with an industry strongly tied to a pioneering past could be widely coopted to the one homegrown company. One by one, firms that had been fixtures of the local commercial landscape were falling by the wayside. Boans, the 'retail emporium', would soon close its doors for the final time, a fate that had also befallen the retailers Foy and Gibson, Bairds and Sandovers. By contrast, Bunnings was going from strength to strength, and during 1986, the centenary of its founding would be observed.[60]

The occasion was marked in a number of ways. Tom found himself at Kings Park to open a jarrah gazebo, right near the giant karri log he had handed over three decades earlier. Locomotives another other old sawmilling equipment were also donated to communities throughout the Southwest, and an ornate jarrah cabinet was presented to the state parliament. A company history was published, *The Timber People*, authored by Jenny Mills, Charlie's daughter, and

Jenny Mills, Charlie's daughter and the author of the Bunnings centenary history, *The Timber People* (1986) (Bunning Family Collection)

launched at the Fremantle Arts Centre by Western Australia's governor. The fact that Robert and Arthur had constructed part of the building was not lost on the audience of 250 people. Extracts from the book were later published as lift-outs in the state's main newspaper, alongside other commemorative items. One of these attempted to put the company's growth in some kind of perspective. A £50 outlay on 100 shares in 1952 would have grown, with bonus issues, to a parcel worth in excess of $9,500 before dividends were included. An investment of $100 in 1975, with dividends reinvested, would have grown to $2,400. Bunnings were actively sponsoring sporting teams, musical and art exhibitions, and initiatives in children's health. For some time, they had also sponsored a weekly television program with a home-handyman or do-it-yourself theme.[61]

The celebrations culminated with a lavish dinner at the Sheraton Hotel in the city. It was thought a nice touch to park a 1928 Chevrolet truck in the foyer, as a nod to the year Charlie and Tom joined Bunning Bros, even if it did take all day to remove enough windows to fit in in. Tom's speech focused on the old timers that were mostly no longer around – men like the stern accountant Collins, from whom he had learnt so much through the tough times of the early 1930s, or the venerable Petherick, who was the natural choice to succeed his father after his shock death exactly fifty years earlier. There were others, like his childhood friend Don Stewart, who had spent a half-century alongside him at head office, or Bruce Johnston, who joined the company after being invalided home from the First World War and rose through the ranks to become a director. Another to have been there through the Depression years and the Second World War was Ron Drysdale, who had built *Suzy Wren* at Charles Street on Saturday afternoons and later been instrumental in the relocation to Welshpool. Old Ron eventually started to get on Tom's nerves due to his habit of switching off his hearing aid whenever he was being told something he would rather not hear, and he had to be coaxed into retiring. It was all forgotten now. Bunnings had always been the sort of place where people were committed to their jobs, with the intention of staying with the company for the long term. There had never been a shortage of characters among them. It was appropriate to acknowledge them on such an occasion.[62]

It was left to Kuba to address the future. He had every confidence, he exclaimed, that the next hundred years would be even more successful than the first.[63] This looked likely: the bulk of the state's timber resources were in their hands, and the company was predominant in timber, hardware and home improvement retailing. A certain excitement was permeating through Western Australia's business circles. The market for commercial and residential real estate had taken off again, with a raft of new developments being undertaken or proposed.[64] During the centenary year, Innerhadden was listed on the Second Board of the Perth stock exchange. It was structured to guarantee 50 per cent of the stock and 51 per cent of the voting rights remained secure in the family's hands via Perth Jarrah Mills. They would contribute three members to its board of four. If the underlying strategy remained sound, Kuba's prediction of a second prosperous century for Bunnings would not be far-fetched.

Tom remained on side, even agreeing to chair Innerhadden's board. The imperative of maintaining family unity had only been growing amid the excitement of the times. Oliver Vincent, for one, had become impatient with what he regarded as a stodgy, out-of-date vision for the Bunnings group. Notwithstanding the growth that had occurred, he saw the fortunes being amassed by the likes of Robert Holmes à Court or Alan Bond and thought that Bunnings also should be venturing into resources, mining, transport and the like.[65] Sharemarket analysts did not agree, and mainly advocated a continuation of the company's 'stick to the knitting' approach.[66] That others held similar notions was about to become apparent, when Innerhadden shares were picked up by entities including Wesfarmers and Sun Securities Ltd. Wesfarmers was a successful Western Australian agricultural, industrials and transport conglomerate that had listed in 1984. Sun Securities was a small Perth-based investment firm, about which little was known. Around the same time, some purchases of Bunnings stock by Citizen Finance, another Perth-based investment firm, appeared in the register. Having lifted its stake in Innerhadden to eleven per cent, Sun Securities suddenly announced that it and Citizen Finance were associates of a small agroforestry company, Tree & Plantation Services, headed by the businessman Wayne Ryder. He immediately began to make it known around Perth's business circles that he had backers in the agribusiness giant Elders, the British bank NatWest, and the New Zealand multinational Fletcher Challenge, and that they were working towards purchasing Hawker Siddeley's shareholding.[67] It was what Tom had long warned about: an attempt at a hostile takeover. The strategy to block it was about to be tested.

Although it was not yet widely known, Ryder was being backed by Ron Brierley, a feared asset stripper from New Zealand.[68] Should he prevail,

Bunnings would be likely to experience mass layoffs in a drive for higher margins or be carved up entirely and sold off to the highest bidder. Hawker Siddeley's obligation and intent had to be clarified. Within the company itself, some thought the best way to hold off this prospective takeover was to embark on a program of expansion with the aim of driving future profits to even higher levels. Bob Bunning had one such proposal. Given $70 million, his division could fully refurbish its sawmills, build new pine sawmills and complete other projects that would drive efficiency and profit to new levels. On top of this, they could expand interstate and develop a national chain of sales outlets for about $30 million, build the long-awaited pulp plant for WACAP for the same amount again, and unlock the potential in Vanimo for about $20 million in capital works. There were different pathways open to this, including loans, a rights issue, the family pumping in more of its collective wealth, or inviting a friendly corporate suitor in.[69]

Although Tom had been remaining out of the way since retiring as chairman, he had been keeping his eye on the accounts, and there was something concerning him. Despite record turnover, profits had fallen by five per cent.[70] In a considered submission to the board, he highlighted ongoing losses in some sections of the company in spite of the significant capital investment since the Millars acquisition. 'All in all, I feel there is a lot to be done to raise the efficiency of our present operation', he cautioned. Until that happened, by which he meant that until management improved its own performance, 'I would be loathe to see them become responsible for the control of any other major operation'. Furthermore, to Tom's way of thinking, strengthening the company against its current and prospective future suitors should involve cutting costs rather than spending more in pursuit of a more attractive bottom line. It was a traditional view, if perhaps a little out of step with the spirit of the times. He made a point of explaining it in his submission:

> In my experience of management I have never rated myself at all highly – I have always been more conscious of deficiencies rather than achievements. I have certainly always considered myself to be a student rather than some sort of teacher or authority. However, my experience has been gained not only in Bunnings, but in my association as a board member of other companies and this has given me the opportunity of

seeing other managers and chief executives at work – some excellent, some good, some bad. There are several key factors adding up to good management amongst which are to organize, to delegate and define responsibilities, to control, and credibility. The paramount factor is "to control" and this of course comes back to the ability to measure the performance in the various operation which make up the whole on a daily, weekly or no longer than monthly basis.[71]

In days gone by, he continued, this had been a fairly straightforward exercise. But as companies became larger, they required sophisticated accounting systems and the expertise to manage them competently. His point, in short, was that their priority should be getting their own house in order.[72]

With the current financial year ending, Tom and Margot headed back overseas. They were intent on travelling as often as possible and the height of winter was as good a time as any to leave all the fuss behind. That July, they went back to Hawaii and California, where they had old friends to catch up with.

Happy family Sunday nights at McNeil Street (Bunning Family Collection)

At Oahu, Tom went around the course in 86. A week later, in Santa Barbara, he played nine holes with Margot. When she returned to the hotel he was sitting on 42, and after playing the back nine alone, Tom finished with a score of 78.[73] By the time they were home, the raid on Bunnings was being discussed openly in the newspapers. Sun Securities had continued to target Innerhadden, lifting its stake to 11 per cent and driving its share price from 48 to 70 cents. Citizen Finance held seven per cent of stock in Bunnings Ltd.[74] One journalist approached Tom for a response to it all. He would not comment, but made it known the family was intent on retaining control. Privately, he knew that holding ranks would only get tougher for as long as the value of their individual stakes in the company continued to rise.[75]

On this, however, he need not have worried; there would be no higher price, not in the short term anyway. Only weeks later, Tom, and everybody else in Perth, awoke to reports the stock exchanges in London and New York had crashed overnight. All of a sudden, the bubble burst, and by the end of the day Australia's share markets had lost a quarter of their nominal value; it became known as Black Tuesday down under, and Black Monday everywhere else. Tom had an appointment in Melbourne that week to attend a dinner for Dampier Salt as an honoured guest. There were old friends to catch up with, some new executives to meet, and a delegation of visiting Japanese businessmen to receive, though along Collins Street it was inevitable there would be one topic dominating their conversations. After he came back, there was a trip to make to the Bunnings mills at Yarloop, Nannup and Pemberton, and to the engineering works and WACAP operations at Manjimup.[76] In between, he had a window of opportunity to speak with his family members to clarify their thoughts and wishes, and to settle upon what to do next.

Bunnings shares had fallen to $4.20, broadly in line with the market's correction. It was unclear what Tree & Plantation Services' next move would be. The secret partner, Brierley, had lost massively in Black Tuesday, although he would go on to rehabilitate his fortunes, for a time. Although his role remained obscure, there were still contingencies to plan for. Even when confronted by massive paper losses, there were investors intent on taking advantage of what they now perceived as bargains on the share market. On the other hand, by continuing to talk up the prospects for a takeover, Ryder and his backers might be able to push the price of Bunning shares back up, before cutting their losses and walking away.⁷⁷ This could open the door to another takeover attempt at some later stage by whomever was the purchaser. The family's defensive strategies in Innerhadden and the arrangement with Hawker Siddeley had not forestalled the designs of an aggressive play at a hostile acquisition, until the worst single-day crash in equities markets since the Great Depression granted this moment of reprieve. The prospect of an offer too good to refuse remained on the cards as a positive outcome for shareholders, and if it came, it could be in the vicinity of one-quarter of a billion dollars.⁷⁸ Collectively, the family remained nervous about the prospects of another raid against Bunnings.

Part of their predicament concerned the status of Hawker Siddeley's shareholding. Tom remained less confident than others in the family that the right of first refusal would be enforceable, should his gentleman's agreement be ignored. The problem was that it was largely an untested matter legally, and all the more so because the *Companies Code* and *Foreign Takeovers Act* had each been updated since the agreement was signed. Crucially, they were also bound by

Party time with friends at McNeil Street (Bunning Family Collection)

their agreement to not sell out of their majority interest without first obtaining Hawker Siddeley's consent, but then again, maybe not. Innerhadden's existence only muddied these waters.[79] Hawker Siddeley was itself hardly immune to takeovers, and their interest in Bunnings had always been marginal to their core business, which remained the manufacture of aircraft and locomotives. In the aftermath of Black Tuesday, the impression that remained in the market was that Bunnings remained in play.

Questions also surrounded the family's own designs for the company. When Millars was taken over, Bunnings had achieved its goal of buying back the farm or restoring the timber industry to local control. The problem now was that the farm was providing diminishing returns and a more challenging climate to operate in. The Environmental Protection Authority (EPA) was carefully scrutinising WACAP's activities for a second time.[80] CALM had unveiled its long-awaited reform to forest management in Western Australia. It marked an attempt to navigate between competing interests, with the timber industry

The Bunning family aboard *Manitoba* at Rottnest Island (Bunning Family Collection)

Tom and Margot aboard *Manitoba*, 1986 (Bunning Family Collection)

gaining improved security of tenure in return for higher royalties, at the same time that some 500,000 hectares of state forest was transitioned into conservation reserves.[81] Tree & Plantation Services might have been an embodiment of 1980s corporate ambition, but it was also a sign of the wider transition taking place in the timber industry. Another reason Tom visited the Southwest in late 1987 was because he was interested in buying land for tree farming. He would soon put some of his own money into land around Bridgetown to plant Tasmanian bluegum.[82] The industry's restructure would continue, and Bunnings needed to stay one step ahead, but it remained to be seen if the Forest Products division could be turned around and deliver a better return on the capital invested.

A third factor to consider was a more personal one. If the centenary had fostered a certain sense of nostalgia, it had also highlighted tangible contributions to Western Australia's social and economic development. There was a certain value in the brand or trading reputation, and a very real sense of pride in what had been achieved across this extended timeframe. But what Tom's full legacy would be remained to be determined. In this sense, the future of the company's workforce loomed at least as large as any monetary figure that might be attached to the value of the company's assets. Neither Tom nor anybody else in the Bunning family wanted to see mass layoffs at the hands of overseas interests intent on turning a quick profit out of the hard work of others; it wouldn't do for all their hard work across so many decades to end this way. Even at the risk of appearing paternalistic, the company had long taken its responsibility as an employer seriously. This, more than anything else, clarified the options for them. To stabilise the company, it was time to seek out a friendly investor or white knight to take on a share of the ownership. On behalf of the Bunning family, it would be Tom's prerogative to make the first move.

11

The end of a dynasty

THE FINANCIAL PRESS had recently taken to describing Bunnings as a 'dynasty'.[1] In an era of transition in business and the economy, it was an apt designation. The 1980s had produced many new corporate empires, fuelled by uninhibited borrowing, aggressive takeovers, an acquiescent state government and seemingly boundless personal ambitions. Along the way, larger family-run firms of a kind that had once been a mainstay of Western Australian commerce became increasingly uncommon, if not anachronistic. Bunnings stood out because it was steeped in the state's past, strongly tied to the Southwest region, and admired for its success in the cut and thrust world of competitive enterprise. Calling the company a 'dynasty' also acknowledged the tight hold of ownership the Bunning family maintained. But in the wake of Black Tuesday, a day of reckoning had come. In his own way, Tom had been preparing for it for many years. He had foreshadowed what was now underway eight years earlier, when he prepared to take over the chairmanship from Charlie. 'The history of takeover bids indicates that once an offer has been made it is most unlikely that the old corporate structure can be maintained', he had observed at this time. 'It is usual that control of the company passes to other interests though in many cases not to the original offeror'.[2] What now lay ahead would prove just how prophetic these words were.

If Bunnings was a dynasty, Tom was its 'patriarch' or 'scion'.[3] This sharpened the contrast between older and newer ways of doing business in Western Australia. Insofar as Perth had an establishment, he was as closely bound up with it as anybody. He had certainly embodied a 'stick to your knitting' style of leadership and strategic approach.[4] Yet he had also been the architect of the decentralised or divisional management structure that had resulted in the rise of the most innovative retail building materials operation in the country. That he valued financial acumen in others, as well as a sense of responsibility to shareholders and employees, was about to be made plain. By contrast, the headlines during the latter part of 1987 were focused very much on the wavering fortunes of entrepreneurs who had made it big only comparatively recently and whom, in their success and now in their failures, lent the 1980s a character all of its own.[5] Some had proceeded immediately into exile, others had seen their paper empires vanish almost overnight, and others still were doubling down on indebtedness and deals with the Burke government, sowing the seeds for the looming bankruptcies, imprisonments, and other indignities of an unravelling WA Inc. By then, the contrast to Bunnings could hardly have been starker, even if the dynasty itself was coming to an end.

The white knight that Tom reached out to was Wesfarmers. Although it had listed publicly only recently, it had origins as a farmer's cooperative dating back seventy years and a corporate identity that also reflected its ties to the Western Australian community. It was now one of the state's most successful businesses, and the largest outside of the resources sector. It had substantial farming, transport and chemical operations, and had recently completed a takeover of the fertiliser manufacturer CSBP.[6] Wesfarmers also operated a dedicated investment division, managed by Michael Chaney. He and Tom had met before. Chaney had cut his teeth working at the AIDC while Tom was on the board, and they crossed paths again when the AIDC worked with Bunnings to bring about the Millars acquisition. He and the other Wesfarmers executives had built reputations for astute and ethical conduct and a long-term vision for their group of companies.[7] It made them the right choice, and all the more so in light of the circumstances that prevailed.

To see Chaney, Tom had to travel a short distance down St George's Terrace from the Bunnings head office to Wesfarmers headquarters. No longer the graceful Edwardian high street of his youth, it nonetheless held landmarks from a lifetime in business with almost every step. One of the first was Government House, where he had received his AO and where he and Margot had been guests on many occasions, most recently when the governor had hosted a garden party for the Prince and Princess of Wales.[8] At Barrack Street he went past the Weld Club, which he still visited regularly, in a building his father and uncle had built in the days in their building trade. It sat behind the offices where Robert would once go to collect the cash that Louis Abrahams loaned him to keep Bunning Bros afloat through the Great War, although that building had long since been demolished. On the next corner, where the Palace Hotel had become the façade for what was, on that day, the city's newest and tallest skyscraper, Tom was at the place where his father had collapsed and died midway through his testimonial speech. His destination was just down the hill. He had a simple proposition to make: that Wesfarmers take up a 10-per-cent placement in Bunnings Ltd.[9]

Tom could be confident his offer would receive serious consideration. What was not entirely clear, and about to be revealed, was just how keen Wesfarmers actually would be. Their small stake in Innerhadden suggested an interest, though it was also a prudent step for any corporation with an investment arm. The fact of the matter, however, was that Wesfarmers had been contemplating their own tilt at Bunnings, but they had decided against it for the time being due to the complicated ownership structure, family cohesion and the agreement with Hawker Siddeley. They had been enticed, above all, by the company's timber assets. Logging rights in state forests, woodchip export contracts and guaranteed access to pine plantations, together with the company's sawmills and timber and other allied manufacturing assets, all held considerable long-term value, and would neatly complement their established rural, dairy, fertiliser and transport businesses.[10] The Bunnings chain of hardware and home improvement outlets was a secondary but still attractive proposition, as Wesfarmers had been looking to diversify into the retailing sector.[11] Chaney told Tom directly that whereas a modest share placement would be given serious consideration, it might also become the first step towards a takeover of their own. In his own mind, this was something Tom had prepared for. 'I could think of worse outcomes' was his reply.[12]

The details were quickly settled, and the deal announced publicly in December 1987. Wesfarmers was taking on a 10-per-cent holding and would fill two places on the Bunnings board of directors. These were occupied by Chaney and his managing director, Trevor Eastwood. Zink, Kuba, Rutherford and Perth businessman Harold Clough remained from the old guard of Bunnings, alongside the Bunning family's Tom, Gavin, Bob and Clive Hovell. With Ron Brierley keen to sell out of his holding, the initial placement soon grew into 19-per-cent stake via on-market purchases for about $5.72 per share. This was in line with Chaney's prediction of increased investment, even though it was occurring rather quickly, and the two companies remained in accord.[13] Backed up by Wesfarmers' finance and expertise, Bunnings continued its expansion, buying up Amtel Holdings, a manufacturer of steel roofing. A second steel products company was added a short time later.[14] The company was also increasing its focus on tree farming. It had established a nursery at Manjimup and by 1990 was producing over six million seedlings annually, with four million of these going into the company's own plantations. That year, the company

Handing out the presents, Christmas 1989 (Bunning Family Collection)

established a new entity, Bunnings Tree Farms, with the objective of buying up land for further plantations.[15]

Tom's move towards a full retirement was reaching its finale. He stepped down as chairman of WA Chip and Pulp (WACAP) during 1988. As he did, it was generating almost $40 million in export income and employed almost 500 people. At Bunnings, the end came formally at the AGM in 1989, when he opted against seeking re-election to the board. After sixty-one years, the curtain had finally closed on his corporate career. As he stepped away, Bunnings employed 3,650 people and had a turnover of $366 million.[16] The ebbs and flows of its fortunes continued. Later that year, a recession took hold nationwide and had an immediate impact on performance, as residential construction was particularly hard hit. However, just as it had done in the early 1970s and again in the early 1980s, the company was able to weather the adverse conditions better than its competitors. In 1990, it purchased the struggling Alco Handyman and WA Salvage chains. The Alco stores were quickly rebranded, leaving the company with 31 Bunnings outlets and an additional 10 WA Salvage stores across Western Australia.[17]

Despite these successes, the road quickly became much rockier for the executive team that had been with Tom throughout the 1980s. Kuba, in particular, was unable to see eye to eye with the Wesfarmers directors, and after a period of rising tension he decided upon an early retirement.[18] His replacement as CEO was Ian Mackenzie. Confronted with all the indications of a looming downturn, he had set about a far-reaching restructure, putting the future of the Forest Products division firmly in his sights. The problems, in a nutshell, remained largely as Tom had identified some years earlier: returns on capital that were too low for a large public company, combined with a lack of confidence in the financial acumen of senior management.[19] Mackenzie was also worried by the ongoing preoccupation with hardwood milling. Decreasing supplies of jarrah and karri had long been anticipated, but the higher royalties of the recent timber allocation strategy were now a reality and would only weigh more heavily against returns in the future.[20] This put him at loggerheads with Bob Bunning, who was more bullish about the company's future in hardwoods. Confronted by an attempt to move him aside, Bob opted to resign from his role, though he would retain his place on the company's board. Privately, Tom accepted the necessity for his departure, though he also recognised his contribution across more than two decades. From the Cable Beach Club in Broome, he wrote to console him on this development: 'I have been thinking a lot about you, and this happening in the family hierarchy and you have my very best wishes for the future'.[21] Bunnings sold out of its Papua New Guinea operation shortly afterwards. Amid the rampant corruption of regional powerbrokers, it had never performed satisfactorily.[22] At home, the company was forced to curtail production and lay-off staff at its sawmills amid sharp falls in residential construction.[23]

Tom continued to play golf, now in a cart, and to keep a diary of his scores each round and the names of his playing partners. At the age of seventy-nine he noted down stroke scores of 40 and 39 on consecutive days, thus equalling his age across eighteen holes. There had been no overseas trips since his retirement, but he did enjoy holidays to Broome, and to Exmouth and Shark Bay aboard *Manitoba*. He did not join Margot on a trip to Spain in 1990, preferring to avoid the overseas flight.[24] That he was suffering from emphysema had become obvious to his family and friends. Although he had not been in the habit of doing so previously, he had begun to attend the Sunday service at St Columba's, a Presbyterian church along Keane Street in Peppermint Grove and the local Bunning family church during his childhood. He had also become interested in his family tree and started corresponding with other Bunnings in the eastern states in the hope of finding common ancestors.[25] The family continued to gather each Sunday at McNeil Street, with the evening barbecue preceded by ramshackle musical performances on a mixed bag of instruments, overseen by Margot. Ever the patriarch, Tom could come across as formal, if not imposing, to the grandchildren, especially the younger ones. To his own children, however, it seemed as if his demeanour had softened, especially whenever his two granddaughters were around.[26]

Apart from his time with family and friends, Tom kept up his contact with the associations representing ex–prisoners of war and the returned servicemen of the 2nd/4th Battalion. The Machine Gun Battalion was to commemorate the half-century of its creation in 1990, and as the most senior surviving officer, Tom was asked to lead a march down St George's Terrace to a service at St George's Cathedral on 25 November 1990. He had become somewhat frail, though so too had the other men he had been with at camps in Northam, at Woodside in the Adelaide Hills and at the Adelaide River, during that furious week of combat in Singapore, and at Changi, where he had remained for three and a half years. He had also been asked to make a speech inside the cathedral:

Ivan Ivancovich, Skipper of *Manitoba* for seventeen years (1984–2001) (Bunning Family Collection)

Geoff Renshaw, Skipper of *Manitoba* for twenty-one years (2001–2022) (Bunning Family Collection)

Manitoba at Parker Point, Rottnest, February 2025 (Bunning Family Collection)

Top and bottom: The 50th Anniversary of the 2/4th Machine Gun Battalion in November 1990. As the Battalion's senior surviving officer, Tom led the march down Adelaide Terrace, before speaking at the service in St George's Cathedral (Bunning Family Collection)

> Those years of 1939–45 were a distinct chapter in the lives of most of us here today. We all experienced occasions and periods which were awful, some weren't so bad, others unforgettable and some were good. Thank God for the vagaries of human nature in that we tend to remember the good things whilst the memory of the bad things seems to fade and for those of us who came out without too many scars, the experience has stood us in good stead. There would be few of us who did not have one big wish that was, that as a unit we did not have another chance to fight again so as to confirm the quality of our battalion. On the lighter side of course, another important wish was to become members of the RSL.[27]

Margot found that he was very tired that night, news that did not surprise Gavin, who had noticed the determinedly robust demeanour he had mustered as he marched proudly ahead of his old fellow servicemen. Among Tom's recent correspondence were letters from military historians researching the battalion's history and exploits in the war. He was happy to cooperate and answer their questions, but the full historical value of his extensive diary and the other records he kept over those years at Changi had not yet been realised.[28]

Tom passed away in his sleep at home on 12 March 1991.[29] Margot was away attending a dinner on his behalf at BP headquarters in Melbourne held in honour of retired directors. He was found by their housekeeper, and Margot found out herself when six-year-old grandson Rory answered the home phone and broke the news to her. He was eulogised widely over the days that followed. Zink wrote on behalf of the company that:

> Tom Bunning personified the best qualities in business and community leadership. He was a man of unwavering integrity, forward looking, sensitive to the emotional needs of others and he possessed a delightful sense of humour. His accomplishments were many but he never lost his characteristic modesty.[30]

The premier, Carmen Lawrence, sent her condolences to Margot; 'The part which your husband played in the development of industry earned for him a place of respect and warm regard in the community over many years.'[31] There were other letters like it. One read 'he achieved a great deal yet he never lost touch with those about him no matter their circumstances. He led by example with a sense of duty and integrity unmatched', and another, 'Tom Bunning was one of those few people about whom it can be genuinely said was one of nature's gentlemen'.[32] Charles Court was among the mourners attending the funeral. 'I thought you Bunnings were Presbyterians', he huffed jokingly at Jenny Mills as he sat down beside her; he had also written privately to Margot upon learning the news.[33] Confined these past few years to a wheelchair, Charlie sat silently and still throughout the entire service. Gavin gave the eulogy; 'He had this insatiable appetite for knowledge, and he recognised that the best means for him to gain knowledge was to listen to and learn about people.'[34]

It was probably inevitable, in light of Tom's authority and the effect of his counsel, that the family's influence in maintaining the independence of Bunnings as a public company became more vulnerable after his passing. About 18 per cent of shares remained spread among them, with another seven per cent held by Innerhadden.[35] Wesfarmers, holding nearly twenty per cent, remained determined to increase its ownership. Chaney and Eastwood had travelled quietly to London to sound out Hawker Siddeley's CEO about its 25-per-cent holding, only to find themselves rebuffed in short order.[36] The catalyst for a takeover came a few months later, after Hawker Siddeley was itself taken over by the Australian businessman Alan Jackson's multinational conglomerate, BTR Plc. By law, Wesfarmers was required to make a bid for the entire company if they wished to purchase Hawker Siddeley's stake, so they decided to push ahead with one. Chaney called at Zink's holiday house on New Year's Day to advise him of their intentions. Their offer, announced the next day, was for $3.55 per share. It was a lowball figure, with shares trading on the exchange for $4 and an independent analyst valuing them between $4.30 and $4.70. There was therefore widespread surprise, and concern, when BTR quickly indicated its acceptance. The Bunning family scarcely had time to develop an alternative placement strategy. Their concern now was that other shareholders might accept a lower price for their holdings, enabling Wesfarmers to effectively steal the company away from them. As it transpired, the only significant acceptance of the bid was from BTR.

Wesfarmers now owned 44.6 per cent of Bunnings, giving it majority control of the board. Gavin, McKenzie and Clough remained as independent directors and were faced with the challenge of resisting pressure from the Wesfarmers

THE END OF A DYNASTY

management team to convey the idea that Bunnings was one of their subsidiaries. In their eyes, they remained accountable to all shareholders as directors of a publicly listed company. Mackenzie, in particular, was able to deftly utilise the benefits of their connection without comprising his accountability and independence.[37] In the meantime, no more significant parcels of shares changed hands. The family, through Bob, pursued a Supreme Court injunction against Wesfarmers, and legal action against BTR was eventually settled out of court without affirming the validity of the claim to pre-emptive rights. If the agreement Tom signed with Hawker Siddeley in 1975 had not thwarted Wesfarmers after his death, it had at least helped the family to shape the terms upon which the company would eventually change hands. Piece by piece, their collective shareholding began to diminish; Oliver and Jane had quit most of their shares during the heady days of the mid-1980s, and after 1991, both Charlie and Bob sold off some of theirs, while Innerhadden parted with its holding altogether.

Charlie Bunning (Bunning Family Collection)

The Bunnings juggernaut continued to roll on. During 1992, the company settled on a joint venture with Wesfi, its former rival in the development of softwood milling, in what was a major rationalisation of the sector within Western Australia. A year later, the company purchased all the assets of the longtime Victoria-based hardware chain McEwans.[38] This gave Bunnings a national footprint and platform for the Wesfarmers-led strategy of interstate expansion. When the Alco chain was acquired, the company had made a point of retaining its highly regarded managing director, Joe Boros. To facilitate this, Gavin moved aside to enable Boros to run the store operations as Managing Director of Bunnings Building Supplies. The appointment meant Wesfarmers were putting Boros in charge of expanding Bunnings outside of Western

Charlie and Betty (Bunning Family Collection)

Australia. Their strategy, modelled closely on the Home Depot stores in the United States, was to develop low-price, bulk-display, warehouse-style outlets. It was underway by 1994, when the first concept store opened in Melbourne.[39] By then, the family retained only about nine per cent of the issued stock. That May, Wesfarmers made a successful play for full ownership at $10.52 per share, a price that valued the 52 per cent of shares outside of their control at about $543 million.[40] For Gavin's family and the other shareholders that had retained their holdings, it was a much happier outcome that the $3.55 per share on offer only two years earlier.

Charlie passed away only weeks later, in June 1994. His achievements in business and community service were as illustrious as any of his contemporaries. These included, among other responsibilities, holding the role of President of the Western Australian Employers Federation and the National Safety Council of Australia, directorships of the Swan Brewery, the Swan Portland Cement Companies, the Town and Country Building Society and National Mutual, positions on the Senate of the University of Western Australia, the National Parks Board, the Zoological Gardens Board and the Metric Conversion Board, and longest-serving president on record at the Western Australian Cricket Association. More than one promising young cricketer found a tolerant employer at Bunnings over the years.[41] Throughout it all, he had remained, as daughter Jenny once wrote, 'essentially a man of the South-West, always approachable, with a humane concern for people and their families'; perfectly at home inside head office or the boardroom, he was always most content to be down in the forest among the sawmillers and timberman he had known since his youth.[42] Bob delivered his eulogy; 'The Old Man was one of the most extraordinary people – one who immediately commanded respect – but one who was also immediately likeable'.[43] Jane passed away a short time later, Flora in 1997 and Angie in 2005.

By the turn of the twenty-first century, Bunnings had become a very different business from what it once had been, even if it retained echoes of the culture and image built over Tom's long career. The interstate expansion of its retail outlets gathered pace in the late 1990s, when over 30 new warehouse stores were established outside of Western Australia. During this period, the decision was made to move out of timber production entirely. Commercial realities were part of the reason, as retailing activity now eclipsed forestry in its

Tom and his siblings (Bunning Family Collection)

share of the company's profits. Environmental politics was another factor. The forest conservation movement had gained traction in Western Australia during the 1990s through its campaign to protect 'old-growth forest' from any form of logging. The executive team at Wesfarmers found themselves confronted by weekend protests outside of Bunnings stores and protestors on the floor of its AGM. Under growing public pressure, Richard Court's state government moved during 1999 to revise its Regional Forest Agreement, reducing the timber industry's allocation of jarrah and signalling the end to logging of karri and tingle forest.[44] Faced with threats of consumer boycotts and the future reduction of access to hardwood resources, Wesfarmers made the decision to divest the timber assets that had attracted it to Bunnings in the first place. WACAP and Bunnings Tree Farms were sold to its main customer, the Japanese multinational Marubeni. Much of what remained of the old Forest Products division ended up in the hands of the Tasmanian forestry company Gunns.[45]

In the meantime, the Bunnings hardware chain was moving from strength to strength. During 2001 Wesfarmers took over BBC Hardware, a long-established

Margot (Bunning Family Collection)

operator and the company's main competitor in the eastern states. It was a significant acquisition. The BBC network, which included Hardwarehouse and Benchmark stores, was a larger operation, with annual sales of $2.4 billion compared to the $1.3 billion of Bunnings.[46] Combining these retail chains raised an immediate quandary – by what name would the merged operation be known? Customer surveys found that the Bunnings brand was well known and respected, whereas BBC's image was comparatively mediocre. So Bunnings it would be. It was a credit to the building up of a local reputation under Robert's initial guidance, its development under the stewardship that passed on to Charlie and Tom, and its maintenance and expansion through the process of diversification that had occurred under Tom's guidance. Wesfarmers continued to nurture the values and identity of the company it had taken over, as Bunnings grew into a chain of more than 380 stores and over 53,000 employees across Australia. In 2025, it was the single most profitable part of the Wesfarmers empire.

Margot passed away in late 2006. She had been among the longest lived of those that had come of age in the 1930s, had lived through the Second World War, and then experienced the good times on the other side. She had felt Tom's loss profoundly but kept up the brave front that was a hallmark of her generation and did not let her loss hold her back after he was gone. 'As much as she loved him and missed him', observed one friend, 'she already had a plan for the future, she had a motivation, a determination and she pursued those relentlessly. She also had a stoicism which she also expected others to have'.[47] The family continued to gather at McNeil Street and to spend time aboard *Manitoba*. She remained committed to her voluntary work at the Art Gallery of Western Australia, serving as Patron of the Gallery Foundation in 1991, and for many years acting as the state's representative on the Australian Federation of Friends of Galleries and Museums. More than two million dollars was raised for the gallery's acquisitions through efforts and initiatives she had spearheaded.[48] There had been a flood of tributes following her passing, as there had been for Tom. In her own way, she had also left an indelible mark on those around her.

Gavin had moved out of the Bunnings management team in 1992, and the board ceased to exist after the final acquisition in 1994. Working with Sue and Clive, his focus turned to managing the diversified family investment portfolio initially developed by Tom. None of Tom and Margot's grandchildren had entered the company after its takeover by Wesfarmers, going on instead to pursue careers elsewhere in hospitality, information technology, property, academia, medicine and the equestrian industry.[49] More recently, this next generation has picked up the reins of the family's shared investments, with each family developing an independent approach for part of their funds and investing jointly with the rest. Today, when Bunnings is one of the nation's most recognised brands, its origins in the Western Australian building trade of the 1880s and its timber industry of the early twentieth century often comes as a surprise to many Australians.

That timber industry, with which Tom had become acquainted in his childhood, no longer exists. More than a million hectares of what was formerly Western Australia's state forest is now part of the conservation estate, and hardwood logging has been phased out entirely.[50] An industry based on a high-quality sustainable resource has disappeared, and with it has gone a workforce committed to its sustainability. The timber sold in Bunnings stores today comes

Gavin and Sue (Bunning Family Collection)

from privately owned plantations or from imports, much of it derived from forests that are not nearly so well-managed as Western Australia's forests formerly were. It is a transition that Tom could hardly have foreseen. He was an industrialist of the twentieth century, who firmly believed that his key responsibilities were to generate returns for investors, to provide work for employees and to pay the appropriate dues to the government in the form of taxation. All of it was done in an ethical manner and he never wavered in these principles and this approach. A consistent set of values lay beneath his efforts to keep the company afloat during the Great Depression, his stand against the attempt to hand over the Milyeannup concession to outside control, and his efforts to support the Trade Bureau in its fight back against the Hawke Government's attack on free enterprise. That the forest resource base was renewable and could sustain production indefinitely, to the collective benefit of the community at large, was a belief that remained unchanged. He had said as much during his chairmanship, when Brian Burke's Labor was threatening to end the long era of Liberal ascendency in state politics and promising a government with very different priorities in its place.[51] If these were old fashioned values, they had also stood up well across a remarkably long period of time.

When Bunnings marked its centenary in 1986, the historian Geoffrey Bolton commented on the company's achievement. 'Bunnings is a rare example of a Perth-based company which, when confronted with competition based on outside capital, managed successfully to fight back', he wrote. 'Part of this success probably results from the manner in which the firm has managed to identify itself with the Western Australian community'.[52] In the second half of his career, Tom oversaw the timber industry's transition from two-thirds offshore ownership to complete local control. In the years that followed, Bunnings went from being a

McNeil Street, Peppermint Grove (Bunning Family Collection)

household name in Western Australia to one that is familiar across the length and breadth of Australia. There have been attempts to account for the expansion overseen by Wesfarmers and apportion credit for the stunning success that Bunnings has become.[53] In truth, it is rooted in a much earlier past, among the strategy and decisions devised by close-knit and hard-working teams of business executives and managers, in their different guises across the years. Tom Bunning was only one among them, and often the quiet one, yet so often at the very heart of it all. Along the way, he had not only helped the company identify with the community, but the community itself to form its own idea about who and what it was, and from whence it came.

Appendix

Tom's letter on the Selarang Barracks incident, Changi, 1942

Changi, 6th Sept 1942

Margot Darling,

After starting to describe to you in my diary the happenings during the past week, I have decided that it would be more discreet to write a separate screed in case the diary may be scrutinised by the Little Yellow Men. You may have noticed that right through my diary I have refrained from any criticism for this reason.

Beyond saying now that I consider temperamentally they can be likened to children – some bullying, some friendly, a lot of them quite likeable, but all capable of absolute thoughtless cruelty and all of them with a childish curiosity and that I admire their efficiency and the apparent simplicity of their army organisation, I will say nothing. My further views, and they are quite strong, I will leave to be discussed at a later date.

Now to return to my narrative. On Monday and Tuesday nothing further was said and on Tuesday afternoon Malaya Comd. submitted a 'Nil' return to the I.J.A. At 3.30 am on the following morning I was awakened by Curly to tell me that there would be a conference at 0400. Naturally I was immediately curious to know what it might be about but did not anticipate the full import of it.

At the appointed time Staff and Area Comds. were assembled and were advised by the Comd. who had just returned from a conference called by

Changi
6th Sept. 42.

Margot Darling,

After starting to describe to you in my diary the happenings during the past week I have decided that it would be more discreet to write a separate record, in case the diary may be scrutinised by the little yellow men. You may have noticed that right through my diary I have refrained from any criticism for this reason.

Beyond saying now that I consider that temperamentally they can be likened to children — some bullying, some friendly, a lot of them normally quite likable, but all capable of absolute thoughtless cruelty and all of them with a childish curiosity and that I admire their efficiency & the apparent simplicity of their army organisation I will say nothing. My further views, and they are quite strong, I will have to be discussed at a later date.

Now to return to my narrative. On Monday & Tuesday nothing further was said and on Tuesday afternoon Malaya Comd submitted a "nil" return to the I.J.A. At 3.30 AM on the following morning I was awakened by Curly to tell me that there would be a conference at 0x00. Naturally I was immediately curious to know what it might be about but did not anticipate the full import of it. At the appointed time Staff & Area Comds were assembled & were advised by the Comd who had just returned from a conference called by Col. Holmes that the I.J.A. had issued an order that all personnel not requiring the Parade would be concentrated in the Barrack Square; they would not move until ordered to do so by IJA & move would be completed by 1800 hrs on Wednesday 2nd Sept.

This meant that 15000 men would be concentrated

A page from Tom's letter, 6 September 1942 (Bunning Family Collection)

APPENDIX

Col. Holmes that the I.J.A. had issued an order that all personnel not signing the Parole would be concentrated in the Barrack Square, they would not move until ordered to do so by I.J.A. and move would be completed by 1800 hours on Wednesday 2nd September.

This meant that 15,000 men would be concentrated in about 9 acres of space, that latrines would need to be built and that all rations also would have to be assembled in the area.

Buildings were allotted and everything organised as far as possible so that a start could be made at daylight to get cracking.

The Comd. was advised further that four escapees who were being held by the Japs would be shot and also that the Hospitals also maybe shifted into the Area.

So at 0900 hours on Wednesday GMB [i.e. Tom] was in the Barrack Square supervising the dumping of tarpaulins, tables and forms and building material. In the meantime Carl Gunther was on the job and banks of latrines for all formations were being spitlocked out and a start made on digging. At 1300 hours we received the order to move in and then the pilgrimage started.

It was amazing to see the gear that was brought into that Barrack Square and the different means used to convey it. Trailers of course were the best form of transport and going down the scale came hand carts, wheel barrows, chairs with castors on them and strips of cane fibre being hauled along. Included in the chattels brought in were two goats and lots of chickens & ducklings. By 1800 hrs there we all were with quite 90% of our worldly possessions.

Our 1900 were distributed 300 per floor in the building and 170 on the roof with the remaining 840 out in the open, including all officers, and as soon as everyone was settled in we issued all the tarpaulins available. In the meantime the Kit store had been dumped out of the building they occupied and there was a net mounted over them doing what it could to save something from the wreck.

Cooking arrangements and sites for kitchen had been rather indefinite as we had hoped to resume possession of a flat area just out from the road and strictly beyond our perimeter. Also the organisation on this side had been relegated until about 1600 hrs when Jim Hardaker had been called in and appointed O.C. Kitchens. At about 1900 hrs we were informed that our perimeter would be the inside of the road and everything outside must be in by 1930 hrs. So cook houses were brought in and lined up in the open north of the building.

I managed to scrounge a big long canopy for AIF. H.Q., which with a tarpaulin over it made quite a water tight show and gradually the sorting out process went on and people settled themselves in.

APPENDIX

Of course the tremendous problems were Sanitation and Hygiene and the outlook in this regard was not made any rosier when 200 diphtheria suspects and contacts were returned to us from the Hospital. No latrines were yet complete, and our only urinals were one per floor to serve 1900 men. It was therefore necessary to form up in a queue about 200 long and of course the effect of this to nervous individuals was that when they found themselves in front of the receptacle they could do nothing about it. About 2100 hrs I was sent to 18 Div. H.Q. and found that they overcame the difficulty by peeing in the gutter. This is an indication of troubles with which we were to be confronted and also of the idea of English troops on Sanitation which I say without fear of contradiction are punk.

The cooks turned out quite a good meal the first night and really did a wonderful job right through the piece. On the first night we all slept out under the stars but fortunately it was a beautiful night and except for the constant stream of traffic past our beds to the latrines we had quite a pleasant night.

In the meantime, patrols of Japs and Sikhs marched around the perimeter whilst we had a patrol moving around the inside directing men to the latrines and generally watching hygiene. Fatigue parties worked on these all night in order that we would have a complete set ready to function as soon as possible. In all seven were dug 20ft long × 3ft wide and twelve feet deep right in the centre of what had been the Gordons very solidly constructed & bituminised Parade Ground.

Another problem at this stage was water. In the whole area there was only one water point and formations were allotted times right around the clock for the drawing of water. The allowance was one gallon per man per day for all purposes.

As soon as we had breakfasted on the second day everyone set to work again sorting out units into areas and erecting whatever shelter was available in the form of tarpaulins and ground sheets. The kit store was restacked in order to avoid pilfering and also so that it could be waterproofed and by the end of the day everyone was as comfortable as they could possibly be under the circumstances and the siege was under way.

On Friday the situation was becoming more acute in that no fuel or rations had been supplied to us at all and the evacuations to hospital were limited to 20 dysentery, 2 diphtherias on the first day and 31 dysentery, 9 dips on the second day. All doors and any available timber was requisitioned for the construction of latrine seats and a nice stench had begun to permeate the area.

However the A.I.F. reserve of rations kept the wolf from the door and the whole show was wonderfully well disciplined.

APPENDIX

Saturday was a big day for me in that I paid my first successful visit to the latrines since Tuesday morning. Strangely enough we were all affected similarly and even allowing for the general delay, the queues were often 70 to 100 men long. This was enough to make one realise just how appalling the situation would become when (and there would be no "if" about it) dysentery hit us properly.

On Saturday morning we had started to pull out all door & window frames for fuel but nothing had come in from outside.

By the time the order to sign had been issued and at 1300 hours we received the order to move back.

It was my job in the afternoon to organise trailers for moving gear & equipment and by 1800 hrs the square was about clear again. It was about like Heaven to return to our spacious bungalow, the only disappointment being that there was no water on and therefore I could not have the much looked forward to shower.

One thing that stood out during the incident was the grand morale of the troops right through. They had a damned hard time from the beginning of the first day but everything was done willingly and well and a cheerful atmosphere pervaded the camp during the whole time. The Comd. did damned good job and on Friday night said his piece on five separate occasions.

I must tell you a little about the execution of the four escapees, which the Comd. was ordered to attend. Each man refused to be blindfolded and Cpl. Brevington when he was led out saluted the British Officers present & told them all "to keep their chins up". The first shot hit him on the arm, the second through the groin & the third finished him off. There was only one man doing the firing.

There are different theories as to why the issue was so strongly forced on us and the most logical appears to be as follows:- When the naval Big Shots were here they did not like the idea of POWs overlooking the Straights. The army pointed out that this was unimportant as no persons could escape but when the Navy investigated this statement they discovered that this was untrue as there had been isolated attempts made. So then the Army said "Well, don't worry we will arrange for them to promise not to escape". Then again another intimation from the I.J.A. was that the forms were printed and sent down from Tokyo and that all POW must serve 6 months servitude before being granted the privilege of parole.

How do I feel about this incident? Although the Comd. unquestionably took the only sensible course and we did force from the I.J.A. a written order to sign, what they were not prepared to give before one can't help feeling a little unsettled in mind about the whole affair. His contention is that in regard to our own force of

APPENDIX

2000 men, if we struck out, then within a month 1000 would be dead and the other 1000 permanently impaired in health and all without inflicting one casualty to the enemy. On the other hand, the time may come when these men will be of use to Australia. Unquestionably he is right, because what he says is absolutely true, but on the other hand every POW on the island has now had an opportunity, given the lead from the Commander of dying a hero, on two occasions. Certainly the material damage to our enemy would have been a small but if tradition is worth building on, perhaps the sacrifice might be worthwhile as an inspiration to our troops in other theatres.

Still we are not yet out of the wood and whether we like it or not we may well have our hardest time ahead of us.

Now for the sequence of events covering the "Incident"

Date	Time	Event
30th August		Formation Commanders were called to Conference House and were informed that all POW would be given the forms to sign.
1st Sept		Col. Holmes was advised that those refusing to sign would be subjected to measures of severity and would be confined to a smaller area.
2nd Sept	0300	AIF Comd. summoned to Conference.
	0400	Area Comds conference at which we were told of concentration.
	1200	Statement went to Malaya Comd. advising no one prepared to sign.
	1300	Received order to move to Square.
	1320	Comd. received order to R.V. in order to witness executions.
	2030	All formation Comds. summoned by Japs to pathway opposite clock tower. Addressed by Lt.Col. Okayange who advised them to order signing.
3rd Sept	1600	Conference of Lt, Cols. D.D.M.S. had advised formation Cmd. that he estimated 1,000 dysenteries before end of week (6 Sept) to Roberts hospital could only accommodate 300 more patients. Japs had threatened reprisals in form of executions and would reduce our rations to one third. During following day M.C. had two or three conferences with Japs suggesting variations to wording of forms, however J states that form was sent down from Japan & no one can alter it.
4th Sept	1700	Comd. advises that Col. Holmes had been taken to Conference House and under orders had taken Jap Order No 17 of

APPENDIX

2 Sept. to effect that those who refused to sign would concentrate. This he handed over and in its place received Order No 17 dated "2 Sept" ordering all personnel to sign.

The form reads:- "I, the undersigned hereby solemnly swear on my honour that I will not, under any circumstances, attempt escape.

Signed...

Dated..

At..

Nationality...

Rank & Position....................................

Following is the order revised to all troops by Comd. A.I.F:
"The extreme duress placed upon us by the I.J.A. compels me to obey a direct order raised from Tokyo, an order which leaves me no option but disease and death to us all; and I therefore order all officers, warrant officers, non-commissioned officers and men of A.I.F. to sign the declaration given to you by the I.J.A. I accept full responsibility."

Notes

1. An unplanned beginning

1. *Western Mail*, 16 July 1910, p. 30; *Bunbury Herald*, 21 July 1910, p. 2.
2. Gavin L. Bunning, interview with the author, 31 May 2019; *West Australian*, 27 July 1910, p. 1.
3. *West Australian*, 26 November 1886, p. 3.
4. Twentieth Century Impressions of Western Australia, Hesperian Press, Victoria Park, 2000 (1901), pp. 413–14.
5. P. de Serville, *3 Barrack Street: The Weld Club 1871–2001*, Helicon Press, Wahroonga NSW, 2003, p. 80.
6. J. Mills, *The Timber People: A History of Bunnings Ltd*, Bunnings Ltd, Perth, 1986, pp. 12–21; *West Australian*, 19 December 2015, accessed 6 February 2025. https://thewest.com.au/business/finance/forrest-buys-cott-mansion-for-16m-ng-ya-134236
7. Mills, *The Timber People*, p. 14.
8. Mills, *The Timber People*, pp. 10–21.
9. *Twentieth Century Impressions of Western Australia*, pp. 413–14.
10. Mills, *The Timber People*, p. 32.
11. Flora Bunning, interview by Ronda Jamieson, July–August 1984, J.S. Battye Library of Western Australian History Oral History Programme, OH628, State Library of Western Australia.
12. R. Marchant James, *Heritage of Pines: A History of The Town of Cottesloe Western Australia*, Town of Cottesloe Council, Cottesloe, 1977, p. 48.
13. D. Black, 'Wilson, Frank (1859–1918)', Australian Dictionary of Biography, National Centre of Biography, Australian National University, 1990 (hardcopy), accessed online 29 December 2022. https://adb.anu.edu.au/biography/wilson-frank-9135/text16115
14. L. T. Carron, *A History of Forestry in Australia*, Australian National University Press, Canberra, 1985, pp. 141–4.
15. See Robert Bunning's remarks, 1 July 1903, in Parliament of Western Australia, *Royal Commission on Forestry: First Progress Report*, Government Printer, Perth, 1903, pp. 100–3.
16. R. Bunning, 1 July 1903, in *Royal Commission on Forestry: First Progress Report*, p. 102.
17. Carron, *A History of Forestry in Australia*, p. 144; J. Mills, 'The impact of man on the northern jarrah forest from settlement in 1829 to the Forests Act 1918', in B. Dell, J. J. Havel et al. (eds), *The Jarrah Forest*, Geobotany, Springer, Dordrecht, 1989, 13:267–8.

18 Mills, *The Timber People*, pp. 39–41.
19 J. S. Battye, *The Cyclopedia of Western Australia*, Hesperian Press, Victoria Park, 1985 [1911], 1:655.
20 Mills, *The Timber People*, pp. 30–1.
21 B. Moore, *From the Ground Up: Bristile, Whittakers and Metro Brick in Western Australian History*, University of Western Australia Press, Nedlands, 1987, pp. 42–7.
22 G. Blainey, *Gold and Paper: A History of the National Bank of Australasia Ltd*, National Bank of Australasia Ltd, Melbourne, 1958, pp. 157–63.
23 Moore, *From the Ground Up*, pp. 43–5.
24 *Swan Express*, 18 December 1914.
25 R. Bunning, 1 July 1903, in Royal Commission on Forestry: First Progress Report, p. 102; Mills, *The Timber People*, pp. 34–7.
26 *Southern Times*, 6 May 1909, p. 4.
27 *Bunbury Herald*, 1 February 1907, p. 2; see also J. S. Battye, *The Cyclopedia of Western Australia*, Hesperian Press, Victoria Park, 1985 (1913), 2:283–9.
28 *Twentieth Century Impressions of Western Australia*, pp. 413–14.
29 Downing & Downing, 'Memorandum and Articles of Association of Bunning Brothers Limited', Bunning Family Manuscript Collection; Mills, *The Timber People*, p. 88.
30 See the contents of 'Bunnings – Various (file 1)', Bunning Family Manuscript Collection; also Mills, *The Timber People*, p. 43.
31 Jamieson, interview with Flora Bunning.
32 Mills, *The Timber People*, p. 46.
33 *Southern Times*, 6 May 1909, p. 4.
34 *West Australian*, 10 November 1908, p. 2.
35 See *Daily News*, 18 November 1908, p. 4; 25 January 1909, p. 9; 30 March 1909, p. 10. For the accident at Lyall's Mill, see *Southern Times*, 1 May 1909, p. 6. For pre-existing problems in the industry, see *Western Mail*, 30 March 1907, p. 18.
36 Mills, *The Timber People*, pp. 48–9.
37 Robert's dealings with the Abrahams brothers are covered by: Mia Mia Pastoral Company Limited; Abrahams Alfred; *Abrahams Emanuel v Bunning Brothers Limited*; Bunning Robert; Bunning Arthur Benjamin, Appeal Book 1 and Book 2, Items 8869219 and 8869220, Series A10078, National Archives of Australia [hereafter Appeal Book 1 or Book 2, National Archives of Australia]; and by Mills, *The Timber People*, pp. 48–9, p. 64.
38 *West Australian*, 20 July 1910, p. 8.
39 *West Australian*, 19 November 1901, p. 7.
40 Battye, *Cyclopedia of Western Australia*, p. 283.
41 *Collie Miner*, 13 March 1909, p. 3.
42 *Evening Star*, 25 January 1911, p. 3.
43 *Sunday Times*, 29 May 1910, p. 4.
44 *Western Mail*, 25 February 1911, p. 31.
45 Moore, *From the Ground Up*, pp. 50–3.
46 Battye, *Cyclopedia of Western Australia*, p. 283.

NOTES

47 'The Law Report 1840–2015' [unpublished family history], Bunning Family Manuscript Collection.
48 Moore, *From the Ground Up*, pp. 47–51.
49 *Bunbury Herald*, 22 July 1911, p. 7.
50 D. Black, 'Party Politics in Turmoil 1911–1924', in C. T. Stannage (ed), *A New History of Western Australia*, University of Western Australia Press, Nedlands, 1981, pp. 386–93.
51 J. R. Robertson, 'Scaddan, John (1876–1934)', *Australian Dictionary of Biography*, National Centre of Biography, Australian National University, 1988 (hardcopy), accessed online 1 November 2019. http://adb.anu.edu.au/biography/scaddan-john-8348/text14651
52 M. Roche, J. Dargavel and J. Mills, 'Tracking the KTC from Kauri to Karri to Chatlee', in J. Dargavel and S. Feary (eds), *Proceedings of the Second National Conference on Australian forest history*, Centre for Resource and Environmental Studies, Australian National University, 1993, pp. 187–94.
53 Mills, *The Timber People*, p. 52.
54 Mills, *The Timber People*, pp. 50–2.
55 *Southern Times*, 26 June 1913, p. 5; *Western Mail*, 20 April 1939, p. 12.
56 Mills, *The Timber People*, p. 57.
57 Moore, *From the Ground Up*, pp. 50–3.
58 *West Australian*, 21 January 1914, p. 7.
59 *West Australian*, 21 January 1914, p. 7.
60 *West Australian*, 22 January 1914, p. 2.
61 *Daily News*, 8 December 1910, p. 3.
62 *West Australian*, 17 April 1914, p. 7; 15 May 1914, p. 8.
63 *West Australian*, 22 May 1914, p. 7.
64 *Daily News*, 15 July 1914, p. 15.
65 Mills, *The Timber People*, pp. 55–7.
66 Mills, *The Timber People*, p. 49.
67 Jamieson, interview with Flora Bunning.

2. Bonza times

1 J. Gregory, *Building a Tradition: A History of Scotch College 1897–1996*, University of Western Australia Press, Nedlands, pp. 126–42.
2 Robert Bunning to the Secretary of Defence, Melbourne, 10 May 1915, and reply, 16 May 1915, 'Bunning Joseph William', Item 3166599, Series B2455, National Archives of Australia.
3 W Olsen, *Gallipoli: The Western Australian Story*, University of Western Australia Press, Crawley, 2006, pp. 43–63.
4 See Statement of Service in 'Bunning Joseph William', Item 3166599, National Archives of Australia.
5 Mills, *The Timber People*, p. 88.
6 *West Australian*, 4 October 1922, p. 6.
7 *Sunday Times*, 17 February 1918, p. 1.
8 Mills, *The Timber People*, p. 64.
9 Mills, *The Timber People*, p. 57.

10 Mills, *The Timber People*, p. 57.
11 L. T. Carron, 'Lane-Poole, Charles Edward (1885–1970)', *Australian Dictionary of Biography*, National Centre of Biography, Australian National University, 1983 (hardcopy), accessed online 24 June 2023. https://adb.anu.edu.au/biography/lane-poole-charles-edward-7026/text12221
12 L. McCaw, F. Batini, J. Bradshaw, J. McGrath and R. Underwood, 'Enduring Themes in Western Australian Forest Management – Marking the Centenary of the Forests Act 1918', *Australian Forestry*, 2018, 81(4):211–13.
13 Mills, *The Timber People*, p. 66; *Daily News*, 31 May 1922, p. 5.
14 S. Hovell, Eulogy for Margot Bunning, 20 November 2006, Bunning Family Manuscript Collection.
15 Gavin L. Bunning, Biographical notes on Tom Bunning, Bunning Family Manuscript Collection.
16 G. C. Bolton, 'Anderson, Peter Corsar (1871–1955)', *Australian Dictionary of Biography*, National Centre of Biography, Australian National University, 1979 (hardcopy), accessed online 14 April 2020. http://adb.anu.edu.au/biography/anderson-peter-corsar-5019/text8349
17 Gregory, *Building a Tradition*, pp. 92–3.
18 P. C. Anderson, 'Principal's Report', *Scotch College Reporter*, 1920, 8(1):6–12.
19 Gavin Bunning, Biographical notes on Tom Bunning.
20 Gregory, *Building a Tradition*, pp. 111–13; *Western Mail*, 27 January 1927, p. 63.
21 *Western Mail*, 12 May 1921, p. 42; *Daily News*, 2 May 1922, p. 3.
22 G. M. Bunning, Diary, 8 and 26 February 1925, Bunning Family Manuscript Collection; see also Gregory, *Building a Tradition*, p. 151.
23 G. M. Bunning, Diary, 10 June 1925, 29 April 1925, 3 and 6 June 1925.
24 G. M. Bunning, Diary, 2 and 30 May 1925; *Call*, 5 September 1924, p. 12.
25 Letter from Charles Lane-Poole, quoted in Forests Department of Western Australia, *Royal Commission on Forestry*, 'Report of Evidence, Part 3', 1922, p. 481; see also *West Australian*, 11 May 1922, p. 8.
26 *Royal Commission on Forestry*, 'Report of Evidence, Part 3', pp. 482–7; Mills, *The Timber People*, p 68.
27 *Royal Commission on Forestry*, 'Report of Evidence, Part 3', pp. 482–7; J. Dargavel, *The Zealous Conservator: A Life of Charles Lane Poole*, University of Western Australia Press, Crawley, 2006, pp. 64–9.
28 *Daily News*, 31 May 1922, p. 5; 1 June 1922, p. 8.
29 *West Australian*, 15 December 1921, p. 2; see also *West Australian*, 4 October 1922, p. 8.
30 *Daily News*, 7 September 1923, p. 11.
31 *Sunday Times*, 13 July 1930, p. 21.
32 Dargavel, *The Zealous Conservator*, pp. 68–76.
33 Mills, *The Timber People*, p.75; see also L. T. Carron, A History of Forestry in Australia, Australian National University Press, Canberra, 1985, p. 149.
34 Mills, *The Timber People*, p. 66, pp. 75–81.
35 Mills, *The Timber People*, pp. 79–81.
36 Gavin L. Bunning, Biographical notes on Tom Bunning.

NOTES

37 G. M. Bunning, Diary, 10 and 12 March, 18 June 1925; Gregory, *Building a Tradition*, p. 188.
38 G. M. Bunning, Diary, especially March 1925 and January 1927.
39 G. M. Bunning, Diary, 22 and 28 March, 28 April 1925.
40 G. M. Bunning, Diary, 1925, end pages.
41 G. M. Bunning, Diary, 15 August 1925.
42 R. Pascoe, *Peppermint Grove: Western Australia's Capital Suburb*, Oxford University Press, Melbourne, 1983, p. 39.
43 J. Gregory, *Building a Tradition: A History of Scotch College 1897–1996*, University of Western Australia Press, Nedlands, p. 44; see also Bolton, 'Anderson, Peter Corsar (1871–1955)'.
44 G. McEachran and P. J. Ryan, *Cottesloe Golf Club, A Centenary History*, Cottesloe Golf Club, Swanbourne, 2010, p. 13, pp. 37–44.
45 G. M. Bunning, Diary, passim, June–November 1925.
46 G. M. Bunning, Diary, 26 September and 15 October 1925.
47 G. M. Bunning, Diary, 22 March 1925.
48 G. M. Bunning, Diary, passim, August 1925.
49 *Daily News*, 18 February 1927, p. 2.
50 G. M. Bunning, Diary, 14 January 1927.
51 *Western Mail*, 28 July 1927, p. 14.
52 G. M. Bunning, Diary, 8 February 1927.
53 Gavin Bunning, Biographical notes on Tom Bunning.
54 G. M. Bunning, Diary, 26 February 1927; G. M. Bunning, interview with S. M. Howroyd [transcript], 1 August 1983, Bunning Family Manuscript Collection (original in Scotch College archives).
55 G. M. Bunning, Diary, 9 April 1927.
56 G. M. Bunning, Diary, 2 April 1927.
57 Sue Hovell, Eulogy for Margot Bunning.
58 Moore, *From the Ground Up*, pp. 48–53.
59 G. M. Bunning, Diary, 12 June 1927.
60 McEachran and Ryan, *Cottesloe Golf Club*, p. 79.
61 McEachran and Ryan, *Cottesloe Golf Club*, p. 67.
62 G. M. Bunning, Diary, 13 March 1925.
63 *Sunday Times*, 15 February 1925, p. 4.
64 *West Australian*, 14 March 1925, p. 12.
65 W. M. Collins, 'Annual Report combining Bunning Bros Ltd, Perth Jarrah Mills Ltd, Wandoo Timber Company Ltd, and Preston Valleys Sawmills Ltd, 1924', cited by Mills, *The Timber People*, p. 57, p. 77.
66 Mills, *The Timber People*, p. 83.
67 Mills, *The Timber People*, pp. 83–5.
68 Mills, *The Timber People*, p. 90.
69 G. M. Bunning, 'Prisoner of War Diary' [typescript of original diary], 12 July 1942, pp. 66–7, Bunning Family Manuscript Collection.

3. The younger set

1. Gavin L. Bunning, Biographical notes on Tom Bunning, Bunning Family Manuscript Collection.
2. J. Mills, *The Timber People: A History of Bunnings Ltd*, Bunnings Ltd, Perth, 1986, p. 88; Gavin L. Bunning, interview with the author, 31 May 2019.
3. See 'Annual application to renew registration of a factory', Department of Labour file 1921/1629, 'Bunning Bros, Charles Street, West Perth', Cons. 749, State Records Office of Western Australia.
4. Mills, *The Timber People*, pp. 66–8, p. 93.
5. Mills, *The Timber People*, pp. 66–8, pp. 88–9.
6. *Daily News*, 18 February 1929, p. 6; *West Australian*, 18 February 1929, p. 15.
7. *Daily News*, 18 February 1929, p. 6.
8. *Daily News*, 18 February 1929, p. 6; see also *West Australian*, 19 February 1929, p. 13.
9. Mills, *The Timber People*, pp. 86–7; WC Thomas, 'Mills and Men in Western Australia', *The Australian Timber Journal*, Part 12, Oct–Nov 1938, pp. 537–8; and Part 16, Jan–Feb 1939, pp. 9–10.
10. G. D. Snooks, 'Depression', *Historical Encyclopedia of Western Australia*, eds J. Gregory and J. Gothard, University of Western Australia Press, Crawley, 2009, pp. 272–3; and G. D. Snooks, *Depression and Recovery in Western Australia, 1928/29 – 1938/39*, University of Western Australia Press, Nedlands, 1974, pp. 61–3.
11. Mills, *The Timber People*, pp. 95–7.
12. G. M. Bunning, Statement on behalf of the Executors of the Estate of the Late Robert Bunning to the Commissioner of Stamps, 18 March 1937, Bunning Family Manuscript Collection; Mills, *The Timber People*, pp. 97–8.
13. *Truth*, 12 October 1930; *Sunday Times*, 9 August 1936, p. 27.
14. *Western Mail*, 22 October 1931, p. 22.
15. P. O'Sullivan, 'Rich Musical Memories', *Local News Cottesloe*, 16 December 1992, p. 14.
16. *Truth*, 4 January 1931, p. 12.
17. *Daily News*, 24 June 1931, p. 9.
18. *Western Mail*, 22 October 1931, p. 22.
19. Gavin L. Bunning, Biographical notes on Tom Bunning.
20. G. McEachran and P. J. Ryan, *Cottesloe Golf Club: A Centenary History*, Cottesloe Golf Club, Swanbourne, 2010, pp. 177–88; see also Gavin L. Bunning, Biographical notes on Tom Bunning.
21. McEachran and Ryan, *Cottesloe Golf Club*, pp. 115–20; *West Australian*, 12 April 1932, p. 8.
22. *West Australian*, 30 May 1931, p. 14.
23. Mills, *The Timber People*, pp. 94–5, p. 100; *South West Tribune*, 20 August 1931, p. 5.
24. *West Australian*, 7 December 1932, p. 15.
25. *Daily News*, 15 June 1933, p. 1.
26. *West Australian*, 15 June 1933, p. 13.
27. *West Australian*, 16 June 1933, p. 19.
28. Patricia Quinn, archivist, Bank of New South Wales to Jenny Mills, 22 February 1978, Bunning Family Manuscript Collection.

29 Mills, *The Timber People*, p. 101.
30 *West Australian*, 2 August 1933, p. 4; Mills, *The Timber People*, pp. 79–82.
31 Gavin Bunning on behalf of the Executors of the Estate of the Late Robert Bunning to the Commissioner of Stamps, 18 March 1937; Mills, *The Timber People*, pp. 97–8.
32 Mills, *The Timber People*, p. 101.
33 Gavin Bunning, Biographical notes on Tom Bunning.
34 *West Australian*, 2 October 1933, p. 5.
35 *Mirror*, 6 July 1935, p. 20.
36 Gavin Bunning, Biographical notes on Tom Bunning.
37 Mills, *The Timber People*, pp. 103–7.
38 *Daily News*, 15 January 1934, p. 7.
39 Robert Bunning to G. M. Bunning, 17 August 1935, Bunning Family Manuscript Collection.
40 Robert Bunning to Bunning Brothers, 7 July 1935, Bunning Family Manuscript Collection.
41 Robert Bunning to G. M Bunning, 18 October 1935, Bunning Family Manuscript Collection.
42 See weekly memos and telegrams to Robert Bunning, April–November 1935, Bunning Family Manuscript Collection.
43 Robert Bunning to G. M. Bunning, 8 November 1935, Bunning Family Manuscript Collection
44 Cited in Mills, *The Timber People*, p. 102.
45 Mills, *The Timber People*, pp. 109–16.
46 Handwritten notes, inside the envelope 'Letters from Robert Bunning', Bunning Family Manuscript Collection; see also *West Australian*, 13 August 1936. A clipping of this newspaper column is inside the envelope.
47 Mills, *The Timber People*, pp. 112–14.
48 Mills, *The Timber People*, p. 115.
49 Mills, *The Timber People*, pp. 108–9; G. Bunning on behalf of the Executors of the Estate of the Late Robert Bunning to the Commissioner of Stamps, 18 March 1937.
50 *Daily News*, 3 February 1930, p. 6; 'Margot Dorothy Bunning, 1914–2006', *West Australian*, 12 January 2007, p. 45.
51 *Daily News*, 5 March 1934, p. 7; *Daily News*, 13 January 1934, p. 12.
52 *Daily News*, 8 December 1934, p. 1.
53 *Western Mail*, 24 September 1936, p. 27.
54 G. M. Bunning, 'Prisoner of War Diary' [typescript of original diary], 31 December 1943, pp. 215–16, Bunning Family Manuscript Collection; *West Australian*, 6 May 1938, p. 6.
55 *West Australian*, 10 December 1937, p. 10.
56 *West Australian*, 6 May 1938, p. 6; see also *Sunday Times*, 2 May 1937, p. 27, and 12 December 1937, p. 29; and *West Australian*, 21 August 1937, p. 8.
57 Gavin L. Bunning, 'Biographical notes on Tom Bunning'.
58 *West Australian*, 30 August 1937, p. 6.
59 *West Australian*, 5 September 1938, p. 16.
60 *Western Mail*, 15 September 1938, p. 4.
61 *West Australian*, 5 November 1938, p. 9; see also *Sunday Times*, 13 November 1938, p. 13.
62 Mills, *The Timber People*, pp. 116–22.

NOTES

63 R. Jamieson, 'An Interview with Flora M. Bunning, July–August 1984: Music in Western Australia' (J. S. Battye Library of Western Australian History, Oral History Programme, 1985, p. 10.
64 Moore, *From the Ground Up*, pp. 95–108.
65 Mills, *The Timber People*, p. 119.
66 *West Australian*, 12 February 1939, p. 10.
67 *Sunday Times*, 30 October 1932, p. 5.
68 *Western Mail*, 11 January 1940, p. 20.
69 G. M. Bunning, 'Prisoner of War Diary', 29 August 1943, pp. 191–2.
70 Gavin L. Bunning, interview with the author, Peppermint Grove, 31 May 2019.
71 Attestation papers in 'Bunning Gavin Macrae, WX3542', Item 6457832 AA Series B883, National Archives of Australia.
72 *West Australian*, 14 March 1939, p. 9.
73 *West Australian*, 22 August 1939, p. 11.

4. Officer, husband, father

1 Attestation Papers in 'Bunning Gavin Macrae, WX3542', Item 6457832 AA Series B883, National Archives of Australia.
2 P. Dennis, J. Grey, et al. (eds), *The Oxford Companion to Australian Military History*, Melbourne University Press, 1995, pp. 371–2.
3 L. Cody, *Ghosts in Khaki: The history of the 2/4th Machine Gun Battalion*, Victoria Park, WA, 1997, p. 8; M. Ewen, *Colour Patch: The men of the 2/4th Australian Machine Gun Battalion*, Victoria Park, WA, 2003, p. 4.
4 Cody, *Ghosts in Khaki*, pp. 7–8.
5 G. M. Bunning to Margot Bunning, undated [late-November 1940], Bunning Family Manuscript Collection.
6 G. M. Bunning to Margot Bunning, 6 January 1941, Bunning Family Manuscript Collection.
7 G. M. Bunning to Margot Bunning, undated [late-November 1940].
8 *West Australian*, 24 December 1940, p. 6.
9 Ewen, *Colour Patch*, see inside cover.
10 *Kalgoorlie Miner*, 24 December 1940, p. 4.
11 *West Australian*, 7 January 1941, p. 4; *West Australian*, 26 November 1940, p. 4.
12 *Western Mail*, 12 June 1941, p. 16
13 Cody, *Ghosts in Khaki*, pp. 12–14.
14 G. M. Bunning, 'Prisoner of War Diary' [typescript of original diary], 26 August 1942, p. 87, Bunning Family Manuscript Collection.
15 Cody, *Ghosts in Khaki*, pp. 18–19.
16 Cody, *Ghosts in Khaki*, pp. 25–6.
17 G. Odgers, *100 Years of Australians at War*, New Holland, Sydney, 2003, pp. 104–11.
18 Cody, *Ghosts in Khaki*, pp. 16–23.
19 G. M. Bunning to Margot Bunning, undated [late July 1941], Bunning Family Manuscript Collection.
20 G. M. Bunning to Margot Bunning, 26 July 1941, Bunning Family Manuscript Collection.

NOTES

21 G. M. Bunning to Margot Bunning, 26 July 1941.
22 G. M. Bunning to Margot Bunning, 1 August 1941, Bunning Family Manuscript Collection.
23 G. M. Bunning to Margot Bunning, 2 August 1941, Bunning Family Manuscript Collection
24 G. M. Bunning to Margot Bunning, 8 August 1941, Bunning Family Manuscript Collection.
25 G. M. Bunning to Margot Bunning, 13 August 1941, Bunning Family Manuscript Collection.
26 G. M. Bunning to Margot Bunning, 5 and 11 August, Bunning Family Manuscript Collection
27 G. M. Bunning to Robert and Pauline Law, 18 August 1941, Bunning Family Manuscript Collection
28 G. M. Bunning to Margot Bunning, telegram, 23 August 1941, Bunning Family Manuscript Collection.
29 G. M. Bunning to Margot Bunning, 25 August 1941, Bunning Family Manuscript Collection.
30 G. M. Bunning to Margot Bunning, 25 August 1941.
31 G. M. Bunning to Margot Bunning, 23 September 1941, Bunning Family Manuscript Collection
32 Cody, *Ghosts in Khaki*, p. 44, p. 56.
33 G. M. Bunning to Margot Bunning, 7 November 1941, Bunning Family Manuscript Collection.
34 G. M. Bunning to Margot Bunning, 19 and 24 October 1941, Bunning Family Manuscript Collection.
35 See Service and Casualty form in 'Brooksbank Albert WX9316', Item 6456871, Series B8883, National Archives of Australia.
36 G. M. Bunning to Margot Bunning, undated [late September 1941], Bunning Family Manuscript Collection.
37 G. M. Bunning to Margot Bunning, 16 November 1941, Bunning Family Manuscript Collection.
38 G. M. Bunning to Margot Bunning, 16 November 1941.
39 G. M. Bunning to Margot Bunning, 10 November 1941, Bunning Family Manuscript Collection.
40 G. M. Bunning to Margot Bunning, 3 December 1941, Bunning Family Manuscript Collection.
41 G. M. Bunning to Margot Bunning, 3 December 1941, Bunning Family Manuscript Collection.
42 G. M. Bunning to Margot Bunning, 10 November 1941, Bunning Family Manuscript Collection.
43 G. M. Bunning to Margot Bunning, 10 November 1941.
44 G. M. Bunning to Margot Bunning, 3 December 1941.
45 G. M. Bunning to Margot Bunning, 16 November 1941.
46 G. M. Bunning to Margot Bunning, 24 November 1941, Bunning Family Manuscript Collection.
47 G. M. Bunning to Margot Bunning, 11 and 14 December 1941 Bunning Family Manuscript Collection.
48 G. M. Bunning to Margot Bunning, 3 December 1941.

NOTES

49 G. M. Bunning to Margot Bunning, 17 and 25 December 1941, Bunning Family Manuscript Collection.
50 G. M. Bunning to Margot Bunning, 27 December 1941, Bunning Family Manuscript Collection.
51 G. M. Bunning to Margot Bunning, 1 January 1942, Bunning Family Manuscript Collection.
52 G. M. Bunning, Transcript of interview with S. M. Howroyd, 1 August 1983, Bunning Family Manuscript Collection (original in Scotch College archives), p. 6.
53 G. M. Bunning to Margot Bunning, 12 January and 18 January 1942, Bunning Family Manuscript Collection.
54 G. M. Bunning, interview with S. M. Howroyd, 1 August 1983, pp. 6–7.
55 L. Wigmore, *The Japanese Thrust*, Australia in the War of 1939–1945, Series 1 – Army, Vol. 4, Australian War Memorial, Canberra, pp. 284–7.
56 Cody, *Ghosts in Khaki*, pp. 99–100.
57 Wigmore, *The Japanese Thrust*, pp. 210–11.
58 Cody, *Ghosts in Khaki*, pp. 101–2.
59 Wigmore, *The Japanese Thrust*, pp. 289–90.
60 Wigmore, *The Japanese Thrust*, pp. 309–12.
61 Wigmore, *The Japanese Thrust*, pp. 314–17.
62 Ewen, *Colour Patch*, p. 179.
63 Wigmore, *The Japanese Thrust*, p. 324.
64 Wigmore, *The Japanese Thrust*, pp. 328–30.
65 Cody, *Ghosts in Khaki*, pp. 134–6.
66 G. M. Bunning, 'Prisoner of War Diary', May 1942, pp. 38–41.
67 Cody, *Ghosts in Khaki*, pp. 156–7.
68 Wigmore, *The Japanese Thrust*, pp. 354–5.
69 Cody, *Ghosts in Khaki*, pp. 152–4.
70 Wigmore, *The Japanese Thrust*, p. 363.
71 Ewen, *Colour Patch*, p. 81, p. 85.
72 Wigmore, *The Japanese Thrust*, pp. 371–81.
73 G. M. Bunning, 'Prisoner of War Diary', 29 March 1942, p. 1.
74 G. M. Bunning, 'Prisoner of War Diary', 29 March 1942, p. 1.
75 G. M. Bunning, 'Prisoner of War Diary', 29 March 1942, p. 2.
76 Margot Bunning to Gavin MacRae Bunning, 27 June 1942, Family Manuscript Collection.
77 G. M. Bunning, 'Prisoner of War Diary', 29 March 1942, pp. 2–4.
78 G. M. Bunning, 'Prisoner of War Diary', 29 March 1942, pp. 4–5.
79 G. M. Bunning, 'Prisoner of War Diary', 29 March 1942, pp. 4–5.
80 G. M. Bunning, 'Prisoner of War Diary', 10 April 1942, p. 21.
81 Odgers, *100 Years of Australians at War*, p. 137.
82 Ewen, *Colour Patch*, p. 4.
83 G. M. Bunning, 'Prisoner of War Diary', 1 March 1942, p. 11.

5. Prisoner of war

1. A. J. Sweeting, 'Prisoners of the Japanese', in L. Wigmore, *The Japanese Thrust*, Australia in the War of 1939–1945, Series 1 – Army, Australian War Memorial, Canberra, 1957, 4:511; L. Cody, *Ghosts in Khaki: The history of the 2/4th Machine Gun Battalion*, Hesperian Press, Victoria Park, WA, 1997, p. 189.
2. G. M. Bunning, 'Prisoner of War Diary', 29 March 1942, p. 10.
3. Sweeting, 'Prisoners of the Japanese', p. 515; Cody, *Ghosts in Khaki*, p. 195.
4. G. M. Bunning, 'Prisoner of War Diary', 1 March 1942, pp. 6–7.
5. G. M. Bunning, 'Prisoner of War Diary', 1 March 1942, p. 10.
6. G. M. Bunning, 'Prisoner of War Diary', 29 March 1942, p. 9.
7. G. M. Bunning, 'Prisoner of War Diary', April 1989, p. 336.
8. G. M. Bunning, 'Prisoner of War Diary', 18 March 1945, p. 304.
9. G. M. Bunning, 'Prisoner of War Diary', 23 August 1942, pp. 84–5.
10. G. M. Bunning, 'Prisoner of War Diary', 1 March 1942, p. 10.
11. Sweeting, 'Prisoners of the Japanese', p. 514; G. M. Bunning, 'Prisoner of War Diary', 1 March 1942, p. 13.
12. Cody, *Ghosts in Khaki*, p. 196.
13. G. M. Bunning, 'Prisoner of War Diary', 1 March 1942, p. 10.
14. G. M. Bunning, 'Prisoner of War Diary', 1 March 1942, pp. 10–11.
15. G. M. Bunning, 'Prisoner of War Diary', 1 April 1942, pp. 13–14; see also Sweeting, 'Prisoners of the Japanese', pp. 515–16.
16. G. M. Bunning, 'Prisoner of War Diary', 1 May 1942, p. 31.
17. G. M. Bunning, 'Prisoner of War Diary', 2 April 1942, p. 15; 4 May 1942, p. 32.
18. G. M. Bunning, 'Prisoner of War Diary', 2 April 1942, p. 15; 3 April 1942, p. 16.
19. G. M. Bunning, 'Prisoner of War Diary', 3 April 1942, p. 17.
20. Margot Bunning to G.M. Bunning, 27 June 1942, Bunning Family Manuscript Collection.
21. G. M. Bunning, 'Prisoner of War Diary', 14 May 1942, p. 36; Sweeting, 'Prisoners of the Japanese', p. 519.
22. G. M. Bunning, 'Prisoner of War Diary', 8 May 1942, pp. 33–4.
23. G. M. Bunning, 'Prisoner of War Diary', 10 June, pp. 53–4.
24. G. M. Bunning, 'Prisoner of War Diary', 24 July 1942, p. 70.
25. G. M. Bunning, 'Prisoner of War Diary', 1 April 1942, p. 16 and passim.
26. G. M. Bunning, 'Prisoner of War Diary', 8 August 1942, p. 76.
27. G. M. Bunning, 'Prisoner of War Diary', 28 June 1942, p. 60.
28. G. M. Bunning, 'Prisoner of War Diary', 31 July 1942, pp. 76–7; 18 August 1942, pp. 81–2.
29. 'Changi', *Encyclopedia of the Australian War Memorial*, accessed 7 February 2025. https://www.awm.gov.au/articles/encyclopedia/pow/changi
30. G. M. Bunning, 'Prisoner of War Diary', 6 September 1942, p. 92.
31. G. M. Bunning, 'Prisoner of War Diary', 2 October 1942, pp. 104–5; 7 October 1942, pp. 106–7.
32. G. M. Bunning, 'Prisoner of War Diary', 14 October 1942, p. 110; and G. M. B. Bunning, 'Ideals of a POW', in files of notes and ephemera from Changi Prison, Bunning Family Manuscript Collection.
33. G. M. Bunning, 'Prisoner of War Diary', 14 October 1942, p. 110.

NOTES

34   G. M. Bunning, 'Prisoner of War Diary', 3 October 1942, p. 106.

35   G. M. Bunning, 'Prisoner of War Diary', 4 November 1942, p. 117.

36   G. M. Bunning, 'Prisoner of War Diary', 8 November 1942, p. 118.

37   G. M. Bunning, 'Prisoner of War Diary', 17 November 1942, p. 121; 30 October 1942, p. 116; 8 January 1943, p. 139.

38   G. M. Bunning, 'Prisoner of War Diary', 11 December 1942, p. 128.

39   G. M. Bunning, 'Prisoner of War Diary', 19 May 1942, p. 40.

40   G. M. Bunning, 'Prisoner of War Diary', 28 December 1942, pp. 136–7.

41   G. M. Bunning, 'Prisoner of War Diary', 15 February 1943, pp. 147–8.

42   G. M. Bunning, 'Prisoner of War Diary', 7 February 1943, p. 145.

43   Margot Bunning to G. M. Bunning, 3 February 1943; and Telegram to Margot Bunning, 8 January 1943, Bunning Family Manuscript Collection.

44   Margot Bunning to G. M. Bunning, 25 August 1942, Bunning Family Manuscript Collection.

45   Margot Bunning to G. M. Bunning, 29 September 1942, Bunning Family Manuscript Collection.

46   Margot Bunning to G. M. Bunning, date removed but March 1943 [marked 'read 1/5/44'], Bunning Family Manuscript Collection.

47   G. M. Bunning, 'Prisoner of War Diary', 17 January 1943, p. 141.

48   G. M. Bunning, 'Prisoner of War Diary', 24 January 1943, p. 142.

49   G. M. Bunning, 'Prisoner of War Diary', 23 March 1943, p. 155.

50   G. M. Bunning, 'Prisoner of War Diary', 22 December 1942, p. 133.

51   G. M. Bunning, 'Prisoner of War Diary', 17 March 1943, p. 154.

52   G. M. Bunning, 'Prisoner of War Diary', 9 April 1943, p. 160.

53   G. M. Bunning, 'Prisoner of War Diary', 21 April 1943, p. 163

54   G. M. Bunning, 'Prisoner of War Diary', 3 July 1943, p. 180; 22 July 1943, p. 185.

55   G. M. Bunning, 'Prisoner of War Diary', 28 December 1942, pp. 134–5.

56   G. M. Bunning, 'Prisoner of War Diary', 21 June 1943, p. 177.

57   G. M. Bunning, 'Prisoner of War Diary', 24 July 1942, p. 69.

58   G. M. Bunning, 'Prisoner of War Diary', 6 July 1943, pp. 180–1.

59   G. M. Bunning, 'Prisoner of War Diary', 14 October 1942, p. 204.

60   G. M. Bunning, 'Prisoner of War Diary', 27 November 1942, pp. 124–5.

61   G. M. Bunning, 'Prisoner of War Diary', 12 September 1942, p. 95; 20 September 1942, p. 100.

62   Margot Bunning to G. M. Bunning, 23 May 1943, Bunning Family Manuscript Collection.

63   G. M. Bunning, 'Prisoner of War Diary', 30 May 1943, p. 172.

64   G. M. Bunning, 'Prisoner of War Diary', 24 September 1943, p. 197.

65   G. M. Bunning, 'Prisoner of War Diary', 4 December 1943, p. 211.

66   G. M. Bunning, 'Prisoner of War Diary', 18 December 1943, p. 214.

67   G. M. Bunning, 'Prisoner of War Diary', 1 April 1942, pp. 14–15.

68   G. M. Bunning, 'Prisoner of War Diary', 18 December 1943, p. 214.

69   G. M. Bunning, 'Prisoner of War Diary', 17 January 1944, p. 220.

70   G. M. Bunning, 'Prisoner of War Diary', 17 January 1944, pp. 220–1.

71   G. M. Bunning, 'Prisoner of War Diary', 17 January 1944, p. 222.

72   G. M. Bunning, 'Prisoner of War Diary', 24 February 1944, p. 228.

NOTES

73 G. M. Bunning, 'Prisoner of War Diary', 27 October 1943, p. 207.
74 G. M. Bunning, 'Prisoner of War Diary', 12 and 18 April 1944, pp. 238–9.
75 G. M. Bunning, 'Prisoner of War Diary', 30 May 1944, p. 250.
76 G. M. Bunning, 'Prisoner of War Diary', 4 June 1944, p. 251.
77 G. M. Bunning, 'Prisoner of War Diary', 7 May 1944, p. 243.
78 G. M. Bunning, 'Prisoner of War Diary', 23 August 1944, pp. 264–5; 29 September 1944, p. 272; 27 October 1944, p. 274.
79 G. M. Bunning, 'Prisoner of War Diary', 16 September 1944, p. 268.
80 G. M. Bunning, 'Prisoner of War Diary', 5 November 1944, p. 276.
81 G. M. Bunning, 'Prisoner of War Diary', 5 November 1944, p. 276.
82 Sweeting, 'Prisoners of the Japanese', p. 531.
83 G. M. Bunning, 'Prisoner of War Diary', 8 June 1945, p. 318; 14 July 1945, p. 323.
84 Sweeting, 'Prisoners of the Japanese', 11 February 1945, p. 298.
85 G. M. Bunning, 'Prisoner of War Diary', 11 February 1945, p. 298; 9 March, pp. 301–2.
86 G. M. Bunning, 'Prisoner of War Diary', 11 July 1945, p. 323; 7 August 1945, p. 326.
87 G. M. Bunning, 'Prisoner of War Diary', 31 July 1945, pp. 325–6.
88 G. M. Bunning, 'Prisoner of War Diary', 26 July 1945, p. 325.
89 G. M. Bunning, 'Prisoner of War Diary', 20 August 1945, p. 328.
90 G. M. Bunning, 'Prisoner of War Diary', 20 August 1945, p. 328.
91 G. M. Bunning, 'Prisoner of War Diary', 23 August 1945, p. 329.
92 G. M. Bunning, 'Prisoner of War Diary', 27 August 1945, p. 330; 31 August, pp. 331–2; 1 September, p. 332; 2 September, p. 333.
93 G. M. Bunning to Margot Bunning, 12 September 1945 and 15 September 1945, Bunning Family Manuscript Collection.
94 G. M. Bunning to Margot Bunning, 7 September 1945, Bunning Family Manuscript Collection.
95 G. M. Bunning to Margot Bunning, 10 September 1945, Bunning Family Manuscript Collection.
96 G. M. Bunning to Gavin Bunning, 12 September 1945, Bunning Family Manuscript Collection.
97 G. M. Bunning to Margot Bunning, 27 September 1945, Bunning Family Manuscript Collection.
98 G. M. Bunning to Margot Bunning, 27 September 1945 and 28 December 1945, Bunning Family Manuscript Collection.

6. Back to work

1 *Sunday Times*, 20 April 1969, p. 41.
2 P. Holmes, interview with the author, 2 May 2019.
3 Lecture notes by G. M. Bunning, undated [but early 1950s], Bunning Family Manuscript Collection.
4 P. Ellery, '1945–1960', in P. Firkins (ed), *A History of Commerce and Industry in Western Australia*, University of Western Australia Press, Nedlands, 1979, pp. 118–22.
5 J. Mills, *The Timber People: A History of Bunnings Ltd*, Bunnings Ltd, Perth, 1986, pp. 144–7.

NOTES

6   G. M. Bunning, 'Prisoner of War Diary' [typescript of the original diary], 12 July 1942, p. 67, Bunning Family Manuscript Collection.

7   G. M. Bunning, 'Prisoner of War Diary', 18 March 1944, pp. 233–4.

8   G. M. Bunning to G. L. Bunning, 12 September 1945, Bunning Family Manuscript Collection.

9   Margot Bunning to G. M. Bunning, 24 November 1942, and Flora Bunning to G. M. Bunning, undated but marked as read on 20 May 1944, Bunning Family Manuscript Collection.

10   Helen Bunning to G. M. Bunning, 24 June 1942, Bunning Family Manuscript Collection.

11   Helen Bunning to G. M. Bunning, 10 August 1942, Bunning Family Manuscript Collection.

12   Charles Bunning to Tom Bunning, undated but c. 1943, Bunning Family Manuscript Collection.

13   G. M. Bunning, 'Prisoner of War Diary', 18 March 1944, pp. 233–4.

14   *West Australian*, 24 January 1946, p. 1.

15   Anon, 'Bunning Profiles', Bunning Family Manuscript Collection.

16   Millars and Bunnings, Shipbuilders, Auditors Report and Accounts, 31 December 1945, Bunning Family Manuscript Collection; see also *West Australian*, 2 July 1946, p. 4.

17   Bunning Timber Holdings Ltd, *The Bunning Story*, Bunning Timber Holdings Ltd, Perth, p. 4.

18   Mills, *The Timber People*, p. 143.

19   B. Moore, *From the Ground Up: Bristile, Whittakers and Metro Brick in Western Australian History*, University of Western Australia Press, Nedlands, 1987, pp. 149–53; Mills, *The Timber People*, p. 159.

20   'Minutes of Meeting of Directors', Bunning Bros, 26 August 1946, Bunning Family Manuscript Collection.

21   Mills, *The Timber People*, p. 147.

22   Mills, *The Timber People*, p. 130, p. 145.

23   'Minutes of Meeting of Directors', Bunning Bros, 26 August 1946.

24   Mills, *The Timber People*, p. 149.

25   'Bunning Brothers Ltd. 27th July 1945' [contains a list of employees who served in WWII, with name, date of enlistment, and date of joining company], Bunning Family Manuscript Collection.

26   Gavin L. Bunning, Biographical notes on Tom Bunning, Bunning Family Manuscript Collection.

27   Mills, *The Timber People*, p. 134, p. 142.

28   Gavin L. Bunning, Biographical notes on Tom Bunning.

29   'Brooksbank Albert WX9316', Item 6456871, Series B8883, National Archives of Australia.

30   Gavin L. Bunning, Biographical notes on Tom Bunning.

31   *Sunday Times*, 22 September 1946, p. 15.

32   Gavin L. Bunning, Biographical notes on Tom Bunning.

33   Sue Hovell, Eulogy for Margot Bunning, 20 November 2006, Bunning Family Manuscript Collection.

34   Moore, *From the Ground Up*, p. 146; see also *West Australian*, 23 September 1947, p. 1.

35   Sue Hovell, Eulogy for Margot Bunning.

36   *West Australian*, 17 December 1951, p. 17; and Gavin L. Bunning, Biographical notes on Tom Bunning.

NOTES

37 Mills, *The Timber People*, pp. 149–50; C. Fox, 'Industrial Welfare in the South West Timber Industry of Western Australia, 1945–1954', *Studies in Western Australian History*, 2024, 36:59–78.
38 Mills, *The Timber People*, p. 148.
39 Mills, *The Timber People*, p. 154.
40 'Minutes of a Meeting of the Directors', Bunning Bros, 10 July 1950, Bunning Family Manuscript Collection.
41 'Minutes of a Meeting of the Directors', Bunning Bros, 28 July 1950, Bunning Family Manuscript Collection; see also *West Australian*, 17 April 1946, p. 11; 28 February 1947, p. 8; *Sunday Times*, 30 December 1951, p. 2.
42 Mills, *The Timber People*, p. 149.
43 'Minutes of an Extraordinary General Meeting', Bunning Bros, 27 September 1949, Bunning Family Manuscript Collection.
44 'Minutes of an Extraordinary General Meeting', Bunning Bros, 27 September 1949; see also Mills, *The Timber People*, p. 154.
45 'Minutes of an Extraordinary General Meeting', Bunning Bros, 27 September 1949.
46 Ellery, '1945–1960', pp. 119–20.
47 'Minutes of a Meeting of the Directors', Bunning Bros, 28 August 1950, Bunning Family Manuscript Collection.
48 'Minutes of a Meeting of the Directors', Bunning Bros, 28 August 1950.
49 Mills, *The Timber People*, p. 158.
50 'Minutes of a Meeting of the Directors', Bunning Bros, 13 March 1950, Bunning Family Manuscript Collection.
51 Mills, *The Timber People*, p. 133.
52 G. M. Bunning, 'Prisoner of War Diary', 18 March 1944, p. 233.
53 Gavin L. Bunning, Biographical notes on Tom Bunning.
54 J. Gregory, *Building a Tradition: A History of Scotch College 1897–1996*, University of Western Australia Press, Nedlands, pp. 425–6.
55 Albert Brunini, interview with the author, 2 May 2019; Gavin L. Bunning, interview with the author, 31 May 2019.
56 *Countryman*, 25 May 1950, p. 18.
57 Mills, *The Timber People*, pp. 159–61.
58 *West Australian*, 1 September 1950, p. 4.
59 *West Australian*, 30 August 1950, p. 1.
60 Mills, *The Timber People*, p. 160–1.
61 *West Australian*, 1 November 1950, p. 3.
62 *West Australian*, 6 October 1950, p. 3.
63 Legislative Council and Legislative Assembly of Western Australia, *Parliamentary Debates* [hereafter WAPD], 31 October 1950, p. 1535.
64 *West Australian*, 31 August 1950, p. 3; see also, *West Australian*, 6 September 1951, p. 2.
65 *West Australian*, 10 October 1950, p. 9. Wild's response appears in *West Australian*, 11 October 1959, p. 10.
66 *West Australian*, 10 October 1950, p. 9.

67	Quoted in Mills, *The Timber People*, p. 161.
68	L. Layman, 'Development Ideology in Western Australia, 1933–1965', *Historical Studies*, 1982, 20(79):240–1.
69	WAPD, 7 November 1950, pp. 1702–3.
70	WAPD, 31 October 1950, p. 1535.
71	*Sunday Times*, 5 November 1950, p. 5.
72	Government of Western Australia, 'Joint Select Committee Report into the Provisions of the Kauri Timber Company Limited Agreement Bill' (First session of the Twentieth Parliament, 28 November 1950).
73	L. T. Carron, *A History of Forestry in Australia*, Australian National University Press, Canberra, 1985, p. 154.
74	*West Australian*, 25 April 1951, p. 5.
75	Minutes of a Meeting of the Directors, Bunning Bros, 2 May 1950, Bunning Family Manuscript Collection.
76	Ralph Bower's letter of resignation, 14 February 1965, Bunning Family Manuscript Collection; see also Mills, *The Timber People*, p. 170.
77	Mills, *The Timber People*, p. 172.
78	Mills, *The Timber People*, pp. 172–3.
79	*West Australian*, 27 March 1952, p. 18.
80	*West Australian*, 29 March 1952, p. 9.
81	G. J. Rodger, *Report of the Royal Commission Appointed to Inquire into and Report upon Forestry and Timber Matters in Western Australia*, Government Printer, Perth, 1952, p. 55.
82	Rodger, *Report of the Royal Commission*, p. 57.
83	Rodger, *Report of the Royal Commission*, p. 55.
84	Mills, *The Timber People*, pp. 162–3.
85	R. Jamieson, *Charles Court: I love this place*, St George's Books, Osborne Park, WA, 2011, p. 47.
86	G. M. Bunning, 'Prisoner of War Diary', 31 July 1945, p. 325.
87	Gavin L. Bunning, interview with the author, 31 May 2019.
88	G. M. Bunning, Travel diary, 18 April 1952, Bunning Family Manuscript Collection.
89	G. M. Bunning, Travel diary, April–June 1952.
90	G. M. Bunning, Travel diary, June–October 1952.

7. Ploughing back the profits

1	H. P. Downing, 'First Report of the Directors', in Bunning Timber Holdings Ltd. First Report and Balance Sheet, Bunning Timber Holdings, 1953, Bunning Family Manuscript Collection.
2	'Notes of Meeting of Senior Staff of Bunning Bros Pty Ltd, Held at Head Office on Friday 4 December 1953', Bunning Family Manuscript Collection.
3	Downing, 'First Report of the Directors'.
4	L. Layman, 'Development Ideology in Western Australia', *Historical Studies*, 1982, 20(79):234–26.
5	P. Pendal, 'Hawke, Albert Redvers (Bert) (1900–1986)', *Australian Dictionary of Biography*, National Centre of Biography, Australian National University, Canberra,

2007 [hardcopy], accessed online 25 May 2021. https://adb.anu.edu.au/biography/hawke-albert-redvers-bert-12608/text22711
6 *Daily News*, 31 August 1950, p. 2.
7 'Notes of Meeting of Senior Staff of Bunning Bros Pty Ltd', 4 December 1953.
8 G. L. Bunning, Biographical Notes on Tom Bunning, Bunning Family Manuscript Collection.
9 Layman, 'Development Ideology in Western Australia, 1933–1965', p. 242.
10 B. Moore, *From the Ground Up: Bristile, Whittakers and Metro Brick in Western Australian History*, University of Western Australia Press, Nedlands, 1987, p. 211.
11 Nor'-West Whaling Company Ltd, Nor'-West Whaling Company, Perth, 1957.
12 H. P. Downing, Second Report of the Directors, in 'Bunning Timber Holdings Ltd. Second Report and Balance Sheet', Bunning Timber Holdings, 1954, Bunning Family Manuscript Collection.
13 C. Fox, 'Industrial Welfare in the South West Timber Industry of Western Australia, 1945–1954', *Studies in Western Australian History*, 2024, 36:59–78.
14 H. P. Downing, 'Chairman's Address, 26 September 1955', Bunning Timber Holdings, 1955, Bunning Family Manuscript Collection.
15 'Minutes, Meeting of Directors of Bunning Bros', 16 May 1955, Bunning Family Manuscript Collection; Gavin L. Bunning, interview with the author, 31 May 2019.
16 J. Mills, *The Timber People: A History of Bunnings Ltd*, Bunnings Ltd, Perth, 1986, pp. 192–3.
17 Mills, *The Timber People*, p. 190.
18 Gavin Bunning, interview with the author, 24 July 2019.
19 G. M. Bunning, 'Prisoner of War Diary', 17 January 1944, p. 221, typescript of original diary, Bunning Family Manuscript Collection.
20 G. Bunning, interview with the author, 24 July 2019.
21 G. L. Bunning, Biographical Notes on Tom Bunning.
22 *Countryman*, 2 June 1955, p. 44.
23 H. P. Downing, 'Chairman's Address, 24 September 1956', Bunning Timber Holdings, 1956, Bunning Family Manuscript Collection.
24 Moore, *From the Ground Up*, pp. 166–7.
25 J. McIlwraith, 'New, Charles Richard (1914–1989)', *Australian Dictionary of Biography*, National Centre of Biography, Australian National University, Canberra, 2012 (hardcopy), accessed online 11 February 2025, https://adb.anu.edu.au/biography/new-charles-richard-14984/text26173; Gavin Bunning, interview with the author, 24 July 2019.
26 H. P. Downing, 'Chairman's Address, 24 September 1956'.
27 C. R. Bunning, 'Chairman's Address, 28 September 1959', Bunning Timber Holdings, 1959, Bunning Family Manuscript Collection.
28 S. Ward, 'The Hawke Government's Unfair Trading and Profit Control Legislation, 1956–59', *Papers in Labour History*, 1999, 22:25–6.
29 D. Black, 'Liberals Triumphant', in C. T. Stannage (ed), *A New History of Western Australia*, University of Western Australia Press, Nedlands, 1981, pp. 451–2.
30 L. T. Carron, *A History of Forestry in Australia*, Australian National University Press, Canberra, 1985, p. 157.

31 H. P. Downing, 'Chairman's Address, 24 September 1956'; C. R. Bunning, 'Chairman's Address, 30 September 1957', Bunning Timber Holdings, 1957, Bunning Family Manuscript Collection.
32 Mills, *The Timber People*, pp. 190–1.
33 C. R. Bunning, 'Chairman's Address, 28 September 1959'.
34 G. L. Bunning, 'Bunnings in Darwin 1950s & 60s', email to author, 7 July 2020.
35 *Canberra Times*, 21 November 1961, p. 5.
36 G. M. Bunning, Travel diary, entries for 3, 4 and 7 July 1959, Bunning Family Manuscript Collection.
37 F. K. Crowley, *State Election: The Fall of the Hawke Government*, the author, Perth, 1959, p. 22; Mills, *The Timber People*, p. 183.
38 Ward, 'The Hawke Government's Unfair Trading and Profit Control Legislation', pp. 24–6.
39 G. M. Bunning's CV, Bunning Family Manuscript Collection.
40 Ward, 'The Hawke Government's Unfair Trading and Profit Control Legislation', pp. 44–5; Layman, 'Development Ideology in Western Australia, 1933–1965', p. 255.
41 A. G. Smith, 'Interim Report No.6 of the Royal Commission of the Western Australian Government Railways', *Royal Commission on the Western Australian Government Railways*, Perth, 1958, p. 3.
42 Legislative Council and Legislative Assembly of Western Australia, *Parliamentary Debates* [hereafter WAPD], 8 October 1958, p. 1325.
43 Crowley, *State Election*, p. 25.
44 Smith, 'Interim Report No.6 of the Royal Commission of the Western Australian Government Railways', p. 16.
45 *West Australian*, 8 October 1958, p. 1.
46 WAPD, 25 September 1958, p. 1120.
47 Crowley, *State Election*, p. 25.
48 Quoted in Layman, 'Development Ideology in Western Australia, 1933–1965', pp. 256–7. The letter appeared in *Financial Times*, 28 May 1958, p. 8.
49 *West Australian*, 9 October 1958, p. 1, p. 10.
50 *West Australian*, 9 October 1958, p. 1, p. 10.
51 C. R. Bunning, 'Chairman's Address, 28 September 1960', Bunning Timber Holdings, 1959, Bunning Family Manuscript Collection; 'Minutes, Meeting of Directors of Bunning Bros', 5 May 1958, Bunning Family Manuscript Collection.
52 Mills, *The Timber People*, pp. 186–7.
53 R. Harris, 'To Market! To Market! The Changing Role of the Australian Timber Merchant, 1945–c. 1965', *Australian Economic History Review*, 2000, 40:33.
54 Minutes, Meeting of Directors of Bunning Bros, 18 November 1958, Bunning Family Manuscript Collection.
55 Mills, *The Timber People*, pp. 192–3.
56 Gavin Bunning, interview with the author, 24 July 2019.
57 Crowley, *State Election*, p. 9.
58 Crowley, *State Election*, p. 9.
59 Gavin Bunning to Tom Bunning, 16 March 1959, Bunning Family Manuscript Collection.

NOTES

60 Crowley, *State Election*, p. 9.
61 Sue Bunning to Margot Bunning, 25 March 1959, Bunning Family Manuscript Collection.
62 G. M. Bunning, Travel diary, entries for late February and March 1959.
63 G. McEachran and P. J. Ryan, *Cottesloe Golf Club: A Centenary History*, Cottesloe Golf Club, Swanbourne, 2010, p. 763.
64 G. L. Bunning, Biographical notes on Tom Bunning.
65 G. M. Bunning, Travel diary, entries for November 1960.
66 Layman, 'Development Ideology', p. 257.
67 L. Layman, 'Dumas, Sir Russell John (1887–1975)', *Australian Dictionary of Biography*, National Centre of Biography, Australian National University, Canberra, 1996 (hardcopy), accessed online 24 July 2021. https://adb.anu.edu.au/biography/dumas-sir-russell-john-10059/text17743
68 D. Lipscombe, '1960–1979', in P. Firkens (ed), *A History of Commerce and Industry in Western Australia*, University of Western Australia Press, Nedlands, 1979, p. 139.
69 J. Mills, handwritten notes on July 1959, Bunning Family Manuscript Collection; Mills, *The Timber People*, p. 194.
70 Tom Bunning to Gavin Bunning, 22 August 1960, Bunning Family Manuscript Collection; G. M. Bunning, Memo, May 1987 (document 7443A, Bunning Timber Holdings), Bunning Family Manuscript Collection.
71 Letter from Tom Bunning to Gavin Bunning [undated, but early 1961], Bunning Family Manuscript Collection
72 J. Mills, handwritten notes on 28 January 1958 and 24 March 1958, Bunning Family Manuscript Collection.
73 C.R. Bunning, 'Chairman's Address, 28 September 1960'.
74 J. Mills, handwritten notes on November 1960, Bunning Family Manuscript Collection.
75 C. R. Bunning, 'Chairman's Address, 25 September 1961', Bunning Timber Holdings, 1961, Bunning Family Manuscript Collection; C. R. Bunning, 'Chairman's Address, 28 September 1960'; Gavin L. Bunning, interview with the author, 24 July 2019.
76 *Timberlines*, December 1968.
77 Layman, 'Development Ideology', pp. 258–9.
78 Lipscombe, '1960–1979', pp. 139–40.
79 Mills, *The Timber People*, p. 195.
80 Black, 'Liberals Triumphant', pp. 460–1; G. Bolton, *Land of Vision and Mirage: Western Australian since 1826*, University of Western Australia Press, Crawley, 2008, pp. 154–5.
81 Moore, *From the Ground Up*, pp. 237–8.
82 C. R. Bunning, 'Chairman's Address, 25 September 1961'.
83 Tom Bunning to Gavin Bunning, 5 May 1961, Bunning Family Manuscript Collection.
84 WAPD, 8 October 1958, pp. 1324–5.
85 Mills, *The Timber People*, p. 195.
86 G. M. Bunning, Travel diary, entries for late June and July 1961.
87 Tom Bunning to Gavin Bunning, 22 August 1960, Bunning Family Manuscript Collection.
88 Gavin L. Bunning, email to author, 14 January 2025.
89 G. M. Bunning, Travel diary, 24 June 1961.

90   G. M. Bunning, Travel diary, 27 June 1961.

91   Moore, *From the Ground Up*, pp. 237–37. *West Australian*, 27 June 1961, p. 1, p.7; *West Australian*, 8 July 1961, p. 2.

92   G. M. Bunning, Travel diary, entries for late July and August 1961.

8. Hard-headed innovation

1   C. R. Bunning, 'Chairman's Address, 25 September 1961', Bunning Timber Holdings, 1961, Bunning Family Manuscript Collection.

2   G. M. Bunning, interview with S. M. Howroyd [transcript], 1 August 1983, Bunning Family Manuscript Collection (original in Scotch College archives).

3   G. M. Bunning, Travel diary, 5 August 1961, Bunning Family Manuscript Collection.

4   C. R. Bunning, 'Chairman's Address, 25 September 1961'.

5   J. Mills, *The Timber People: A History of Bunnings Ltd*, Bunnings Ltd, Perth, 1986, p. 204.

6   G. M. Bunning, interview with Jenny Mills, c. 1983 [handwritten notes], Bunning Family Manuscript Collection; Mills, *The Timber People*, pp. 203–4.

7   C. R. Bunning, 'Chairman's Address, 25 September 1961'.

8   *South Western Times*, 24 October 1963, pp. 31–8.

9   *Timberlines*, September 1968.

10   *Albany Advertiser*, 18 May 1962, p. 2.

11   *Albany Advertiser*, 18 May 1962, p. 2.

12   *West Australian*, 27 June 1962.

13   B. Moore, *From the Ground Up: Bristile, Whittakers and Metro Brick in Western Australian History*, University of Western Australia Press, Nedlands, 1987, pp. 198–202.

14   G. M. Bunning, interview with Jenny Mills, c. 1983; see also R. Harris, 'To Market! To Market! The Changing Role of the Australian Timber Merchant, 1945–c. 1965', *Australian Economic History Review*, 2000, 40:15–32.

15   'Timber Industry Review', *Countryman*, 2 June 1955, pp. 29–52.

16   *Timberlines*, December 1969.

17   G. L. Bunning, interview with the author, 24 July 2019.

18   Mills, *The Timber People*, p. 202; Bunning Timber Holdings Ltd, *The Bunning Story*, Bunning Timber Holdings Ltd, Perth, p. 6.

19   G. M. Bunning, Memo on meeting with Main Roads Department, 24 July 1962, in 'West Perth Resumption', Bunning Family Manuscript Collection.

20   C. R. Bunning, 'Chairman's Address, September 1964', Bunning Timber Holdings, 1964, Bunning Family Manuscript Collection; Mills, *The Timber People*, p. 202.

21   J. Seward to G. M. Bunning, 21 November 1966, in 'Bunning Park Estate', Bunning Family Manuscript Collection; C. R. Bunning, 'Chairman's Address, 27 September 1965', Bunning Timber Holdings, 1965, Bunning Family Manuscript Collection.

22   G. M. Bunning, interview with Jenny Mills; Mills, *The Timber People*, pp. 195–6.

23   J. Hutton, *Manufacturing Industry and Western Australian Development*, University of Western Australia Press, Nedlands, 1966, pp. 121–2.

NOTES

24 Bunning Timber Holdings, *The Bunning Story*, Bunning Timber Holdings, Perth, 1964, p. 16; *Albany Advertiser*, 28 May 1962, p. 2; *South Western Times*, 29 October 1963, special feature on 'WA's One Stop Building Supply Centre'.

25 *West Australian*, 11 October 1966, p. 64; A Kerr, *The South-West Region of Western Australia*, University of Western Australia Press, Nedlands, 1965, pp. 57–66.

26 *West Australian*, 11 October 1966, p. 64.

27 Memorandum to C. R. and G. M. Bunning on desirable set-up for Bunning Bros Pty Ltd Head Office, 24 July 1962, in 'West Perth Resumption', Bunning Family Manuscript Collection.

28 J. Gregory, *City of Light: A History of Perth Since the 1950s*, City of Perth, 2003, pp. 105–6.

29 F. Downing, 'Some aspects of Compensation', c. 1966, in 'West Perth Resumption', Bunning Family Manuscript Collection.

30 C. R. Bunning, 'Chairman's Address, 27 September 1965', Bunning Timber Holdings, 1965, Bunning Family Manuscript Collection; Bunning Timber Holdings, board minutes, 21 February 1966 [handwritten notes], Bunning Family Manuscript Collection.

31 G. M. Bunning, 'Notes on the History of the Cliffe', Bunning Family Manuscript Collection.

32 G. L. Bunning, interview with the author, 31 May 2019.

33 J. J. Taylor, 'Mervyn Henry Parry (1913–2006)', *Western Australian Architect Biographies*, accessed 30 December 2021. http://www.architecture.com.au/i-cms?page=13453; G. L. Bunning, Biographical notes on G. M. Bunning, Bunning Family Manuscript Collection.

34 House plans in '41 McNeil St', Bunning Family Manuscript Collection.

35 G. L. Bunning, Biographical notes on G. M. Bunning.

36 *Beverley Times*, 27 September 1963, p. 1.

37 G. L. Bunning, Biographical notes on G. M. Bunning.

38 G. L. Bunning, Biographical notes on G. M. Bunning.

39 Moore, *From the Ground Up*, 1987, pp. 193–6.

40 *Fisheries Newsletter*, August 1963, 22(8):19.

41 Bunning Timber Holdings, board minutes, 16 December 1965 [handwritten notes], Bunning Family Manuscript Collection; Mills, *The Timber People*, p. 206.

42 Bunning Timber Holdings, board minutes, 21 October 1965 [handwritten notes], Bunning Family Manuscript Collection.

43 C. R. Bunning, 'Chairman's Address, 27 September 1965'.

44 *Australian Financial Times*, 29 July 1964.

45 C. R. Bunning, 'Chairman's Address, 28 September 1964', Bunning Timber Holdings, 1964, Bunning Family Manuscript Collection; Mills, *The Timber People*, p. 206.

46 G. L. Bunning, interview with the author, 24 July 2019; *West Australian*, 11 October 1966, p. 64.

47 Bunning Timber Holdings, board minutes, 16 February 1965 [handwritten notes], Bunning Family Manuscript Collection.

48 Interview with Gavin Bunning, 24 July 2019.

49 Interview with Gavin Bunning, 24 July 2019.

50 C. R. Bunning, 'Chairman's Address, 3 October 1966', Bunning Timber Holdings, 1966, Bunning Family Manuscript Collection.

51 *West Australian*, 11 October 1966.

52 Associated Sawmillers and Timber Merchants of Western Australia, 'Forestry Matters', notes of meeting with Conservator of Forests, 2 May 1966, Bunning Family Manuscript Collection.

53 L. T. Carron, *A History of Forestry in Australia*, Australian National University Press, Canberra, 1985, pp. 159–60.

54 C. R. Bunning, 'Chairman's Address, 2 October 1967', Bunning Timber Holdings, 1967, Bunning Family Manuscript Collection.

55 R. Underwood, 'Harris, Allan Cuthbert (Bluey) (1904–1996)', *Australian Dictionary of Biography*, National Centre of Biography, Australian National University, published online 2020, accessed 10 January 2022. https://adb.anu.edu.au/biography/harris-allan-cuthbert-bluey-18448/text37061

56 Associated Sawmillers and Timber Merchants of Western Australia, 'Forestry Matters', notes of meeting with Conservator of Forests, 2 May 1966, Bunning Family Manuscript Collection.

57 G. M. Bunning to Charles Bunning, no date but mid-1966, Bunning Family Manuscript Collection.

58 G. M. Bunning, Travel diary, entries for May–August 1966, Bunning Family Manuscript Collection.

59 Bunning Timber Holdings, 'Board Minutes for 26 August and 26 September 1966' [handwritten notes], Bunning Family Manuscript Collection.

60 Bunning Timber Holdings, 'Board Minutes for 21 July 1966' [handwritten notes], Bunning Family Manuscript Collection.

61 D. Lipscombe, '1960–1979', in P. Firkins (ed), *A History of Commerce and Industry in Western Australia*, University of Western Australia Press, Nedlands, 1979, pp. 141–2.

62 C. R. Bunning, 'Chairman's Address, 2 October 1967'.

63 *The Bunning Story*, p. 6; Bunning Timber Holdings, 'Board Minutes, 21 February 1966' [handwritten notes], Bunning Family Manuscript Collection.

64 Bunning Timber Holdings, 'Board Minutes for October 1966' [handwritten notes], Bunning Family Manuscript Collection.

65 C. R. Bunning, 'Chairman's Address, 2 October 1967'.

66 Charles Court, Minister for Industrial Development, to John McEwan, Minister for Trade & Industry, 14 August 1967, in Forests Department item 005422F1506 'Use of Wood Utilization – Reconstituted Wood – Paper Pulp and Chip Japan [FD19670083]', cons. 5607, State Records Office of Western Australia [hereafter SROWA].

67 M. R. Jacobs, Director-General, Department of National Development, Forestry and Timber Bureau, to Allan Harris, Conservator of Forests, 2 May 1967; and Harris to Stewart Bovell, Minister for Forests, 14 June 1967, in Forests Department Item 005422F1506, SROWA.

68 Lipscombe, '1960–1979', pp. 156–7.

69 Charles Court to John McEwan, 14 August 1967, in Forests Department item 005422F1506, SROWA.

70 Roger Bryce, Managing Director, Hawker Siddeley Building Supplies, to Charles Court, Minster for Industrial Development, 3 July 1967, in Forests Department item 005422F1506, SROWA.

71 G. M. Bunning, Bunning Bros Pty Ltd, to Alan Harris, Conservator of Forests, 1 August 1967, in Forests Department item 005422F1506, SROWA.

NOTES

72 Mills, *The Timber People*, pp. 216–18.
73 Roger Bryce to Alan Harris, 18 July 1967, in Forests Department item 005422F1506, SROWA.
74 Roger Bryce to Alan Harris, 14 August 1967, in Forests Department item 005422F1506, SROWA.
75 G. M. Bunning to Alan Harris, 1 August 1967, in Forests Department item 005422F1506, SROWA.
76 Notes of Jenny Mills's interview with Tom, Bunning Family Collection.
77 G. M. Bunning to Alan Harris, 1 August 1967, in Forests Department item 005422F1506, SROWA.
78 G. M. Bunning, interview with Jenny Mills.
79 Alan Harris to G. M. Bunning, 9 August 1967, in Forests Department item 005422F1506, SROWA.
80 G. M. Bunning to Alan Harris, 17 August 1967, in Forests Department item 005422F1506, SROWA.
81 Alan Harris to G. M. Bunning, 9 August 1967, in Forests Department item 005422F1506, SROWA.
82 Press Statement, August 1967, in Forests Department item 005422F1506, SROWA.
83 *West Australian*, 15 August 1967.
84 Millars Timber and Trading Company Ltd to Alan Harris, Conservator of Forests, 22 September 1967, in Forests Department item 005422F1506, SROWA.
85 G. M. Bunning to Alan Harris, 22 September 1967, in Forests Department item 005422F1506, SROW; Warren and Manjimup Times, 25 October 1967, p. 1.
86 C. R. Bunning, Bunning Bros Pty Ltd, to Charles Court, 26 October 1967, in Forests Department item 005422F1506, SROWA.
87 Court to Bovell, 30 October 1967, in Forests Department item 005422F1506, SROWA. The advertisement appeared in the *Sunday Times*, 12 November 1967.
88 Bunning Timber Holdings Ltd, Toyo Menka, Kaisha Ltd & The Kokusaku Pulp Industry Co. Ltd, 'Clarification of Proposals for Western Australian Wood Chip – Paper Pulp Project, as required following briefing from The Minister for Industrial Development on 10th April, 1968', Perth, 29 May 1968, Bunning Family Manuscript Collection; see also *West Australian*, 8 December 1967.
89 Bunning Timber Holdings Ltd, Toyo Menka, Kaisha Ltd & The Kokusaku Pulp Industry Co. Ltd, 'Clarification of Proposals for Western Australian Wood Chip – Paper Pulp Project'.
90 C. R. Bunning, 'Chairman's Address, 1 October 1968', Bunning Timber Holdings, 1968, Bunning Family Manuscript Collection.
91 C. R. Bunning, 'Chairman's Address, 2 October 1967'.
92 *Timberlines*, September 1968.
93 Bunning Timber Holdings, board minutes, 25 January 1968 [handwritten notes], Bunning Family Manuscript Collection; Mills, *The Timber People*, pp. 205–6.
94 'Bunning Bros Pty Ltd West Perth – Yard & Head Office Compensation Claim', Bunning Family Manuscript Collection.
95 *Sunday Times*, 20 April 1969.
96 *Bulletin*, 24 August 1968, p. 56.

97 Legislative Council and Legislative Assembly of Western Australia, *Parliamentary Debates*, 2 October 1968, p. 1401.
98 *West Australian*, 3 October 1968, p. 1, p. 8.
99 Channel 7 historical news collection, 'Segment 14/10, Wood chips agreement', TVW Channel 7, Perth, 28 June 1969, accessed 12 January 2022. https://encore.slwa.wa.gov.au/iii/encore/record/C__Rb6549672
100 Bob Bunning, interview with the author, 22 May 2019.
101 Lipscombe, '1960–1979', pp. 155–8.
102 *The Bunning Story*, p. 3.
103 *Sunday Times*, 20 April 1969, p. 41.
104 *Sunday Times*, 20 April 1969, p. 41.
105 G. McEachran and P. Ryan, *Cottesloe Golf Club*, p. 187.
106 G. L. Bunning, interview with the author, 24 July 2019.

9. Buying back the farm

1 G. M. Bunning, Travel diary, 28 November to 13 December 1968 (and following pages of notes on visit to Japan), Bunning Family Manuscript Collection.
2 Malcolm Fraser, 'Australian Industry Development Corporation', 24 May 1970, University of Melbourne, Malcolm Fraser Radio Talks Transcripts, accessed 8 February 2023. https://digitised-collections.unimelb.edu.au/items/c217d3d1-2db5-5edd-8b3c-ae00c9dfff80
3 G. M. Bunning, 'The Merger with Hawker Siddeley Group Ltd', 22 November 1988, in *G. M. Bunning, Bunnings–Hawker Siddeley Merger* [unpublished manuscript], Bunning Family Manuscript Collection.
4 G. M. Bunning, transcript of interview with S. M. Howroyd, 1 August 1983, Bunning Family Manuscript Collection (original in Scotch College archives).
5 G. M. Bunning to Sue Bunning, 5 December 1970, Bunning Family Manuscript Collection.
6 G. M. Bunning, 'Conclusion', in *G. M. Bunning, Bunnings–Hawker Siddeley Merger*, p. 3.
7 G. M. Bunning, travel diary, 26 May 1970.
8 G. M. Bunning, 'Presidential Address', The *West Australian* Chamber of Manufacturers, 6 October 1969, printed copy in Bunning Family Manuscript Collection.
9 Charles Court, Minister for Industrial Development, to director, Department of Industrial Development, 15 June 1970, in Department of Industrial Development file 1970/454, 'Bunning Timber Holdings & Hawker Siddeley Building Supplies – proposed merger of timber interests', Cons. 1687, State Records Office of Western Australia [hereafter SROWA].
10 D. Lipscombe, '1960–1979', in P. Firkins (ed), *A History of Commerce and Industry in Western Australia*, University of Western Australia Press, Nedlands, 1979, p. 158.
11 Minute on Hawker Siddeley Building Supplies/Bunnings for the Minister for Industrial Development, 11 June 1970, in Department of Industrial Development file 1970/454, SROWA.
12 C. R. Bunning and R. A. Bryce, 'Bunnings–Hawker Siddeley Merger', 1 July 1970, in G. M. Bunning, Bunnings–Hawker Siddeley Merger.
13 C. R. Bunning to the manager, Australian Broadcasting Corporation, 12 June 1970, in G. M. Bunning, Bunnings–Hawker Siddeley Merger.

NOTES

14 'Conclusion', in *G. M. Bunning, Bunnings–Hawker Siddeley Merger*.
15 G. M. Bunning to G. L. Bunning, 8 October 1970, Bunning Family Manuscript Collection.
16 Tom Dawson, 'Recollections of Tom Bunning', Bunning Family Manuscript Collection.
17 *Timberlines*, June 1971, p. 3.
18 G. M. Bunning, 'Conclusion', in *G. M. Bunning, Bunnings–Hawker Siddeley Merger*, pp. 5–6.
19 'The Timber Industry in Western Australia' [undated typescript], Bunning Family Manuscript Collection.
20 Senior Assistant Crown Solicitor to Downing & Downing, 7 January 1971, Bunning Family Manuscript Collection; see also *West Australian*, 30 June 1971.
21 C. R. Bunning, 'Chairman's Address, 4 October 1971', Bunning Timber Holdings, 1971, Bunning Family Manuscript Collection.
22 *Timberlines*, August 1973, p. 4.
23 *Canberra Times*, 20 November 1971, p. 22.
24 L. Purcell, 'Millars in Western Australia: Ninety Productive Years', in J. Dargavel (ed), *Sawing, Selling and Sons: Histories of Australian Timber Firms*, Centre for Resource & Environmental Studies, Australian National University, Canberra, 1988, p. 249.
25 L. T. Carron, *A History of Forestry in Australia*, Australian National University Press, Canberra, 1985, pp. 169–76.
26 Carron, *A History of Forestry in Australia*, pp. 169–76.
27 J. Mills, *The Timber People: A History of Bunnings Ltd*, Bunnings Ltd, Perth, 1986, p. 238, pp. 246–7.
28 Gavin L. Bunning, interview with the author, 24 July 2019.
29 Dolph Zink, interview with the author, 10 April 2019; *Timberlines*, spring 1984, pp. 3–4.
30 Gavin L. Bunning, interviews with the author, 31 May and 24 July 2019.
31 G. M. Bunning to C. R. Bunning, 7 April 1972, Bunning Family Manuscript Collection.
32 *Bulletin*, 8 September 1973, p. 28.
33 G. M. Bunning to G. L. Bunning, 8 October 1970, Bunning Family Manuscript Collection.
34 Sue Hovell, Eulogy for Margot Bunning, 20 November 2006, Bunning Family Manuscript Collection.
35 Sue Hovell, interview with the author, 6 September 2019; and Clive Hovell, interview with the author, 12 September 2019.
36 Merry & Merry accountants, valuation report on Perth Jarrah Mills, 29 May 1972, Bunning Family Manuscript Collection.
37 *West Australian*, 10 July 1973; *Bulletin*, 28 July 1973, p. 56.
38 B. Moore, *From the Ground Up: Bristile, Whittakers and Metro Brick in Western Australian History*, University of Western Australia Press, Nedlands, 1987, p. 209.
39 G. M. Bunning, 'An Executive Story', Bunning Timber Holdings internal memorandum, 21 October 1977, Bunning Family Manuscript Collection.
40 G. M. Bunning to C. D. MacQuaide, 12 June 1970, and C. D. MacQuaide to G. M. Bunning, 13 July 1970, in Bunnings–Hawker Siddeley Merger.
41 Mallesons Stephens Jacques to Bunnings Ltd, 6 August 1987, Bunning Family Manuscript Collection.

42 C. R. Bunning, 'Chairman's Address, 15 October 1974', Bunning Timber Holdings, 1974, Bunning Family Manuscript Collection.
43 C. R. Bunning, 'Chairman's Address, 10 October 1972', Bunning Timber Holdings, 1972, Bunning Family Manuscript Collection.
44 *West Australian*, 16 October 1974.
45 Carron, *A History of Forestry in Australia*, pp. 161–2.
46 Carron, *A History of Forestry in Australia*, pp. 171–3.
47 *Australian Fisheries*, 1973, 32(9):9.
48 C. R. Bunning, 'Chairman's Address, 15 October 1974'.
49 G. M. Bunning, 'Bunnings Forest Products Pty Ltd', Bunnings Ltd internal memorandum, May 1987, Bunning Family Manuscript Collection.
50 Gavin L. Bunning, interview with the author, 24 July 2019.
51 Gavin L. Bunning, interview with the author, 24 July 2019.
52 Gavin L. Bunning, interview with the author, 24 July 2019.
53 C. R. Bunning, 'Chairman's Address, 9 October 1973', Bunning Timber Holdings, 1973, Bunning Family Manuscript Collection.
54 *Timberlines*, June 1976, p. 2.
55 Legislative Council and Legislative Assembly of Western Australia, *Parliamentary Debates*, 24 August 1976, p. 2056.
56 *Bulletin*, 25 April 1978, pp. 36–7.
57 R. Chapman, 'The 1970s as a time of transition for Western Australian native forests protest', in M. Calver, H. Bigler-Cole, et al. (eds), *Proceedings of the 6th National Conference of the Australian Forest History Society*, Millpress Science Publishers, Rotterdam, 2005, pp. 247–50.
58 *West Australian*, 20 July 1976, p. 3.
59 Gavin L. Bunning, interview with the author, 24 July 2019.
60 J. Mills, *The Timber People*, pp. 248–9.
61 G. M. Bunning, Travel diary, entries for May 1976.
62 C. R. Bunning, 'Chairman's Address, 25 October 1976', Bunning Timber Holdings, 1976, Bunning Family Manuscript Collection
63 Mills, *The Timber People*, p. 241; handwritten notes on Bunning Timber Holdings board minutes, 6 May 1977, Bunning Family Manuscript Collection.
64 J. Mills, *The Timber People*, pp. 241–2.
65 'Analysis of Strategy: *Westralian* Forest Industries Ltd', Bunning Family Manuscript Collection.
66 Handwritten notes on Bunning Timber Holdings board minutes, 24 June 1977, Bunning Family Manuscript Collection.
67 Moore, *From the Ground Up*, pp. 225–6.
68 Grant Wark and Kerry Wark, interview with the author, 12 March 2019.
69 Gavin L. Bunning, interview with the author, 31 May 2019.
70 P. N. Hewett and J. B. Sclater, 'The development of pine logging in Western Australia', in M. Calver, H. Bigler-Cole, et al. (eds), *Proceedings of the 6th National Conference of the Australian Forest History Society*, Millpress Science Publishers, Rotterdam, 2005, p. 436.

NOTES

71 G. M. Bunning, 'Diversification as an element of Bunnings Development Strategy', Bunning Timber Holdings internal memorandum, December 1977, Bunning Family Manuscript Collection.
72 J. Craig MLA, speech notes at opening of Bunning Bros Welshpool Complex, 1 March 1978, Bunning Family Manuscript Collection.
73 G. M. Bunning, 'Diversification as an element of Bunnings Development Strategy'.
74 C. R. Bunning, 'Chairman's Address, 15 October 1978', Bunning Timber Holdings, 1978, Bunning Family Manuscript Collection.
75 G. M. Bunning, 'Diversification as an element of Bunnings Development Strategy'.
76 G. M. Bunning, 'Diversification as an element of Bunnings Development Strategy'.
77 P. Johnston, interview with the author, 15 May 2019.
78 G. L. Bunning, interview with the author, 24 July 2019.

10. Raiders and white knights

1   G. M. Bunning, 'Chairman's address, 27 October 1980', Bunnings Ltd, 1980, Bunning Family Manuscript Collection.
2   G. M. Bunning, 'To All Directors' [Bunnings Ltd internal memorandum], 16 April 1982, Bunnings Ltd, Bunning Family Manuscript Collection.
3   P. Johnston, 'Recollections of Tom Bunning' [undated typescript], Bunning Family Manuscript Collection; J. Mills, *The Timber People: A History of Bunnings Ltd*, Bunnings Ltd, Perth, 1986, p. 255.
4   G. M. Bunning, 'Where do we go from here?' [Bunning Timber Holdings internal memorandum], 4 January 1979, Bunning Family Manuscript Collection.
5   G. M. Bunning, 'Where do we go from here?'.
6   G. M. Bunning, 'Industrial Relations: Where are we going?' [Bunning Timber Holdings internal memorandum], 12 August 1979, Bunning Family Manuscript Collection.
7   C. R. Bunning, 'Chairman's address, 25 October 1978', Bunning Timber Holdings, 1978, Bunning Family Manuscript Collection.
8   Bunning Timber Holdings, 'Bunnings Ltd Group of Companies, Annual Report to Employees 1980–81', Bunnings Ltd, 1981, p. 3, Bunning Family Manuscript Collection.
9   Bunning Timber Holdings, 'Bunnings Ltd Group of Companies, Annual Report to Employees 1980–81', p. 1.
10 *Timberlines*, spring 1984, p. 23; Mills, *The Timber People*, p. 253.
11 'Bunnings Ltd Group of Companies, Annual Report to Employees 1980–81', p. 1; *Timberlines*, summer 1982, p. 2.
12 G. M. Bunning to G. L. Bunning, 'Report on visits to branches, 29 December 1980', Bunning Family Manuscript Collection.
13 'Bunnings Ltd Group of Companies, Annual Report to Employees 1980–81', pp. 1–3; and G. M. Bunning, 'Questionnaire to Directors' [Bunning Ltd internal memorandum], 16 February 1981, Bunning Family Manuscript Collection.
14 Press release, Bunning Bros, 23 April 1980, Bunning Family Manuscript Collection.
15 'Bunnings Ltd Group of Companies, Annual Report to Employees 1980–81', p. 2; *Timberlines*, summer 1982, p. 11.

16 'Bunnings Ltd Group of Companies, Annual Report to Employees 1980–81', p. 2; Bunnings Ltd, 'Bunnings Limited welcome you to the opening of the new Bunnings Engineering Works' [pamphlet], 11 March 1981, Bunning Family Manuscript Collection.
17 G. M. Bunning, 'Chairman's address, 26 October 1981', Bunnings Ltd, 1981, Bunning Family Manuscript Collection.
18 P. N. Hewett and J. B. Sclater, 'The development of pine logging in Western Australia', in M. Calver, H. Bigler-Cole, et al. (eds), *Proceedings of the 6th National Conference of the Australian Forest History Society*, Millpress Science Publishers, Rotterdam, 2005, p. 436.
19 G. Vitale, 'Bunnings – quality medium to long term growth stock', Hartley Poynton & Co, 1985, Bunning Family Manuscript Collection.
20 Gavin L. Bunning, interview with the author, 24 July 2019.
21 G. M. Bunning, back pages of diary covering 1980–89/90, Bunning Family Manuscript Collection.
22 Australian Government, Department of the Prime Minister and Cabinet, Australian Honours list, accessed 6 November 2023. https://honours.pmc.gov.au/honours/awards/871112
23 Gavin L. Bunning, interview with the author, 24 July 2019.
24 'Invitation from His Excellency the Governor to an Investiture', 20 March 1980, Bunning Family Manuscript Collection.
25 Itinerary, Board of The British Petroleum Company of Australia Limited, visit to Perth, 9th – 13th October 1982, Bunning Family Manuscript Collection.
26 S. Christie, Comalco & Dampier Salt, to Sir Charles Court, Premier of Western Australia, 8 May 1975, Bunning Family Manuscript Collection.
27 G. M. Bunning, 'Chairman's address, 25 October 1982', Bunnings Ltd, 1982, Bunning Family Manuscript Collection.
28 G. M. Bunning, 'A Review of the Business and Financial Scene' [Bunning Ltd internal memorandum], 13 August 1981, Bunnings Ltd, Bunning Family Manuscript Collection.
29 G. M. Bunning, 'Chairman's address, 26 October 1981'.
30 G. M. Bunning, 'Chairman's address, 25 October 1982'.
31 G. M. Bunning, 'Chairman's address, 25 October 1982'.
32 G. M. Bunning, 'Questionnaire to Directors'.
33 *Timberlines*, summer 1982, pp. 6–7.
34 G. M. Bunning, 'To All Directors'.
35 G. M. Bunning, 'Chairman's address, 25 October 1982'.
36 Peter Johnston, interview with the author, 15 May 2019; Michael Chaney, interview with the author, 31 May 2019.
37 *Financial Times*, 9 March 1983.
38 G. M. Bunning, 'Letter to the shareholders of Bunnings Ltd, 8 March 1981', Bunning Family Manuscript Collection; I. Kuba, interview with the author, 10 April 2019.
39 *Sunday Times*, 20 March 1983, p. 33.
40 Bunnings Ltd, 'Report of 1983–84 Operations', Bunnings Ltd, 1984, pp. 6–7, Bunning Family Manuscript Collection; Bunnings Ltd, 'Welcome to the Bunnings Group of Companies', Bunnings Ltd, 1985, Bunning Family Manuscript Collection.

41 Bunnings Ltd, 'Bunnings Ltd 33rd Annual Report', Bunning Ltd, 1984, pp. 1–9, Bunning Family Manuscript Collection.
42 G. E. Rundle, 'History of conservation reserves in the south-west of Western Australia', *Journal of the Royal Society of Western Australia*, 1996, 79(4):225–40.
43 Bunnings Ltd, 'Report of 1983–84 Operations'.
44 Extract from 1984 annual report in file of Tom Bunning's board papers, Bunning Family Manuscript Collection.
45 *Timberlines*, winter 1984, p. 6.
46 *Timberlines*, winter 1984, p. 6.
47 Barry Stanley and Herb Williams, interview with the author, 13 March 2019.
48 G. McEachran and P. J. Ryan, *Cottesloe Golf Club*, Cottesloe Golf Club, Swanbourne, 2010, pp. 186–9, 415–16, 429–30.
49 Richard Alder, interview with the author, 10 April 2019.
50 Bunnings Ltd, 'Schedule of Bunning Family Interest' [internal document], 7 July 1987, Bunning Family Manuscript Collection.
51 Vitale, 'Bunnings – quality medium to long term growth stock'.
52 'The Bunnings Family' [facsimile], 10 September 1987, Bunning Family Manuscript Collection.
53 Peter Johnston, interview with the author, 15 May 2019; Gavin L Bunning, interview with the author, 24 July 2019.
54 Gavin L. Bunning, interview with the author, 24 July 2019.
55 'Bunnings Ltd 33rd Annual Report', pp. 1–9; Bunnings Ltd, 'Bunnings Ltd 34th Annual Report', Bunnings Ltd, 1985, pp. 4–9, Bunning Family Manuscript Collection.
56 G. M. Bunning, 'Timber Marketing' [Bunnings Ltd internal memorandum], 16 January 1984, Bunning Family Manuscript Collection.
57 Vitale, 'Bunnings – quality medium to long term growth stock'; Mills, *The Timber People*, p. 258.
58 Mills, *The Timber People*, p. 250.
59 Ian Kuba, interview with the author, 10 April 2019.
60 G. Bolton, 'Foreword', in J. Mills, *The Timber People: A History of Bunnings Ltd*, Bunnings Ltd, Perth, 1986, p. v.
61 *West Australian*, 30 May 1986, pp. 110–11; *Timberlines*, centenary issue, 1986.
62 *Timberlines*, centenary issue, 1986, p. 14; A. Brunini, interview with the author, 2 May 2019.
63 *Timberlines*, centenary issue, 1986, p. 14.
64 Bolton, 'Foreword'.
65 Gavin Bunning, interview with the author, 24 July 2019; Peter Johnston, interview with the author, 15 May 2019.
66 Vitale, 'Bunnings – quality medium to long term growth stock'.
67 *Australian Financial Review*, 11 September 1987.
68 R. Sayer, *The CEO, the chairman and the board: Trevor Eastwood*, Hardie Grant, Prahran, Vic, 2009, pp. 162–5.

69 B. Bunning, 'Bunnings Ltd Discussion Paper' [Bunnings Ltd internal memorandum], 11 September 1987, Bunning Family Manuscript Collection; Mallesons Stephens Jacques to Bunnings Ltd, 6 August 1987.
70 *Australian Financial Review*, 11 September 1987.
71 G. M. Bunning, 'Bunnings Forest Products Pty Ltd', Bunning Ltd internal memorandum, May 1987, Bunning Family Manuscript Collection.
72 For context, see D. Zink, *An Unrepentant Dilettante: Reminiscence and Reflection*, Mayfair Press, Crawley, 1995, p. 134.
73 G. M. Bunning, Travel diary, entries for July–August 1987, Bunning Family Manuscript Collection.
74 'The Bunnings Family' [facsimile], 10 September 1987, Bunning Family Manuscript Collection.
75 *Australian Financial Review*, 11 September 1987.
76 G. M. Bunning, Travel diary, entries for December 1987.
77 Sayer, *The CEO, the chairman and the board*, pp. 164–5.
78 B. Bunning, 'Bunnings Ltd Discussion Paper'.
79 Mallesons Stephens Jacques to Bunnings Ltd, 6 August 1987.
80 The *West Australian* woodchip industry: WA Chip & Pulp Co Pty Ltd: report and recommendations of the Environmental Protection Authority, Environmental Protection Authority, Perth, 1988.
81 S. Shea and R. Underwood, 'Forests for the Future', *Landscape*, 1990, 6(1); Rundle, 'History of conservation reserves in the south-west of Western Australia', p. 238.
82 Clive Hovell, interview with the author, 12 September 2019.

11. The end of a dynasty

1 *Australian Financial Review*, 15 September 1987; *Australian Financial Review*, 24 September 1987.
2 G. M. Bunning, 'Where do we go from here?', Bunning Timber Holdings internal memorandum, 4 January 1979, Bunning Family Manuscript Collection.
3 *Australian Financial Review*, 15 September 1987; *Australian Financial Review*, 24 September 1987.
4 G. Vitale, 'Bunnings – quality medium to long term growth stock', Hartley Poynton & Co, 1985, Bunning Family Manuscript Collection.
5 G. Bolton, *Land of Vision and Mirage*, University of Western Australia Press, Crawley, 2008, pp. 178–83.
6 *Australian Financial Review*, 21 January 1988.
7 P. Thompson, *Wesfarmers 100: The People's Story*, University of Western Australia Publishing Custom, Crawley, 2014, p. 207.
8 'Invitation to G. M. and Mrs Bunning to a garden party at Government House', 7 April 1983, Bunning Family Manuscript Collection.
9 Michael Chaney, interview with the author, 31 May 2019; Thompson, *Wesfarmers 100*, pp. 2078.
10 Michael Chaney, interview with the author, 31 May 2019.

NOTES

11 Thompson, *Wesfarmers 100*, p. 207.
12 Michael Chaney, interview with the author, 31 May 2019.
13 *Australian Financial Review*, 23 March 1988.
14 *Timberlines*, January 1990, p. 17.
15 See Bunnings Ltd, 'Investment in the Future: The Story of WA's Biggest Tree Farming Venture', and 'Pines the Growing Alternative: The Story of WA's Biggest Pine Plantation', reprints from *Timberlines*, c. 1990, Bunning Family Manuscript Collection.
16 Bunnings Ltd, 'Bunnings Ltd, 39th Annual Report', Bunnings Ltd, 1990, pp. 2–4.
17 Bunnings Ltd, 'Bunnings Ltd, 40th Annual Report', Bunnings Ltd, 1991, pp. 4–6.
18 Ian Kuba, interview with the author, 10 April 2019.
19 Ian Mackenzie, 'Recommendations Arising out of the PA Report on Bunnings Organisational Structure'. Bunnings Ltd internal memorandum, 25 July 1990, Bunning Family Manuscript Collection.
20 Shea and Underwood, 'Forests for the Future'.
21 G. M. Bunning to Bob Bunning, 10 August 1990, Bunning Family Manuscript Collection.
22 Gavin L. Bunning, interview with the author, 24 July 2019.
23 Bunnings Ltd, '39th Annual Report'.
24 G. M. Bunning, Travel diary, entries for 1990, Bunning Family Manuscript Collection.
25 See correspondence in the file 'Tom's Siblings', Bunning Family Manuscript Collection.
26 Grandchildren of Tom Bunning (Rob, Devika, Rory, Duncan and Kirsty), interview with the author, 10 April 2019.
27 A copy of Tom's speech is in the file '2nd/4th Machine Gun Battalion', Bunning Family Manuscript Collection, and is reproduced in 'Borehole Bulletin', 1991, 2(14):14–16.
28 Margot had the diary properly conserved, and a printed version was presented to the Australian War Memorial.
29 *West Australian*, 13 March 1991, p. 13.
30 D. Zink, company memorandum, Bunnings Ltd, 12 March 1991, Bunning Family Manuscript Collection.
31 Carmen Lawrence, Premier of Western Australia, to Margot Bunning, 13 March 1991, Bunning Family Manuscript Collection.
32 Chamber of Western Australian Industry, Chairman's board notes, 21 March 1991, Bunning Family Manuscript Collection.
33 Jenny Mills, conversation with the author in October 2019.
34 Gavin Bunning, Eulogy for Tom Bunning, 15 March 1991, Bunning Family Manuscript Collection.
35 Gavin Bunning, interview with the author, 24 July 2019; *Australian Financial Review*, 21 October 1991.
36 R. Sayer, *The CEO, the chairman and the board: Trevor Eastwood*, Hardie Grant Books, Prahran, Vic, 2009, pp. 168–9.
37 G. Bunning, interview with the author, 24 July 2019.
38 *Australian Financial Review*, 18 February 1993.
39 *Australian Financial Review*, 10 May 1999.

40 *Australian Financial Review*, 26 May 1994. The figure of $543m for the takeover bid was reported in The *West Australian*: see undated newspaper clipping 'Wesfarmers bid puts a $543m tag on Bunnings', Bunning Family Collection. Peter Thompson puts the purchase price at $594 million: Thompson, *Wesfarmers 100*, p. 216.
41 Interview with Peter Johnston, 15 May 2019.
42 *Timberlines*, summer 1982, p. 4.
43 Bob Bunning, Eulogy for Charles Robert Bunning, Bunning Family Manuscript Collection.
44 Thompson, *Wesfarmers 100*, p. 233.
45 *Age*, 9 July 2004; *WA Business News*, 28 August 2000; *Australian Financial Review*, 1 September 2000.
46 Wesfarmers Ltd, 'Wesfarmers Announces $2.2 Billion Offer For Howard Smith', press release, 13 June 2001, accessed 22 February 2025. https://www.wesfarmers.com.au/docs/default-source/asx-announcements/wesfarmers-announces-2-2-billion-dollar-offer-for-howard-smith.pdf?sfvrsn=aa5698ba_0
47 Sue Hovell, Eulogy for Margot Bunning, 20 November 2006, Bunning Family Manuscript Collection; Sue Hovell, interview with the author, 6 September 2019.
48 *West Australian*, 12 January 2007, p. 45.
49 'The Law Report 1840–2015' [unpublished family history], Bunning Family Manuscript Collection.
50 *West Australian*, 1 January 2022.
51 G. M. Bunning, 'Chairman's Address, 25 October 1982', Bunnings Ltd, 1982, Bunning Family Manuscript Collection.
52 G. Bolton, 'Foreword', in J. Mills, *The Timber People: A History of Bunnings Ltd*, Bunnings Ltd, Perth, 1986, p. v.
53 For example: Thompson, *Wesfarmers 100: The People's Story*, 2014; and R. Sayer, *The CEO, the chairman and the board: Trevor Eastwood*, Hardie Grant Books, Prahran, Vic, 2009.

Index

11th Infantry Battalion, 22
18th Division, 77
1914 fire, 43
2/26th Battalion, 76
2/29th Battalion, 77–78
2/30th battalions, 79
2/4th Battalion
    as prisoners, 84, 99
    formation and training, 63–64, 67–68, 74, 77, 102, 256
    in combat, 69, 72, 76, 78, 80–81, 83, 94, 104
    postwar association, 117
22nd Brigade, 76–78
25th Light Horse Regiment, 62, 64
27th Brigade, 76–79, 90
44th Indian Brigade, 76
8th Division, 69, 72, 76, 78, 80–81, 84, 87, 94

A.I.F., 272, 275
Abrahams brothers
    as financiers, 12–13, 19, 24–26, 251
    in litigation, 30, 54
Abrahams, Emanuel, 12
Abrahams, Louis, 24, 30, 251
Adelaide
    as city, 70
    as company, 69, 71–73, 95, 113, 144, 147, 152, 160, 193, 233, 254, 256
    as river, 74
Adelaide Club, 70–71

Adelaide Timber Company, 147
AGM, 159, 176, 192, 214, 253, 262
AIDC, 189, 192, 198, 224, 228, 250
AIF
    as soldiers, 63, 65, 69, 72–74, 77, 79, 83, 85–87, 89–90, 94, 271
    in command, 274
Aintree Circuit, 156
Air Force, 69, 72, 79, 100
Albany, 2, 38, 53, 67, 161, 209
Alco chain, 237, 260
Alco Handyman, 253
Alcoa, 154
Alexandria, 22, 24
Alice Springs, 72
Alliance Française, 44
AMP, 121, 170, 224
Amtel Holdings, 252
Anderson, Bill, 26, 33, 35, 37, 46, 59
Anderson Peter Corsair (PC), 33, 35, 46
Anderson, Wally, 143, 150, 162, 171
Anglo-Iranian Oil Company, 135
Anketell, Michael, 64, 67, 71, 79, 81
Anzac Cove, 22
Anzac Day, 21
Anzac Memorial Chapel, 170
AO, 224–225, 251
Aquatania, 75
Arab oil embargo, 203
Argyle, 8–9, 12–13, 19, 29, 31, 42–43, 46, 51
Armadale, 8–9, 16, 142, 155, 184

INDEX

Armistice Day, 21
Army Medical Corps, 103
Army's Western Command, 68
Art Gallery of Western Australia, 264
Ascot Racecourse, 132, 174–175
Associated Sawmillers & Timber Merchants of Western Australia, 146, 155, 173
Atkins, William, 7, 214
Attlee, Clement, 174
Australia Club, 75
Australian Federation of Friends of Galleries and Museums, 264
Australian High Commissioner, 45, 132
Australian Imperial Force, see AIF
Australian Industry Development Corporation, 189
Australian Lumber Company, 31
Australian Open, 50
Australian Paper Manufacturers (APM) Ltd, 181
Australian Society of Accountants, 46
Australian timber industry, 102
Austria, 52

B Company
    casualties and transfers, 74, 99
    in camp life, 73, 84, 87, 93–94
    in combat, 76–79, 81, 85
Bairds, 138, 238
Balcatta, 222–223
bank nationalisation, 121
Bank of New South Wales, 26, 48–49
Banksiadale, 155
Barber, Elizabeth Blair, 128–129
Barrack Square, 271
Barrier Reef, 98
Battle of Britain, 63
Battle of Muar, 76
Battle of Singapore, 84
Battle of Sunda Straits, 74
bauxite mining, 154, 173, 194, 226, 229
BBC Hardware, 262–263
Bedfordale, 9

Benchmark, 119, 263
Bennett, Gordon, 81
Bentley, 164, 184
beri-beri, 88, 99, 105
BHP, 115, 127, 135, 152, 154
Birmingham, 22
Black Monday, 243
Black Tuesday, 243, 245, 249
Blackboy Hill, 22
Blackwood, 98
Boan Brothers, 7
Boans, 51, 138, 238
Boddington, 53, 60, 137, 150, 160, 171, 195, 209, 212, 229, 231
Boddington Pine Plantation, 231
Bolshoi Ballet, 156
Bolton, Geoffrey, 266
Bond, Alan, 240
Borneo, 87, 105, 160, 164
Borneo Timber Company, 164
Boros, Joe, 260
Boston, 174
Bovell, William, 177
Bower, Ralph, 129, 143, 162, 172
Brand, David, 152, 183
brickmaking, 16, 36, 60, 139, 201
brickworks
    as private enterprise, 7, 12, 16, 119
    as state facility, 2, 8, 36, 142, 155
Brierley, Ron, 240, 252
Brisbane, 105
Brisbane, David, 167
Brisbane and Wunderlich, 162, 201, 210
Bristile, 223
British Amateur Golf Championship, 33
British Grand Prix, 156
British Open, 156
British Petroleum (BP), 135, 139, 152, 165, 168, 170, 212, 224, 257
Broken Hill Pty Ltd, 115
Brooking, Pauline Bertha, 15
Broome, 54
Broome, 54, 88, 253–254

Bruce, Stanley, 37
Bruce, Stanley Melbourne, 174
Brussels, 52
Bryce, Roger, 177, 192
Buckland House, 4
Buick, 33–34, 40, 45, 115
building industry, 2–3, 7, 9, 137, 138, 139, 142–143, 154, 172, 204, 207, 209, 250
Building Supplies
    as company division, 17, 127, 142, 147, 155–156, 160–161, 165, 180, 190, 192–193, 230, 237, 260
    as product category, 162
building trade, 10, 17–18, 24, 110, 123, 161–162, 193, 222, 251, 264
Bunbury, 8–9, 14, 17, 19, 49, 58, 109, 122, 144, 160–161, 164, 181, 184, 186, 200, 208
Bunbury harbour, 181
Bunbury railway line, 8
Bunning, Arthur
    as family member, 1, 3, 40
    as manager, 2, 7, 12, 31, 39, 55
    as public official, 9, 76, 127, 239
Bunning Bros 9, 130, 192
    as employer, 18, 41, 111, 117, 127
    as family firm, 1–2, 9, 16–17, 26, 37, 39–40, 42, 53–54, 60, 100, 109–110, 114, 119–120, 125–126, 130, 148, 161, 192
    in financial distress, 10, 12, 19, 24–25, 29–30, 43, 48–49, 121
    in operations, 11, 13, 31, 46, 51, 63, 88, 97–98, 113, 122–123, 129, 149, 239, 251
Bunning Family
    as owners, 11, 24, 36, 60, 69, 115, 120, 130, 137, 164, 168, 183, 191, 195, 202, 213, 215, 222, 245, 247, 249, 252, 255, 258–260, 263, 266
    in biography, 21–22, 27–28, 38, 54, 58, 71, 82, 85, 103, 111, 134, 154, 196, 201, 229, 232–234, 238, 254, 256, 270
Bunning Timber Holdings
    in finance, 159, 184, 198, 214
    in operations, 130, 133, 138, 165, 170, 192, 204, 209, 221
    in ventures, 131, 181
Bunning, Charlie
    as chairman, 46, 109, 114, 125, 138, 163, 171, 186, 190, 198, 206, 208, 217, 220–221, 249, 258, 260
    as youth, 4, 28–29, 32–33, 94, 100, 113
    in business, 19, 26, 42, 44, 71, 111, 119, 123, 130, 146, 159, 161, 164–165, 167, 180, 191, 193, 215, 238–239, 259, 261
    in community, 55, 166
    in industry, 40–41, 51, 65, 122, 136–137, 143, 149, 174, 178–179, 184, 192, 216, 219, 224, 263
Bunning, Gavin MacRae,
    in business, 27, 40, 72–73, 88, 104, 111, 150, 153, 156, 163, 167, 173, 188, 194–196, 206, 220–221, 223, 230, 252, 260–261, 264
    in collection, 8, 140–141, 265
    in family, 1, 28, 71, 74, 80, 87, 93–94, 97, 100–101, 105, 107, 118, 123, 131, 139, 151, 185, 198–200, 210, 257–258
Bunning, Gordon
    as family member, 15, 57, 81, 135, 200, 202
    as public figure, 170, 229
Bunning, Helen, 1, 112
    as daughter, 9, 19, 51, 235
    as mother, 11–12, 112
    Gavin's wife, 1, 4, 6, 10, 22, 35, 40, 93–94, 104, 199–200, 210
Bunning, Jane, 59
Bunning, Joe, 109
    as family member, 3, 10, 44, 113, 188
    in business role, 24, 50, 55, 109, 114, 163, 200, 235, 260
    in military service, 21–22, 26
Bunning, Margot,
    as mother, 15, 26, 68, 70, 72, 91, 118, 139, 210
    as wife, 55, 57, 59, 61–62, 67, 93, 168, 233, 264

in business, 64, 73, 117, 167, 174, 190, 196, 200, 209, 214, 242, 251, 263

in correspondence, 35, 63, 69, 71, 74, 80, 84, 87, 94–95, 97, 99, 101–102, 105, 107, 131–132, 151, 156, 184, 198, 243, 254, 257–258, 269

in family collection, 56, 113, 115, 164, 175, 185, 202, 224–225, 234, 246

Bunning, Robert

as businessman, 3, 6–7, 9–14, 17–19, 24–26, 29–31, 33, 37, 39, 41–43, 46, 48–49, 51–52, 54, 55, 60, 110, 122, 142, 146, 150, 184, 193, 216, 235, 240, 251, 263

as descendant, 21, 137, 200, 239

in family, 1–2, 4, 8, 15–16, 22, 32, 34–36, 40, 44, 53–54, 57, 61, 64, 93, 113, 117, 139, 197, 214

Bunning, Sue, 118, 131, 139, 151, 156, 184–185, 188, 200–201, 210, 224, 234, 264–265

Bunning, Tom

as family member, 1, 3, 12, 15, 22, 32, 34, 53, 55, 57, 61, 93, 107, 113, 117–118, 123, 152, 166, 175, 185, 225, 232, 246, 258, 270

in business, 2, 7–8, 11, 16–17, 19, 26, 31, 40–42, 44, 48–49, 52, 60, 65–66, 88, 109–110, 114–115, 119, 121–122, 125–127, 129–131, 133–139, 143, 145–147, 150–151, 153, 155, 157, 159–160, 162–165, 167–168, 170–174, 176, 178–184, 186–196, 198, 200–204, 206, 208–210, 213–217, 219–223, 226–230, 235–236, 238–242, 244, 247, 249–253, 259, 261–263, 265–267

in golf, 27, 29, 33, 37–38, 43, 45–47, 50–51, 58–59, 132, 148, 211–212, 233–234, 243, 254

in military service, 21, 28, 35, 62, 64, 67–87, 89–92, 94–99, 101–106, 111–112, 144, 149, 156, 224, 256–257, 264, 269, 271

Bunning, Will, 45, 132

Bunnings

as retail chain, 42, 143, 195–196, 206–207, 222, 226–227, 238, 243, 260–264

as timber company, 4, 6, 12, 14, 16, 18, 24, 26, 30, 40, 48, 50, 52, 58, 60, 74, 76, 80, 84, 88, 94, 98, 102, 104, 110, 114, 120, 122, 126, 130, 132, 134, 136, 138, 142, 144, 146–149, 152–153, 155–157, 159–165, 170, 173, 176, 178–182, 184, 186, 188, 190, 192–194, 198, 202–204, 208–210, 212–214, 220, 223, 228–230, 234–235, 237, 242, 247, 251, 253

Bunnings group

as corporate actor, 192, 219

in industry development, 149, 180–181, 194, 240

Bunnings Ltd

as corporate entity, 221, 228, 230

in ownership, 229, 235, 243, 251

Bunnings Manufactured Homes, 184

Bunnings outlets, 253

Bunnings Super Centre, 207

Bunnings Tree Farms, 253, 262

Burke, Brian, 266

Burma, 76, 99

Burt, Septimus, 3

Busselton, 16, 64, 125, 156

Cable Beach Club, 253

Cairns, 113

California, 206, 234, 242

Californian redwood, 4

CALM, 230, 245

Calsil Ltd, 201

Campbell, G. G. 'Bull', 27

Campbell, Sally, 5, 10, 22

Canning Dam, 63

Canning Timber Company, 6

Cannington, 182, 193, 200

Cape Town, 174

Cardiff, 9

Cardup, 8, 11–12, 16

Carlisle, 192

INDEX

Carnac, 40
Casey, Richard, 166
Catlidge Cup, 46, 50, 118
cement
    as industry, 36, 60, 119, 125, 135, 146–147, 152, 162, 165, 261
    as material, 117
Ceylon, 31, 60, 143
chairman, 37, 138, 159, 168, 170, 189, 208, 217, 219–224, 227, 228, 230, 233, 241, 249, 253, 266
Chamber of Manufacturers, 182–184, 189, 191
Chaney, Michael, 250–252, 258
Changi, 80–81, 83–84, 87–89, 94–99, 101–102, 104–105, 111–112, 117, 131, 151, 254, 257, 269
Changi POW Camp, 96, 98
Charles Street
    as disaster site, 18, 48, 239
    as head office, 31, 49, 55, 74, 165, 187, 190, 193
    as public site, 122, 166
    in distribution
    in manufacturing, 25, 39–40, 42–43, 51, 114, 119–120, 123, 134, 137, 149, 160, 163, 171, 176
Chartwell Towers, 132
Chicago, 57, 174
Christian Brothers College, 29
Christmas Cards, 92
Christmas Cup, 118
Christmas Day, 91, 102
Churchill, Winston, 132
Citizen Finance, 240, 243
Claremont, 61
Clarkson, Helen, 199–200
Clifton, Joan, 33
Clough, Harold, 252
Clyde School, 35
coal mines, 117
Cockatoo Island, 115, 127
Cockburn Cement, 146–147, 152, 165
Colin Street
    as family home, 15, 26, 35–36, 70, 93
    as social venue, 55, 57, 59

Collie, 7, 9, 49, 117, 122, 176, 180
Collins, Walter, 9, 31, 39, 48
Cologne, 52
Colombo, 59, 157
Colonial Sugar Refinery, 113
Commemoration Cup, 58
Commonwealth Bank, 43, 48, 152
Commonwealth Employment Service, 111
Commonwealth Forestry Conference, 119
Commonwealth Games Committee, 170
Commonwealth Government, 13, 17, 121, 172
Commonwealth Insurance Company, 60
Commonwealth Military Force, 62
Commonwealth railways, 51, 136
Commonwealth Timber Control Board, 122
Commonwealth Timber Control Organisation, 65
Confederation of Western Australian Industry, 224
conservation, 6, 194, 203, 226–227, 230, 233, 237, 247, 262, 264
Conservator of Forests, 25, 30, 51, 127
Conservatorium, 44
consumer boycotts, 262
Cosmo Club, 51, 57
Cotswold
    as company, 63, 69, 139, 235
    as home, 61, 67, 88, 107, 115–116, 118, 122, 167
Cottesloe
    as golf club, 32–33, 37, 45–47, 50, 58–59, 117–118, 145, 151, 163, 188, 212, 233–234
    as suburb, 3, 9, 24, 57, 61, 75, 139
Cottesloe Beach, 9, 32, 117
Cottesloe Golf Club, 33, 37, 45, 58, 145, 188, 212, 233
Country Party, 150, 192
Court of Arbitration, 18
Court, Charles
    as premier, 125, 152, 208, 226
    in business, 131, 176, 258
Court, Richard, 262
Croatia, 211

CSBP, 250
CSR, 113, 127, 160, 210
Cullity family, 210
Cunderdin, 64
Curtin, John, 80
Cyclone Tracy, 209

Dalkeith, 200
Damascus, 176
Dampier Salt, 209–210, 224, 243
Daniel, 200, 225
Dardanup, 210
Darling Range, 3, 227
Darling Ranges, 8
Darling scarp, 167
Darwin
    as military site, 60, 72–74, 80, 88, 107
    in business, 105, 144, 153, 172–173, 184, 188, 195, 200, 209, 223, 228
Davies, Mary, 197
day-labour system, 142, 147, 152
Deanmill, 17, 192, 204
Democratic Labor Party, 150
Depression, 8, 41, 43, 48, 53, 60, 110, 126, 239, 244, 265
Donnelly River, 114, 119–120, 127, 129, 149, 204
Donnelly River Mill, 120, 127, 129
Douglas Fir, 3
Douglas Jones Pty Ltd, 194
Downing, Henry, 54, 114
Drysdale, Ron, 122–123, 239
Duke of Edinburgh, 198
Dumas, Russell, 152, 156
Dunbrick, 60, 119
Dutch East Indies, 83, 91
Dutch vessels, 75
Dwellingup, 147, 155, 192

East Perth, 2, 214
Eastwood, Trevor, 252
Education Endowment Trust, 212
Edwards, Keith, 212
Elders, 240

Empire Forestry Conference, 51
employees, 153, 187, 192, 209, 214, 216, 221, 228, 250, 263, 265
engineering works, 114, 119, 130, 193, 223, 226, 243
England, Robert, 8, 12
Environmental Protection Authority (EPA), 194, 203, 245
environmentalism, 203
ES&A Bank, 53, 181
Esperance, 172
Esplanade, 35, 167
Eucalyptus diversicolor, 6
Eucalyptus jacksonii, 160
Exmouth, 254

farm
    as industry asset, 117, 189–191, 193, 195, 203, 207, 209, 213, 215, 217, 245
    as rural estate, 4, 33, 88, 95, 100, 192, 201
Fish Protein Concentrate Pty Ltd, 204
Fitzhardinge, BR, 48–9
Fletcher Challenge, 240
Flinders Bay, 181
Forbes, Reg, 58
Foreign Takeovers Act, 244
Forest Products Association, 226
Forest Products division, 221, 237, 247, 253, 262
forests
    as industry, 51, 119, 127, 139, 162, 261–262
    as plantations, 113, 150, 176, 229
    as resource, 6, 13, 123, 126, 149, 155, 173, 179, 180, 209, 213, 226, 251
    dieback, 173
    in conservation, 25, 127, 194, 203, 226, 237, 262
    in management, 25, 26, 29–30, 51, 125, 130, 131, 174, 177–178, 216, 227, 230, 245, 265
Forests Act, 25, 29, 125, 127
Forests Department
    as regulator, 26, 30, 131, 173, 177, 180, 213, 230

    in industry relations, 126, 174, 178, 216
    in plantation development, 150, 209
Forests Forever, 226
Forrest, Andrew, 3
France, 63, 69, 86, 132
Fremantle, 2–4, 7, 9, 11, 17, 24, 32, 39, 42, 49–50, 58, 70, 75, 107, 113, 123, 153, 159, 168, 239
Freshwater Bay, 29, 167

Gage Roads, 75
Gallery Foundation, 264
Gallipoli, 22
Garden Island, 39–40, 55
Geraldton, 2, 54, 88
Germany, 22, 52, 62, 132, 151
Gibson, 238
GJ Rodger, 130
Glulam, 149, 152, 176
Goland, Billy, 29
goldfields, 2, 7, 9, 16, 43, 51, 53, 64
golf
    as competition, 33, 46, 59
    as leisure, 32, 45, 50, 95, 117–118, 145, 151, 174, 184, 188, 211, 233–234, 254
    in club life, 37, 58, 131–132, 212
Gorton, John, 183, 192
Government House, 224, 251
Governor-General, 166
Graham, Herb, 149
Great Britain, 51, 62
Great Depression, 41, 53, 126, 244, 265
Great War, 53, 251
Greenbushes, 210
Grimwade, 210, 223
Guards Division, 77
Guildford, 2, 62
Gunns, 262
Gurkha battalion, 77
Guy Fawkes Day, 102

hardware
    as products, 53, 122, 138, 150, 156, 160, 162–163, 221, 240, 262
    in retail, 137, 143, 161, 171, 188, 195, 206, 222–223, 228, 237, 251, 260
Hardwarehouse, 263
hardwood
    as commodity, 60, 121, 177, 193, 223, 227, 237, 253, 262
    in conservation, 179, 194, 226, 230, 264
    in production, 4, 6, 17, 25, 42, 132, 136–137, 212
Harris, Allan, 173
Harvard Business School, 145
Hawaii, 131, 145, 151, 242
Hawke Administration, 151
Hawke Government, 142, 146, 265
Hawke, Albert, 135, 230
Hawker Siddeley
    as investor, 155, 177, 179–180, 186, 204, 251
    as parent, 178, 203, 259
    as shareholder, 159, 165, 196, 202, 210, 213–214, 216, 220, 235–236, 240, 244–245, 258
    in mergers, 156, 181, 190, 192–193, 209, 241
Hawker Siddeley Building Supplies, 190, 192–193
Hawker Siddeley Group, 159
Heart Foundation, 184, 189
Hejaz railway, 176
Helena Vale works, 36
Hemingway and Robinson, 41, 131
Henry Martin and Co, 130
HG Godden, 50
High Court of Australia, 30, 216
Highgate Golf Club, 132
Hill, Geoff, 37, 47, 58, 74
Hiroshima, 104
His Majesty's Theatre, 4
HMAS Canberra, 75
HMAS Perth, 74
HMS Arawa, 105
HMT Aquitania, 74
Hoar, Brian, 160
Hobbs, Talbot, 53

INDEX

Holden, 117
Holmes, Col., 240, 271, 274
Holmes à Court, Robert, 240
Holmes, Bob, 59, 109
Home Depot, 223, 261
Hong Kong, 151, 235
Honolulu, 145, 174
Honorary Royal Commission, 146–147
Hovell, Clive, 200–201, 252
HQ Company, 79
Hume Pipe Company, 36
Hunt, Bruce
    as friend, 54, 104, 117, 131
    as physician, 88, 94, 103

I.J.A., 269, 271, 273, 275
Inchcape Group, 194, 227
India, 31, 48, 60, 143, 149
Indochina, 72, 77, 87
Industries Advisory Committee, 152
Innerhadden
    as company, 235, 240, 243–245, 251, 258–259
    as family home, 1, 4–5, 9, 17, 26, 32, 34–35, 44, 57, 93, 112–113, 236
International Whaling Commission, 156, 170
iron-ore mine, 60, 115, 121
Italy, 69, 191
Ivancovich, Ivan, 255

Jackson, Alan, 258
Jackson, Lawrence, 127
Japan
    in trade, 57, 102, 154, 177–181, 203, 208, 224, 237, 262
    in whaling, 152
    in World War II, 69, 72, 74, 76–81, 83, 85–86, 88–89, 90, 97, 99, 101–104, 151, 178, 274
Jardanup, 14
jarrah
    as timber, 4, 6–9, 11, 14, 17, 23–26, 31, 55, 60, 86, 110, 114, 123, 125, 137, 152, 155, 163–164, 176–177, 181, 194, 213, 224, 229, 236, 238, 240, 253, 262
    in conservation, 173, 226
    in industry, 22, 109, 200, 235
jarrah dieback, 194, 226
Jarrah Mills
    as family enterprise, 7, 9, 22, 55, 60, 109–110, 200, 235–236, 240
    as industrial operation, 23, 163
Java, 80, 83, 86
Jesus College, 156
JM Johnston Pty Ltd, 113, 160
Johannesburg, 174
Johnston, Bruce, 31, 109, 172, 196, 239
Johore Strait, 76
joinery, 4, 25, 42–43, 51, 114, 120, 133, 137, 163, 171, 176
Joinery Manufacture, 133

Kailis, Michael, 204–205, 212
Kalgoorlie, 2, 43, 49, 153, 163, 188, 228
Kambalda, 182
Karrakatta, 113
karri
    as exhibit, 238
    as raw material, 6, 14, 17, 114, 144, 152, 160, 165, 172, 181, 194, 213, 229, 253
    in conservation, 26, 148–149, 226, 262
    in industry, 153, 155, 177
Kathleen, 15, 35
Kauri, 4, 16, 51, 113, 122, 125–127, 130, 136, 147, 155, 164–165, 194
Kauri Timber Company
    in industry, 16, 122, 125, 127, 136, 147, 155, 194
    in transactions, 51, 130, 164
Kendrew, 198
Kessell, Stephen, 51, 174
kilns, 16, 17, 25, 39, 119, 125, 163, 176, 184, 192
Kimberley, 2, 174
Kimberleys, 205
King's Park, 32, 148–149
Kinloch Rannoch, 4

Kirkwood, Joe, 50
Kobeelya, 35
Kojonup, 35
Kokusaku Pulp Company, 181, 189
Koolyanobbing, 121, 154
Kosciusko, 98
Kranji, 76–77
Kwinana, 135, 152, 154, 161

Labor Party
    in government, 16, 121, 135, 142, 150, 151, 227–228, 230, 250
    in opposition, 150, 157, 226, 266
labour shortages, 65, 120, 126, 136, 171, 193
Ladies Championship, 168
Lake Karrinyup, 55, 58, 118, 168
Lake McCleod, 224
Lancashire, 132, 156
Lancelin, 68
Lane-Poole, Charles Edward, 25, 30
Law Family, 185, 197, 202
Law, Bertha, 15, 57, 134, 185, 197
Law, Dudley, 15, 134–135, 170, 200, 202
Law, Gavin, 71
Law, Margot, 56
Law, Robert
    as industrialist, 7, 12, 14, 17, 36–37, 60, 117, 214
    in family life, 8, 61, 93
Lawrence, Carmen, 257
Legacy, 21, 110, 117, 192, 247
Legislative Assembly, 2, 30, 53
Leinster, 80
Leonora, 51, 80
Lexbourne House, 15, 35–36
Liberal Party, 16, 121, 131, 150, 227, 266
Liberal–Country Party coalition, 121, 150
Lieutenant-Colonel Anketell, 79
Lion Mill, 7–9, 17, 24, 31
Locke, Bobby, 132
logging
    as company operations, 6, 8, 110, 119, 123, 192, 208, 212, 223, 251
    in conservation, 194, 204, 213, 262, 264
logging concessions, 6, 123, 192
logging rights, 251
Lombok, 80
London Stock Exchange, 187
Lyall's Mill
    as industrial site, 9, 17, 19, 25, 39, 43, 51, 53, 123, 176
    in setbacks, 11–12, 42

Macedon, 35
Mackenzie, Ian, 253
Mackinnon, Charles, 235
MacQuaide, 190–192, 202
MacQuaide, Desmond, 190
Major General George Barber, 44
Malay units, 77
Malaya, 72, 76–77, 144, 269, 274
Malaya Comd., 269, 274
Malayan peninsula, 76
Mandai, 78
Manitoba
    as place, 184, 204–205
    as vessel, 168, 212, 215, 224, 245–246, 254–255, 264
Manjimup
    as company base, 119, 193
    for community events, 208
    in timber industry, 14, 17, 60, 114, 122, 130, 133, 136, 152, 178, 180, 186, 192, 212, 223, 243, 252
Manjimup plant, 136
marri, 177–181
Marubeni, 262
Mary, 8, 15, 26, 59, 197, 202
Master Builders and Contractors' Association, 15
Maungakiekie, 234
Mauritius, 31, 60, 171
Maxwell, Brigadier Duncan, 78, 81–82
Maylands, 36, 48, 72
McEwen, John, 192
McEwin, Oswald, 64, 79

INDEX

McIntyre Trophy, 233
McLarty, 126–127, 131
McLarty, Ross, 126
McNeil Street, 167–168, 185, 196–197, 200, 242, 244, 254, 264, 266
McNeil, Neil, 167
Medina, 176
Meecham, Bert, 37
Melbourne
    as commercial hub, 7, 12, 16, 31, 125, 170, 243, 261
    as destination, 1, 51, 174, 257
    in education, 27, 34, 40–41, 44
Melville, 63, 153, 163, 176, 193
Memorial Grounds, 21
Metric Conversion Board, 261
Metro Brick 36
    as successful firm, 60, 135, 142, 170, 200–201
    in decline, 203, 214
Metropolitan Brick Company, see Metro Brick
Metropolitan Region Planning Authority, 167
Metropolitan Timber Workers Union, 221
Miami Club, 57
Midland, 2, 7, 133, 228
Midland Brick Company, 142
Midland Railway Company, 7
mill
    as company asset, 8, 25, 39, 127, 182, 186, 203, 223, 229–230
    as industrial site, 6–7, 9, 11, 13, 16, 23–24, 42, 51, 53, 113, 128, 135, 162, 176, 179, 184, 204
    as workplace, 12, 43, 46, 114, 120, 129, 138–139, 180, 216
    in management, 163, 215
    in pulping, 4, 17, 19, 23–24, 29, 31, 60, 119, 123, 125, 133, 137, 162, 178–179, 181, 210
mill workers, 119, 137, 180, 216
Millars
    as dominant firm, 6, 16, 43, 113, 157, 162, 165, 180, 227, 237
    as landholder, 13, 17, 30, 51, 53, 190

    in industrial relations, 18, 37, 132, 147
    in joint ventures, 122, 136, 203, 210, 250
    in mergers, 194, 228–230, 241, 245
Millars Bunning Shipbuilders, 113
Millars Timber and Trading Company, 30, 157, 194, 227
Millars' Jarrah and Karri Company, 6
mills
    as assets, 25, 192, 235–236, 240
    as modern sites, 7, 173
    as workplaces, 11, 42, 49, 53, 163, 171, 193, 238, 243
    in family life, 1, 22, 93, 100, 139, 200, 258
    in production, 8–9, 17, 23, 39, 51, 55, 60, 109–110, 113–114, 119, 122, 126, 133, 136, 146, 152, 155, 160, 162, 177–178
Milyeannup, 123, 125–127, 131, 134, 155, 164, 190, 265
mining
    and environment, 173, 194, 208, 226
    as industry, 2, 165
    in business, 3, 8, 31, 43, 51, 144, 152, 154, 182, 184, 223, 229, 240
Minister for Forests, 123, 149, 177, 213
Ministry of Munitions, 65
Minnewarra, 57
Miss Annie's, 26
Mitchell, James, 30, 46
Mitre 10, 162, 172, 237
Monier Patent Propriety Company, 14
Moore, Newton, 12
Morley, 228
Mosman Park, 1
Mount Helena, 31
MRPA, 167, 176, 184
MS Duntroon, 70
Mt Newman, 182
Mt Tom Price, 182
Muja, 17, 19, 25, 31, 42, 122
Mullaloo, 68
Mundijong, 212, 229–230
Munster, 135
Muriel, 15, 202

318

Nagasaki, 104
Nannup, 16, 123, 125–126, 243
Napoleon, 102
National Australasian Bank, 8
National Mutual, 261
national parks, 208, 230, 261
National Safety Council of Australia, 261
Nationality, 275
NatWest, 240
Navy, 69, 72, 74, 76, 273
Nedlands, 131, 185, 212
New York, 131–132, 174, 243
New Zealand, 4, 16, 31, 98, 127, 234, 240
New, Rick, 142
Noble, Mollie, 59
Noggerup, 17, 19, 29, 31
Nor'West Whaling Company, 136, 170
North Africa, 63, 69
North Dandalup, 3, 6
North Fremantle, 2, 11
North Perth, 48
North Queensland, 113, 119, 130, 149, 160
North West, 42, 153, 170, 224
North West Shelf, 224
Northam
    as training camp, 63–64, 67–68, 70, 254
    as transport hub, 2
Northampton, 54
Northcliffe, 125–126, 165, 173, 182
Northern Territory
    as military theatre, 67, 72–73
    in economic development, 113, 144, 153, 172–173, 184, 237
Nyamup, 60, 110, 119–120, 128, 152, 155

O'Connor, 222
Officer of the Order of Australia (AO), 224–225
One Stop Centre, 161, 163, 184, 195
Open Championship, 132
Operation Wattle, 228
Order No 17, 274–275
Order of Australia, 224–225

Order of the British Empire, 224
Osborne Parade, 61, 116, 122
Osborne Park, 153, 209, 222

Pacific Coast, 1, 151
Pacific Northwest, 151
Pacific Ocean, 80
Pacific region, 145
Palace Hotel, 53–54, 251
Palm Beach, 139
Papua New Guinea, 60, 74, 88, 99, 153, 212, 223, 226, 237, 254
Parker Point, 255
Parry, Mervyn, 167
Pasir Panjang, 79
Pearce, 60
Pearl Harbour, 74
Pemberton, 17, 155, 180, 192, 243
Peppermint Grove, 26, 167, 254, 266
Percival, 76–79, 81
Percival, Arthur, 76
Perth Jarrah Mills
    as holding company, 9, 163, 200, 235–236, 240
    as sawmill, 7, 22–23, 55, 60, 109–110
Perth Mint, 7
Perth Sawmills, 2–3, 6, 8
Perth stock exchange, 240
Perth–Fremantle Road, 4
Perthshire, 4
Peters Ice Cream, 136, 165, 170, 224
Petherick, 31, 39, 42, 53, 55, 73–74, 109, 114, 138, 143, 239
Petherick, Arthur, 31, 55
Pilbara, 2, 176, 184
pine
    as timber, 4, 19, 137, 160, 162, 171, 209–210, 212, 223, 227, 229–230, 241, 251
    in plantations, 231
pine mill, 230
pine plantations, 137, 171, 209, 223, 227, 229, 231, 251

INDEX

pine sawmilling operation, 212
Pinnacles Station, 51, 80, 87
Pinus pinaster, 210
Pinus radiata, 137, 150, 209
Pix, Keith, 59
plantations
    as corporate asset, 171, 195, 229, 240, 243
    as tree farms, 252–253
    in state forestry, 137, 209–210, 223, 227, 229, 251, 265
plywood, 119, 162, 210
Port Adelaide, 70
Port Hedland, 170, 172, 176, 184
Port Moresby, 74
Postmaster General's department, 160
Prague, 52
prefabricated housing, 51, 130, 136, 142, 154, 171, 182
Premier of Western Australia, 12–13, 16, 30, 46, 68, 125–127, 151–152, 161, 183, 191, 208, 226, 230, 257
Premier Brand, 161
Presbyterian church, 254, 258
Preston Valley, 17
Prices Justification Tribunal, 203
Prime Minister, 37, 80, 132, 174, 183, 192
prisoner of war (POW), 83, 84, 85, 87, 89, 91, 93, 95, 96, 97, 98, 99, 101, 105, 107, 117, 122, 151, 188, 198, 273–274
Prisoner of War Association, 198
Public Works Department, 122, 142, 147
pulp production, 162, 177, 178, 181, 186, 241
Punchbowl Cup, 58
PWD, 122–123

Queensland
    as military origin, 76, 119
    in timber industry, 113, 123, 130, 149, 160, 237
Queensland maple, 113, 123

RAAF, 76
RAF, 76

railways
    as engineering project, 11–12, 14, 186
    as infrastructure, 7, 134
    as market, 13, 31, 46, 51, 121–122, 136, 144, 147, 149, 176
    in administration, 30, 146
    in operations, 2, 7–9, 19, 51, 54, 71, 99, 122, 133, 153, 167, 176, 182, 192
    in supply chains, 3–4, 16–17, 42, 203
Randall, Len, 168
Raphael & Co, 143
rations, 72, 84, 89, 93, 94, 99, 100, 102, 115, 271–272, 274
Red Cross, 67, 87–88, 94, 102, 104
Reddish, Halford, 147
Regional Forest Agreement, 262
Renshaw, Geoff, 255
Reporter, 35
Repulse, 74
retail
    as outlets, 138, 162–163, 165, 192, 207, 222, 228, 238, 261, 263
    in merchandising, 110, 127, 194–195, 206, 221, 226, 250
Rigg, Kathy, 211
Rio Tinto, 154
Riverton, 207
Rivervale, 36–37
Rockingham, 7, 62–63
Rogers, Kelly, 47
Roleystone, 7
Rottnest, 139, 184, 245, 255
Royal Adelaide, 233
Royal and Ancient Golf Club, 45
Royal Australian Engineers, 65
Royal Birkdale, 156
Royal Cinque Ports Golf Club, 174
Royal Commission, 6, 30, 119, 127, 130, 146–148, 157
    as honorary inquiry
Royal Fremantle, 50, 58
Royal Military College Duntroon, 170
Royal Navy, 74, 76

Royal Perth, 58
Royal St George, 174
Royal Sydney, 117
royalties, 26, 29, 31, 46, 125, 173–174, 213, 247, 253
RSL, 257
Russia, 69, 86, 104
Ryder, Wayne, 240

safety officer, 120, 136, 163
Samson, Lionel, 4
Sarawak, 160
Sarich, Ralph, 235
Sawmillers Association, 46, 146
sawmilling
    and safety, 8, 120
    as industry, 6–7, 13, 16, 51, 119, 212, 238
    as modernized facility, 9, 51, 60, 123, 125, 173, 176, 233
    as state operation, 16–17, 114, 147, 204
    as technology, 31
    in company operations, 3, 25, 42, 55, 110, 113, 126, 129, 160, 162–163, 193–194, 213, 223, 226, 233
    in community life, 19
    in politics, 30, 146–147, 150, 155, 261
sawmills
    as company assets, 3, 8, 110, 113, 119, 130, 135, 137, 155, 159, 165, 179, 192, 204, 227–228, 237, 241, 251, 254
    as modern capacity, 17, 126
    as state enterprise, 16, 122, 136, 142, 147, 190
    in industry/labour, 2, 6, 18–19, 30, 46, 131
sawn timber, 19, 46, 60, 113, 119, 123, 126, 160, 173, 213
Scaddan, John, 16
Scandinavia, 52
Scarborough Beach Road, 153, 206
Scotch College
    as school, 21, 26–28, 33–35, 37, 41–42, 62, 131, 150
    in governance, 123, 170

Seaview, 33, 46
Second World War, 136, 146, 152, 188, 239, 264
Selarang Barracks, 83, 89, 269
Seward, Justin, 163–164, 167–168
Shannon Basin, 213
Shannon River, 204, 208, 226
shareholders
    as controlling owners, 121, 135, 170, 187, 192, 244, 259, 261
    as investors, 213–214, 220, 250
    as recipients, 12, 134, 221, 258
Shark Bay, 254
Sheraton Hotel, 239
Sikhs, 85, 272
Sims Products Pty Ltd, 222
Singapore
    as military base, 72, 76–78, 80, 104
    as POW site, 59, 79, 81, 83–84, 95, 99, 102, 105, 111–112, 146, 254
    in trade, 143, 151
Sleeper Mills, 133
sleepers
    in export trade, 3, 7, 13, 14, 16–17, 31, 41, 51, 53, 60, 121, 136–137, 143, 146, 148–149, 182
    in production, 176
Smith, Peter Stuart, 59
Smith, Ted, 173
Smith, William, 7
softwood
    as company, 4, 17, 25, 229
    as timber, 18, 65, 137, 177, 209, 212–213, 260
    in milling, 114, 210, 212, 223, 229, 260
Softwoods Products, 210, 213, 229
Solomon Islands, 99
South Africa, 31, 51, 60, 88, 174
South America, 136, 142, 165
South American hardwoods, 132
South Australia, 7, 70, 72, 136
South Pacific, 74, 127
South Perth, 207
South Pole, 152

South West Forest Holdings, 223
Southeast Asia, 136, 142, 165
Southwest
    as community, 53, 120, 209, 238
    as direction, 76, 78, 249
    in environment, 203, 227
    in industry, 7, 9, 13, 65, 119, 123, 161, 208, 210, 247
Spearwood, 163
SS Canberra, 156, 159
SS Elderslie, 1
St Andrews, 45, 190, 234
St Anne's, 132
St George's Cathedral, 59, 254, 256
St George's Terrace, 2, 39, 68, 250, 254
St Hilda's Anglican School for Girls, 4, 5, 113
St James, 174
St John's Church, 18
St Johnston, Eric, 156
St Lawrence's Church, 200
St Mary's, 26
Stanford, 188, 198, 200, 206
state brickworks, 16, 142, 155
State Building Commission, 136
State Building Supplies
    as public enterprise, 142, 147, 155, 159, 161, 165, 180
    in privatization, 156
state forest 251
    as resource, 26, 155, 192, 194
    for conservation, 227, 247, 264
state government
    as political actor, 249
    as regulator, 6, 143, 191–192, 229, 262
    in economic development, 123, 127, 154, 163, 180, 213
State Housing Commission, 122–123, 126, 133
State Library of Western Australia, 112, 118, 207
State Sawmills
    after privatization
    as public enterprise, 16, 46, 113, 122, 135–136, 142, 147, 155, 159, 190, 192, 204, 237

    in government contracts, 17, 30
State Shipping Service, 16, 144, 150
Stoneware Pipe and Pottery Company, 14, 214
strike, 12, 18, 88, 127, 133, 221
structural timber, 4, 17, 110, 133, 154, 177
Stubbs, Sydney, 53
Subiaco, 24, 29, 71
succession, 171, 201, 214, 227
Sumitomo Shoji Kaisha Ltd, 178
Sun Securities, 240, 243
Sunda Strait, 75
Sunday Times, 37
Super Centres, 207, 209
Supreme Court, 30, 127, 259
Swan Barracks, 62
Swan Brewery, 165, 261
Swan Portland Cement, 36, 60, 125, 261
Swan River Colony, 8
Swan Timber Company, 164
Swanbourne, 26, 46, 58, 212, 234
Swanton, Jim, 190
Swarbrick family, 160
Switzerland, 132, 191
Sydney, 53, 74, 76, 105, 107, 117, 131, 170

Taiwan, 81
takeover
    as acquisition, 143, 201, 220, 228, 237, 241, 243, 249, 258
    as defensive concern, 210, 213, 222, 236, 244, 250–251, 264
    as hostile bid, 240
Tasmania, 8, 127, 204, 212
Tasmanian bluegum, 247
Taylor, Gena, 3
Telegram, 22, 52, 71, 93
Temperley, Norman, 53, 113
Tengah airfield, 78
tennis, 4, 15, 28, 32, 35, 43, 122, 168, 184
Texada Salt Company, 224
Thai–Burma Railway, 99
The Cliffe, 167

INDEX

The Timber People, 238
Thomson, Peter, 132
timber
    as raw material, 4, 9, 12, 17, 21, 43, 48, 149, 206
    in industry, 1, 3, 6–8, 10–11, 13, 15–16, 19, 24–25, 39, 41, 46, 51, 53, 60, 102, 113, 115, 119–121, 123, 125–127, 129–134, 136–139, 142–144, 146–147, 150, 152–154, 157, 159–160, 163, 165, 171, 173, 176–181, 184, 187–188, 190, 194, 203–204, 208–210, 212–213, 216, 221, 223–224, 226, 229, 238, 240, 245, 247, 251, 261, 264, 266
    in manufacturing, 42, 110, 114, 122, 161–162, 191, 193, 237
    in resource management, 30, 65, 148, 155, 164, 170, 192, 198, 214, 220, 227–228, 230, 239, 253, 262, 272
Timber Control Board, 113, 122
Timber Merchants' Association, 9, 30, 39, 146
Timber Regulation Act, 39
Timber Trades, 132
Timber Workers Union, 12, 221
Timor, 83
tingle, 160, 262
Tokyo, 104, 151, 178, 189, 209–210, 273, 275
Tone River
    as mill site, 120, 129, 133, 152, 155, 204
    for housing, 136
Town and Country Building Society, 261
Townsville, 228
Toyo Menka Kaisha Ltd, 178
Toyo Menko, 180–181, 189, 203
Trade Bureau, 146, 150, 265
Tree & Plantation Services, 240, 243, 247
Trinity Church, 2
Tukurua, 3
Tullis, 60

Unfair Trading Act, 146–147
Unfair Trading Control Commissioner, 146–147

United Kingdom, 33, 60, 77, 117, 156, 174, 176
United States
    as ally, 33, 80, 151, 174, 209, 234
    as industrial supplier, 3, 30, 51, 119, 160, 177–178, 206, 223, 261
University Club, 75
University of Cambridge, 156
University of Edinburgh, 27
University of Hawaii, 145
University of Melbourne, 34, 41
University of Western Australia, 151, 261
Uppingham, 10
USS Houston, 74

Vale, Helena, 7, 16, 36
Vanimo Timber Company, 223, 241
VDC, 113
Vermont, 234
Vichy French government, 72
Vickers Australia, 170, 224
Vickers Hoskins Ltd, 139
Vickers machine guns, 67, 77, 79
Victoria Falls, 174
Victoria Park, 24, 48, 122
Vienna, 52, 156
Vincent, Oliver, 59, 67, 69, 240

WA Chip and Pulp, 224, 253
WA Inc, 250
WA Salvage, 237, 253
Wagon Timber Company, 122
Walpole, 160
Walton Heath, 174
wandoo, 17, 53, 60, 137
War Precautions Act, 25
Waratah Avenue, 185
Warwick, 209, 222
Watts, Arthur, 127
Weld Club, 2, 60, 139, 168, 170, 251
Wellington Street, 3, 17, 19, 24–25, 31, 42, 193
Welshpool, 121–122, 163, 176, 182, 184, 188–189, 193–195, 209, 213, 223, 239

Wesfarmers
    as parent company, 212, 240, 250, 252–253, 258–264
    in retail expansion, 251, 267
West Australian Club, 39
West Australian Portland Cement Company, see Swan Portland Cement
West Perth, 15, 26, 34, 36, 139, 153, 163, 171, 182, 188
Western Australian Chamber of Manufacturers, 182–184
Western Australian Chip and Pulp Company Ltd, 184
Western Australian Cricket Association, 216, 261
Western Australian Employers Federation, 261
Western Australian Government Railways, 122, 136
Western Australian Institute of Technology, 196
Western Australian Newspapers, 165
Western Australian Trade Bureau, 146
Western Front, 64, 67
Western Mining Corporation, 154, 182
Westralian Forest Industries, 210
Wharncliffe, 210, 212, 223
Whitakers, 136
Whitby House, 113
White City, 35
White, Joseph, 9
Whittaker Bros, 17
Whittakers, 18, 113–114, 122, 203, 210
Wild, Gerry, 123
Wilgarup Karri and Jarrah Company, 14, 17
Williamson, Frederick, 9
Wilson, Frank, 6, 16, 32
Wimbledon, 132, 156, 174
Windsor Castle, 174
Wittenoom, 127
Woodchip Agreement, 186, 188
woodchips, 178, 179, 180, 184, 186, 189, 190, 203, 208, 224, 237, 251
Woodside, 70, 72–73, 254
workers' compensation scheme, 137
World Expo, 57
World Rally Championship, 231
World War II, 62
Worsley Timber Company, 147, 203
Wren, Suzy
    as person, 140, 169–170, 239
    as vessel, 123–124, 139, 168
Wright, James William, 4
Wundowie, 121

Yampi Sound, 60
York, 2, 54, 131–132, 174, 243
Yornup, 31, 42, 46, 51, 60

Zink, Dolph 196, 198, 204, 230, 252, 257–258
Zoological Gardens Board, 261

www.ingramcontent.com/pod-product-compliance
Lightning Source LLC
Chambersburg PA
CBHW082315230426
43667CB00034B/2739